THE
EASTERNMOST
SKY

Also by Juliet Blaxland

The Easternmost House

THE EASTERNMOST SKY

Adapting to Change in the 21st Century

JULIET BLAXLAND

SANDSTONE PRESS

First published in Great Britain in 2021 by
Sandstone Press Ltd
PO Box 41
Muir of Ord
IV6 7YX
Scotland

www.sandstonepress.com

ISBN: 978-1-913207-56-4
ISBNe: 978-1-913207-57-1

Sandstone Press is committed to a sustainable future.
This book is made from Forest Stewardship Council ® certified paper.

Cover design by Two Associates
Typeset by Iolaire, Newtonmore
Printed and bound by CPI Group (UK) Ltd, Croydon, CR0 4YY

The Easternmost House was dedicated to 'all the people who have been physically involved in the making of the British landscape in the past, and to those who still live and work in the countryside or on the land today', followed by a long list of rural jobs, starting: farmers, fishermen, shepherds . . .

The Easternmost Sky is also dedicated to those who still live and work in the countryside or on the land today . . . but to these I would now add other key workers, including but not limited to: crop pickers, greengrocers, village shop and corner shop workers, supermarket shelf-stackers, till and checkout workers, lorry drivers, van drivers, bus drivers, train drivers, petrol station people, postal workers, warehouse workers, factory workers, mechanics, plumbers, electricians, power and power-cut-repair workers, sewage workers, rubbish collectors, cleaners, ambulance drivers, paramedics, surgeons, doctors, nurses, vets, emergency services, armed forces, care workers, pub and kitchen workers, and anyone similarly essential not yet mentioned.

ACKNOWLEDGEMENTS

Many thanks go to the many people who have helped either in the living on the edge or in the conveying of the spirit of the place to a wider world, in no particular order: Jane Graham Maw and Jennifer Christie of Graham Maw Christie literary agency, Bob Davidson and Moira Forsyth of Sandstone Press, John Lewis Stempel, Andrew Gimson, Mary Miers and Richard Hopton of *Country Life*, Mary and Johnnie James of Aldeburgh Bookshop, India Knight, Janice Turner, Simon Heffer, Jilly Cooper, Patrick Galbraith of *Shooting Times*, Emma Barnett of *Radio 5 Live*, The Reverend Richard Coles of *Radio 4 Saturday Live*, and closer to home, Lesley Dolphin of *BBC Radio Suffolk*, Kevin Burch, Wendy Holden, Emma Shercliff, Abbie Clements of Halesworth Bookshop, Irene Pitcher and Steph of Southwold Books, John Barber, Peter Boggis, John Uden and Ivan Moore, Tony Westlake and Stephen Westlake at Easton Bavents, the Benacre estate, everyone at St Margaret South Elmham and the 'Old Rec Oval', and easternmost of all of us ... Bob the Coastal Engineer.

DISCLAIMER

Several of the more rural places mentioned in *The Easternmost Sky* are individual private farms or old agricultural settlements of only a few houses, rather than villages in the conventional sense. Please be aware that there are no public 'facilities' – car parks, shops, pubs, cafes, loos, bins etc. – in these places. (See below for places *with* car parks, shops, pubs, loos, bins etc.)

Some of the farm tracks and land marked on maps may be signed as having no public right of way or no public access, usually for reasons such as being part of a network of SSSIs, conservation areas and national nature reserves. At nesting times some of the beaches may have roped-off areas which are intended to help protect vulnerable ground-nesting birds (terns, plovers, avocets etc.) from unintentional disturbance by dogs, walkers, riders etc.

The beaches, tides, creeks, estuaries, marshes, broads, bogs, reedbeds and crumbling farmland cliffs along this coast are also inherently dangerous to humans, dogs and the unwary.

Emergencies

Lifeboats	Dial 999 and ask for the coastguard
Erosion	Stay away from the bottom of cliffs to a distance equal to the height
Cold water	RNLI advice is to 'float to live', i.e. float on your back if you fall in
Dogs in sea	Dogs usually save themselves, but owners trying to rescue them often don't
Cows	Make no eye contact, and let go of dogs if cows become protective of calves

The Country Code

Please	Leave gates as you find them and respect signs, footpaths etc.
	Leave animals alone and do not feed them
	Keep dogs on short leads near livestock
	Take litter home
	Leave no trace

Suffolk coast places *with* car parks, shops, pubs, cafes, loos, bins etc. (north to south): Kessingland, Southwold, Walberswick, Dunwich, Minsmere, Sizewell, Thorpeness, Aldeburgh, Snape, Orford, the Suffolk Punch Trust at Hollesley, Felixstowe, Pin Mill.

Where laws, statistics, places and/or cultural norms etc. are referred to, they relate to what was current at the time of writing. Some of these facts, places, norms etc. may change over the lifetime of a printed book, especially one about and written during a time of great change.

CONTENTS

AUTHOR'S NOTE

The recurring theme of *The Easternmost Sky* is 'adapting to change'. It was written on the Suffolk coast, in a place known for its farmland, its nature reserves and some of the most startlingly visible coastal erosion in Europe. By exploring how climate change and social change are already affecting this agriculturally important part of the world, it is possible to imagine a very different landscape, to glimpse what is to come and to understand how these changes will affect us all in the near future. *The Easternmost Sky* is part memoir, part elegy and part warning.

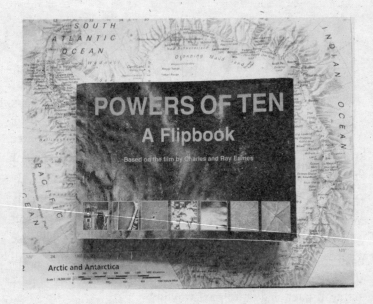

INFLUENCES

Powers of Ten and *Easternmost Sky* thinking

For the purposes of introducing what might be called 'Easternmost Sky thinking', please imagine for a moment that you are one of several people sitting around the table at an informal lunch in the garden of a cottage on the edge of an eroding cliff. The sun is out, and we are at roughly the easternmost edge of England, the easternmost edge of the whole of the UK. The sea crashes constantly onto the beach at the bottom of the cliff, although we have all become so used to the sounds of sea and susurration that we no longer notice it.

The table itself is big and old and has a certain shipwreck chic about it. The food is Mediterranean in spirit, but most of it was grown within sight of the house, with only a few food miles and zero air miles involved in bringing it from the fields to your fork. The mood is of a picnic, but without any of the inconveniences that so often plague picnics in real life (as distinct from picnics in story books). There is none of the 'sand in the sandwiches, wasps in the tea' disgruntlement that niggled John Betjeman's Cornish picnics. Not here. This picnic scene is important, because it is the reference point of the whole of what follows. The lunch table is point X on the globe, and each of us here is a 'picnic man', at rest at distance 0.

Powers of Ten (1977), by Charles and Ray Eames, is the book which sparked the idea for *The Easternmost Sky* and provides an ongoing visual and conceptual hook on which to hang it. *Powers of Ten* is a flipbook based on a short film about the effects of thinking at scale and distance, and of notionally or literally 'zooming in and out' in a manner now familiar from Google Earth. *Powers of Ten* holds as its central reference point an aerial photograph of a man asleep on a picnic rug in a park in Chicago. There is also a woman on the picnic rug, but she is less clear in the photo, so it is 'the picnic man' who is the point of reference. 'The picnic man' is at rest at point X, at a notionally neutral reference distance of 0. The film examines the effect of adding a 0, zooming out x10, x10, x10, and so on . . . to $x10^{+23}$. It doesn't really matter how many times we zoom out, because repeatedly zooming out, any number of times x10, quickly takes us into outer space.

Taking *Powers of Ten* as the generating concept, the lunch table in the garden of the clifftop cottage is our personalised and updated reference point, our equivalent of the picnic, placed at X on the globe, which is now in 2020s Suffolk and not 1970s Chicago. The picnic man represents 'us', any of us, all of us, you, at rest at 0 distance in space.

Our lunch in the clifftop cottage garden gives us somewhere specific to use as an anchoring point, relatable in scale, distance and detail, point X at distance 0. The cottage is our former home, described in *The Easternmost House*.

Starting at close-up 'picnic man' range in the cottage garden, I can then notionally zoom out a bit to explore and guide you around the Benacre estate of 7,000 acres (where we now live) which includes a significant area of productive farmland, as well as wildlife habitats and protected national nature reserves. I then zoom out to the whole UK crumbling east coastline and the 461,400 acres of farmland estimated to be lost to the sea in the foreseeable future (which I explain later), zoom out a bit more and see how this fits into climate change . . . and so on.

The *Powers of Ten* film then zooms back to the original Chicago picnic man, now zooming *in* x10, x10, x10 . . . to $x10^{-15}$, which takes us into the molecular level of the man, which is where we can return to the intensely local, in terms of farming, then food, at which point our private decision-making about what we eat starts to affect the wider world.

Powers of Ten first fascinated me as an architecture student and has continued to do so for years. It is the conceptual hook on which I hang a particular view of the world, which for the purposes of brevity and in this specific context is called *Easternmost Sky* thinking: zooming out and back in, thinking at scale and in 4D, meaning including not only the vastness of space but of time as well. One of the characteristics of *Easternmost Sky* thinking is that it doesn't take itself too seriously, and while the evidence of coastal and other change is explored, it can be zoomed in and out of at will, from a layman's viewpoint rather than that of the dedicated climate scientist. The *Powers of Ten* film is easily found on YouTube (just search for *Powers of Ten*) but I still have my old copy of the *Powers of Ten* flipbook, so can happily flip in and out and pause on an image in a more satisfyingly analogue way than the film ever could . . .

To me, the most interesting frames of *Powers of Ten* are the ones where we can comprehend the vastness of our situation, yet scale is still relatable. This is the core of *Easternmost Sky* thinking.

The knowledge acquired during the life and writing of *The Easternmost House*, in particular on the subject of living with coastal erosion, has led to *The Easternmost Sky* as an exploration of 'adapting to change', especially change which is nature-related and imminent. The starting point of my experience of living in a rural area affected by ongoing coastal erosion leads naturally to an examination of other aspects of change, including 'coastal change', climate change, changes in food, farming and landscape, and associated social change. All this of course is not confined to rural life: such widespread change impacts on all of us.

Those of us living on the crumbling edge of the land may be seen as the twenty-first-century equivalent of the canary down the coal mine, or the prophetic dove foreseeing the coming flood. *The Easternmost Sky* may be read as the gentle warnings of a rural futurologist, but it is also a portrait of the modern countryside in an urban age.

Beginning at the end

Everyone has a cliff coming towards them. The difference is that we can see ours. The thing about it is, though, that when our part of this nature-wrought and romantic place goes, the memory of life here will go with it. Where once Chuffy the brindle greyhound bombed about the beach, and Cockle the cockerel gently heralded the dawn with his rural sounds, and our Skyline hens laid beautiful blue eggs, and our vegetable garden thrived, and we loved the place so much, one day, where all that had been, there will be only a particular volume of sky over the sea which will hold all these memories in its air, and the people on the beach below will not know.

The Easternmost House (2019)

0

DECEMBER

This extract from the last page of *The Easternmost House* closes a book about life in and around a house on the edge of a crumbling cliff, at the easternmost edge of England. On a map, the place is marked as Easton Bavents, but on the ground it isn't really a findable 'place' now, as most of it has been lost to coastal erosion. This non-place used to be the easternmost parish in the whole of the UK, before its nose, Easton Ness, fell into the sea. This final paragraph imagines an unspecified time in the future, without the house as it sits there, loved and lived in, threatened with coastal erosion but still standing strongly against the waves and the weather.

The local forces of nature and the greater uncertainties of climate change were by then encircling and gathering around their prey, but without yet having delivered the final *coup de grâce*. That happened earlier than we had expected, only a few months after the book was published.

The house in question (actually a row of three but always referred to and appearing as if one) was a testament to

7

the good work of the Victorian, or late-Georgian, cottage builders who must have laboured hard against the clifftop elements to build it; yet even as soon as these unknown people had completed their admirable work, the mighty natural forces of its destruction were already mustering, unseen and unstoppable, in the churning sea close by.

For more than twelve years, we lived in this windblown house, at the end of a farm track which leads only into the sea. The farm track looks as if it wants to continue for a mile or two, but it has been hacked off roughly and many times by the wind and sea and erosion. In the summer of 2015, an innocuous enough event happened, for a community accustomed to centuries of coastal erosion, summarised in a sentence broadcast on Radio 4's *iPM*: 'The house on the edge of the cliff was demolished this week, which means we are now the house on the edge of the cliff.' We felt suddenly more vulnerable without the buffer of another generation, or of another house between us and the abyss.

That summer, it seemed as if we had plenty of time. Sunny lunches around the shipwreck table in the garden were habitual. We hadn't yet started zooming out and thinking about the bigger picture.

We are environmental evacuees, by which I mean that Nature caused us to move house when we would have preferred not to. I believe the term 'environmental evacuee' will become more common in the near future, affecting many people in the UK and across the globe, as climate change and the movement of water predictably causes places to become unviable, eventually to be decommissioned and abandoned, more of which later.

We were forced by coastal erosion to move from a house and a place we loved. This was a foreseeable process, but

8

nevertheless a sad one, and it represented the end of an era, not just for us but for the house and the wider world, locally and further afield, who took an interest in the story. The immediate territory of *The Easternmost House* (the house and the book) was and is almost at the easternmost edge of East Anglia, where the land pokes out into the North Sea on the map, to the north of Southwold in Suffolk, amid constantly changing natural boundaries of reedbed, river and sea.

The territory of the life which follows our evacuation, and of *The Easternmost Sky*, is centred around the old ship-wreck lunch table in the garden of the house, zooming out to include the wider territory of Covehithe and the Benacre estate, Britain's 'easternmost estate', currently an area of about 7,000 acres but losing about thirty acres of land a year to the sea. The estate extends approximately from the Hundred River just south of Lowestoft to the north, to the Easton Bavents 'low' and reedbeds to the south, bounded by Henstead to the west and by the sea to the east. Benacre estate land dovetails neatly with the territory of the Easternmost House, the latter sold off by the estate in the 1920s. The high point of the Benacre estate is by a wood called Easton Home Covert, which acts as a natural pivot between the two tracts of land. With typical Suffolk logic, Easton Home Covert was always referred to as Benacre Woods when viewed 'back to front' from the Easton Bavents vantage point of the Easternmost House.

Our natural range reaches other rural territories inland, especially the 'empty quarter' beyond Halesworth on the map, a collection of remote hamlets known as The Saints, where my childhood home, known locally as 'the Old Rec' (rectory), is still a personal epicentre. All of this feels like 'my patch'. Further afield, some of my extended family are farmers in Norfolk or involved in the racing industry orbiting around Newmarket. This area is characterised by ancient land-based and sea-based preoccupations.

This easternmost patch of England may seem globally trivial and geographically tiny, but it is agriculturally important while also being geologically fragile. The east of England is home to some of the most productive farmland in the world, as well as having the fastest rate of coastal erosion in Europe. The land that produces our food is falling into the sea. This is not some abstract calculation of arable acreages or wheat and barley yields. You can literally pick seawater-washed onions and parsnips off the beach between Benacre and Covehithe after a local cliff fall. Wheat and barley are somehow less relatable than bread, beer and biscuits, so people tend not to notice when the 'combinable crops' are washed away, which they are, bit by bit, all the time, every year. Visitors, unused to the sight of recognisable 'supermarket crops' on the beach, often find it amusing. What this means when looked at from a more 'zoomed out' global food supply perspective is less amusing. This lovely but unfashionable part of the world is therefore something of a bellwether. Our crumbling cliffs are a good place from which to peer into the future of food and farming, among other things.

The experience of environmental evacuation is still unusual enough to attract the curiosity of the press, but is likely to become more commonplace. Pedestrian would be an insensitive word to use in this context, given the fact that millions of environmental evacuees will almost certainly be walking across continents before the end of this century, if not this decade. Bangladesh and Myanmar are particularly vulnerable to rising sea levels, but so is Suffolk and much of eastern England.

Living with coastal erosion becomes quite normal, if you live with it all the time. For months or even years on end, it may be barely noticeable, and people can live a pleasantly healthy coastal life with no disruption at all. But the erosion is always there in the back of your mind, lurking, waiting to make its presence felt, or more pertinently waiting to make its absences felt: the visible absences of tree, hedge, farmland, dune and cliff.

'How long have you got?' became our familiar variation on the 'How long have I got?' directed at doctors tasked with delivering uncomfortable diagnoses. People often asked us this question, even at the beginning of our time on the crumbling cliff when there was still plenty of land and time left, for the time being. The truth is one can never know, so the cliff-dweller and the doctor concoct a plausible estimate, based on science, observation, averages, means, medians and a keen eye on recent changes to any of the above. Then they take a stab in the dark in order to satisfy their inquisitor, and say out loud something like, 'Well, given current conditions and based on my previous experiences of these conditions, you (we) could reasonably expect perhaps five years, but I must emphasise that while the prognosis is foreseeable, and in the long term ultimately fatal, there may be unknown unknowns, good and bad, so you may have a longer or shorter time.'

At risk of stating the obvious, nature is by its very nature unpredictable. Long periods of stability can be followed by sudden cataclysmic events: structural collapse; pandemic; eruption. 'All I can advise is to make the most of the time you have...' Just as in the back of your mind you know that your dog will probably die about twelve years from when you first meet, but you don't like to think about it as it would spoil the everyday joy of being with the dog, so the cliff-dweller, or the patient, keeps 'everything as normal as possible for as long as possible', like in the film *Love Story*.

Until one day, the sudden cataclysmic event happens.

It is probably wise to mentally rehearse the certainties in life, the things we know will happen unless something worse happens to us first, to acclimatise and imagine the scenes before they occur in real life. The death of a dog, of a parent, then another parent, a partner or spouse, the end of the reign of a stabilising monarch, the evacuation and demolition of a much-loved house before it is lost to the sea. These are all imaginable scenes.

It is less easy to imagine the exact circumstances, such as the time of day, the time of year, the weather, amount of warning, the reactions of other people around us, or the googlies we neglected to imagine in the first place.

People have to move house for many reasons. In the twelve years we lived in our clifftop idyll, in a magical parallel world of light and sky and water, many terrible things happened to friends 'in the midst of life'. Any of these terrible things could so easily have happened to us: untimely deaths by cancer (several people, of our generation and younger); complete spinal cord neck injury as a result of an accident with a horse causing catastrophic tetraplegic paralysis; circumstances leading to suicide (two people); and various unexpectedly sudden and/or untimely deaths by natural causes such as heart attack, asthma and drowning.

Taken within the context of this sobering emotional landscape of the Something that Might Happen to us all, to have to move only as an environmental evacuation due to coastal erosion may be considered literally *the best reason* to have to move from such a house, akin to a marriage being put asunder only by Fate's chosen scenario re 'til death us do part'. But we always wondered in the back of our minds how it would physically happen, and as we gradually entered the endgame, our observations became more wary. Our visual assessments and pacings became more frequent. The elephant, or rather the woolly mammoth whose fossilised bones were potentially being purloined from the newly exposed face of our crumbling cliff with every tide, had entered the room.

How does it happen? Who decides? Do they just let the houses fall into the sea? Who are 'they' in this context anyway? Who pays for the demolition? Is there any compensation? What will happen in the future when many more people may be evacuated for environmental reasons? How much warning or notice is given? Where will you go? We had airily answered these questions whenever they were asked, or whenever we asked them ourselves, without ever really knowing the answers. Without the specific circumstances, you can only plan in principle, when the realities and details are infinitely variable, just as they are with death. There are echoes of that oddly fascinating aphorism, 'Man anticipates all, save that which befalls him'.

The prospect of such upheaval seems appalling, yet it stalks the seasons. Perhaps one more summer. Perhaps one more Christmas. Not because we particularly care about Christmas, but because it is a noticeable landmark date, a visible buoy to steer towards, a marker of change in mood and season, a harbinger of imminent spring. One more summer was always the imagined end point, since it would seem sensible for the farm to maximise their rent, and to demolish the house (or houses) in late summer or autumn, perhaps August or September, after the various enterprises of the summer holidays, and after the barley harvest on the ever-diminishing arable land of the farm, but while there was still plenty of daylight and time, and a probability of working in the sunshine.

So, as another August and September crept quietly past, with no mention of any of the e-words, no exceptional erosion events or environmental change necessitating evacuation, we hunkered down for another winter. October was 'unremarkable', a reassuringly uneventful word familiar to anyone who has ever had the opportunity to read a post-mortem report, as in, 'The liver was unremarkable'. 'Unremarkable' roughly equates to no news being good news, nothing to see here, or failure of this particular organ probably didn't cause the demise of the person in this particular body.

In the context of living with coastal erosion, with a cliff edge which has gradually moved from being a hundred-plus paces away when we first began pacing and counting, to fifty paces away in 2015, to twenty paces away in the summer, to really quite near now, 'unremarkable' is good. It is the erosion equivalent of 'in remission', but not the same as 'all clear', and certainly not 'cured'.

In early winter, when the landscape still felt autumnal, on 4th November 2019, there began a sudden phase of deep scouring of the beach at Easton Bavents, exposing great dark lumps of flat peat and signs of reedbeds under the usual sand and shingle. The 'seaside' was suddenly stripped away to reveal a glimpse of our ancient ancestors and their archaeology. The beach level dropped by a metre or so, varying all the way along the coastline but still serving as a warning. The churning waves kept churning, and bit by bit the cliff was nibbled away, noticeably. At that stage the loss of land became alarmingly evident, even to seasoned cliff-crumbling-watchers accustomed to startling change. Where before it was normal, within the unusual definitions of normal in this context, in early November our landscape appreciably altered.

At the top of the cliff, a small tree here, a scruffy bramble hedge line there, fell onto the beach below. Individually these didn't amount to much, but they were mini landmarks: the sentinel tree; the chicken house tree; the bramble hedge; the wild yellow lupin on the edge, and so on.

Local people used to fish for bass (sea bass) off the beach, parking their cars on a particular patch of grass between the houses and the cliff-edge, before they enjoyed a dark night or an afternoon of quiet solitude in private communion with nature and their own thoughts, the whole arrangement a typically rural system of loose connections, official and unofficial permissions, friendships and mild antagonisms, tolerated trespasses, erring and straying, and the exercising of ancient rights to the foreshore. For all the years we lived there, this was a habit of the place.

Then one day, our friend and ally Wild Nature paid a final visit and put an end to this quietly convivial co-operation. The indifferent sea advanced as usual, gouging out trenches at the bottom of the cliff, exposing the ineffective old concrete sea defences which had marked the bottom of the cliff when we first arrived. The waves carved downwards and inwards.

After only a night or two, the erosion destroyed the unofficial farm car park, carving a line diagonally from the now-abandoned chicken shed and run I had once laboured to rebuild from dereliction, to the corner fence post from which all our visual assessments and scientific pacings of land loss over the years had been measured. The erosion sliced across the productive vegetable garden I had created while Giles, my husband, had been on tour with the Army in Afghanistan in 2010. That summer, I lived entirely off that patch of land for six months, eating courgettes, tomatoes, lettuces, herbs and eggs in various combinations, and only going shopping for more varied and interesting ingredients when other people came for 'lunch and a swim' in the horrendously freezing North Sea, or invited themselves to stay for a weekend, as people tend to do if you live in a cottage by the sea.

The unusually active and violent phase of erosion in November 2019 removed in one great swoop all the land, and therefore the time, between us and the sea. But it could not be seen as 'destructive' any more than the work of a beaver could be seen as 'destructive', since it was just nature eating away at a cliff, the cliff to become sand and beach and seabed, everything changed but not absent, like the beaver's leaky dam. There were faint echoes of the basic science learnt at school, 'matter is not created or destroyed, it just takes a different form . . .'.

Coastal science professionals, such as the National Trust's flooding and coastal erosion specialist, Phil Dyke (also a nominative determinism specialist), are always careful to use their preferred phrase for the often personally devastating effects of coastal erosion: 'coastal change'. If ever you overhear someone talking about 'coastal change' rather than (or in relation to) coastal erosion, you can infer that they may well be a coastal or climate scientist. They will probably know better than most what they are talking about, and what is to come in the near and far future. They will also have a good idea about what is realistically possible or wise to do about it, and what is not. Often, the same professional water-people who use the phrase 'coastal change', will also use the phrase 'managed retreat'. What this phrase actually means in practice is that in the foreseeable future, certain places will be overwhelmed, inundated, lost, abandoned.

Easton Bavents is one of the places where 'coastal change' becomes very evident as the cliffs crumble and are washed away. Easton Bavents is often cited as the best location in the UK to find Pliocene mammal remains and fossils (the Pliocene epoch being approximately 5.3 million to 2.5 million years 'BP' ('Before Present', according to the professionals), and the only publicly accessible site where mammal remains from the Norwich Crag can be found. The never-ending process of erosion ironically allows these remains to be simultaneously appreciated while also creating the circumstances in which the fossils and bones are lost and washed away.

The menagerie of interesting animals found in the far cliff at Easton Bavents includes, but is not limited to: gazelle (Gazella anglica), beaver (Trogontherium), walrus (Alachtherium cretsii), horse (Equus robustus) and 'hound', i.e. wolf (Canis etruscus).

The author of The Water Will Come, Jeff Goodell, brought this book to my attention when Venice suffered unusually high *acqua alta* and extreme flooding on and around 13th November 2019, around the time of our own coastal erosion *coup de grâce*. I record these dates here in case they later seem significant in the grander scheme of things. Potential environmental evacuees are a tribe who tend to keep an eye on the global situation, not just their own patch, watching with interest anything untoward that is nature-related, and we share the common camaraderie that all people and peoples do when threatened by a foe beyond our control.

It strikes me that the author of *The Water Will Come* has slightly shot himself in the foot with the title, since the entire thesis and/or hypothesis of the book is encapsulated in those four words. Like *Snakes on a Plane*, you comprehend the entire situation straight away, and also that it is likely to escalate exponentially. In the blink of an eye, the whole scenario seems clear. *The Water Will Come*. Yes, it will. There are maps and computer models, areas described as under threat and those which are due to be formally de-commissioned, but in the title *The Water Will Come* alone, we can immediately grasp the gist of the situation.

The point is, everyone has a 'cliff' coming towards them. Whether in the form of melting ice caps, higher sea levels, flooding and water lying more permanently in our estuaries and flood plains, or some other 'unknown unknown' natural phenomenon, an Act of God, or even the Wrath of God, has visited almost every generation and every century in the past, and will surely visit us, sooner or later. The flooding in Venice coinciding with our exaggerated phase of coastal erosion seemed to be a warning of sorts, of more and greater to come. We might not call these natural phenomena 'the Wrath of God' these days. But it is slightly sobering to note that the phrase 'Act of God', or its fellow, *force majeure*, still enjoys a working conversational usage and valid legal meaning in British law.

However accustomed people may become to living in a landscape defined by perpetual change, whether from coastal erosion or flooding, sandstorms or snow-melt, it is still fascinating and slightly alarming how swiftly such sweeping natural changes can occur, and how vast and permanent their legacy. Many of us on the Suffolk coast have seen storms and tidal surges where a whole dune has disappeared overnight, or a salty lake was created in the reedbeds in one tide, so we are seasoned and habitual change-accepters, normally without much ado.

To return to *Powers of Ten* and *Easternmost Sky* thinking, and the idea of zooming out to see the bigger picture, there is a famous photograph called *The Pale Blue Dot*, taken from Voyager 1 on Valentine's Day in 1970. Within that tiny blue speck is all of us, Earth, home, all our troubles, all our history, all our art and architecture, all our joys, all our collective hoards of string and elastic bands, all our drawers of rarely-used kitchen utensils. This 'vast scale' view of Nature puts our crumbling cliff and our coastal erosion crisis into perspective. From further away, it all seems so trivial, an unnoticed blip in the grand scheme of things.

Unless, just possibly, our erosion, and the apparent recent acceleration of its processes, might be seen alongside the finger in the wind, the dove returning to the ark, the tip of the iceberg... as an early indicator of something greater, something unseen, some as-yet perhaps unimagined 'change'. Then, it might not be so irrelevant. It could be a localised but *important indicator* that, without our witnessing it, would have gone unnoticed. On the other side of the world, a butterfly may be beating its wings.

We are now bona fide environmental evacuees, in the sense that we were eventually and inevitably forced by nature to move from a house in which we would otherwise have lived for the foreseeable future. It is exhausting to refer to Nature with a capital N all the time (as in Byron's 'I love not man the less, but Nature more' etc.), and comforting to tone it down to the more tameable 'nature', although at certain key moments the capital N gesture serves to heighten the sense of Nature's indifferent power, and by contrast, our ludicrous, almost comical, powerlessness in its orbit. Ants.

We knew this would happen, eventually, at some point, just as it is predictable that the people of low-lying areas of Bangladesh and other identifiable places will also be forced by nature to evacuate. For many, it will be devastating. At best, environmental evacuation was, and is, and will be, hugely inconvenient and disruptive for many people, including us, largely because of the unpredictability of the timing. If we all evacuated earlier than we needed to, millions of perfectly decent houses or 'homes' of various kinds would be unnecessarily wasted and abandoned, and that would leave its own unwelcome environmental (and economic) footprint.

We chose to live in an existing house that had been there a long time, knowing that it would 'one day' be taken by coastal erosion, and we didn't mind. We knew we would one day just have to move and adapt, and we did, but the speed and ferocity of the conditions in which we eventually did move were startling, and rang distant alarm bells in my mind about the enormity of nature's sweep.

Fate and Nature played their part in the timing of our eventual environmental evacuation. After 200 years or so of the cottage existing and being lived in full time, all year round and in all weathers, by an unbroken chain of farm workers and long-term tenants like us, it was on 4th December 2019 that we received our formal two months' notice to leave 'by 4th February 2020'. On 5th December

2019 we received verbal notice of demolition and on 6th December 2019 we received written notice of imminent demolition.

Having a 1/365th chance, meaning in racing and bookies' terms long odds of 365 to 1, of any given date being the date of the house's 'death', it was place-appropriate and an incredible coincidence that the date of formal demolition notice happened to be 6th December, St Nicholas's Day, the saint of 'our' church. The church of St Nicholas, Easton Bavents, was once the easternmost church in the whole of the UK, hence Easton Bavents being the easternmost parish, but it fell into the sea in about 1666. It seemed quietly fitting and precise that in the run up to Christmas, St Nicholas's Day should be the exact date when the sea formally claimed the old trinity of cottages.

The Christmas symbolism was further enhanced when three wise men from Southwold came to say goodbye to the cottage where they had been so happy as children in the 1940s and 1950s. They told us how in winter they walked home from school in Southwold, aiming for the cosy lights of the cottage in the distance, following their own little 'bright star' in the east. They also told us, with a degree of amused relish at the memory of rural Suffolk's attempts at high drama, that when Easton Bavents babies were born up there on the cliff, one Mrs Flowerdew was summoned to deliver them. The older children were 'taken for a long walk', up to Covehithe and Benacre, a country mile or three to the north up the beach, with plenty of extra 'time-buying miles' available in the circular walks and ample footpaths and byways of the Benacre estate, depending on the antici-pated ease of delivery of the baby, and perhaps the previous experience of the mother (and Mrs Flowerdew). Although a mere rural anecdote and enjoyable memory, this story was also satisfying as a modern Nativity scene, evidently sent by Fate to occur during the closing-in phase of Advent, when the waiting is over and the Baby Jesus imminently due, in the twenty-first century.

At any rate, it added a certain ancient folkloric appropriateness to our Christmastide plight.

I hadn't felt so moved by the spirit of Christmas since feeling the mysterious weight and hearing the scrunching sound of the full stocking on the end of my bed as a child on Christmas mornings, when the magic still hung in the air. As children at the Old Rec, our stockings were always one of my father's gigantic shooting socks, knitted by Granny. And they still are. These giant stockings of thick wool in earthily rural colours have survived both their creator and their wearer by several decades, and this is after several decades of use. They are still deployed for duty as stockings at Christmas, and they are one of the few objects from childhood that hasn't disappointingly shrunk as we have grown bigger. These socks still seem comically giant.

Who makes the decision that this or that house must be demolished, its people displaced? How does it physically happen? How much notice will you be given? Where will you go? The perennial questions seemed more immediate now. We had naturally kept a weather eye on the presumed time we had left, based on our previous observations and measurements, and conversations with occasional experts who came to make more official measurements on behalf of officialdom. Those habitual pacings-from-the-post showed clearly that the edge of the cliff was coming closer, yet the timescale never seemed 'imminent'. Up until recently the pacings had been done largely out of interest and curiosity rather than for any real need to start actively making plans. Coastal Erosion Prediction is an imprecise science. 'Erosionology' follows unpredictable patterns of prolonged stability followed by intense activity. The official consensus had been until recently that we still had a year or two left.

How it actually happened was quite sudden. It was a Wednesday, 4th December, when we received our formal written two months' notice to leave, which would have been annoying, as long-term tenants of the farm, but was entirely reasonable, legal, and logistically doable. Two months would in theory be plenty of time to find another house via the most obvious property websites and/or tapping up a bit of local knowledge, friends, estates and so on. We might not like whatever house we could find, or its location, but we would find a house or an abode of some kind, and we'd be lucky to be able to move into it, and it would have to do. We rued the fact that our time actively loving the place where we lived was probably over. That privilege already seemed episodic, as if we had experienced by chance something dreamlike and other-worldly, then had been rudely awakened from an ethereal trance, and would now have to reintegrate back into the grit and grind of the normal day.

The following day, on Thursday 5th December, we had verbal notice of demolition and the need to leave, not in two months' time but imminently, now. The Coastal Engineer, who up until now had been a distant figure, talked about but never met, and probably part of what I might refer to as 'officialdom', had apparently paid a final fatal visit and found that we were now officially nine metres from the cliff edge, and as such 'our safety was paramount'. Although we had nothing yet in writing, it was suggested that the

23

house would have to be demolished 'as soon as possible'.

On Friday 6th December, we received our formal written notice of demolition. Later that day it was suggested that we should try and move out 'at the weekend if possible'. Then we were told that the water was going to be cut off.

With the best will in the world and a lifetime of local knowledge, there are not many people or households who could move everything out of their house with a day or two's notice after twelve years. We had had enough foresight to have thinned out some of our clutter, and had stacked boxes in the brick shed. Considering that until recently we had been told we had another year or two, this was quite efficient. But we had also looked after my mother-in-law for the last four years of her life, and had absorbed a whole lifetime's worth of her treasures. While many of these treasures were beautiful, useful things like antiques and paintings, furniture and bookshelves, we were also overwhelmed with china and books and unknown 'old things'. Moving out at two days' notice was not a realistic option. Moving out in two months seemed hard enough. Even with the local knowledge of auction rooms and removals firms, and with a fleet of friends' horseboxes accessible as a last a resort, it would be a mammoth task to pack and move in such short order. Plus, we had nowhere to go.

It is worth mentioning that we were in what I am the first to admit is the enormously privileged position of having family (my mother) living not far away, in a remote old house with outbuildings including a barn in which we could have put at least some of our furniture and other things. These spatial privileges are slightly more hard-won than they might at first appear as, since my father died in 2003, and longer if you count working house-sitting holidays since

1997, I have been helping my mother remain in her own home (my childhood home), by on-and-off doing many jobs that other people might assume were done by paid workers: feeding sheep, lambing, planting, pruning, picking, strimming, amateur building maintenance, painting outbuilding doors, and so on. The enjoyable 'job' of keeping my mother remaining *in situ* at the Old Rec also involves helping to host and man various annual events held there, most notably a garden open day and a week of cricket. Nevertheless, I wholly concur with the view that access to such space is itself a great privilege, even though I do not personally own one brick or acre of the Old Rec and its curtilage.

Moving into the Old Rec as a permanent solution to our imminent erosion-enabled homelessness was not a realistic option. Even if eventually we might need to do so, it would only ever be if we became specifically necessary and helpful to my mother (for instance in her dotage), at her invitation, perhaps with me working the kitchen garden and growing vegetables for the comrades in the newly-formed family commune. We had to find a house, a lorry and storage space, and soon.

I searched Rightmove, which to be fair must be praised as a saintly presence at such times, as it immediately yielded several perfectly liveable houses within our chosen area and price range, if not a single one with any sense of remoteness. One cottage was up a track, but with the landlord living cheek-by-jowl next door, and with quite a number of unusually draconian rules. This was by far the most appealing, and I made an appointment to view it.

I also contacted the local estate offices (as in country estates), all of whom would have cottages and farmhouses in various sizes, with the added appeal of likely remoteness, but probably would not have any available. I had long ago put us on notional waiting lists, but without a clear idea of when we would need to move, and it seemed unlikely that this fatalistic foresight would ever bear fruit at the time we needed it to. People in estate cottages tend to be long-term tenants, and estates tend to bend over backwards to keep their long-term tenants for many years.

One of the more specific ways of attracting and keeping long-term tenants is allowing (or perhaps encouraging) all manner of livestock and gardening eccentricities, hence the many dogs, ducks, hens, geese, guinea fowl, ponies, donkeys and so on seen in the gardens and small paddocks around these estates, although Sandringham famously has a 'no cats' policy on all its tenancies. The success of all country estates has always been their focus on *the long term*, so the quirks of long-term tenants tend to be tolerated.

With Benacre, Somerleyton, Henham and Sotterley estate offices alerted, I eyed up alternative rural removals transport ideas in more detail. Horseboxes, farm vehicles and possibly manpower were available in theory through friends. At an absolute pinch, perhaps we could call on the Household Cavalry, off-duty (Giles being ex-HCav). Coming out of our farm track at Easton Bavents preoccupied by such vehicular thoughts, I had to wait while an enormous Peddars Pigs lorry hurtled past on the road, and I bore it in mind as a potential removals van. This is what adapting to change meant in practice. I was already mentally assessing pig lorries and seeing alternative uses for all sorts of things.

In the not-too-distant future, I genuinely believe that we might have to collectively become more adaptable, because of unseen natural forces, probably connected with climate change and rising sea levels, but also possibly connected with unknown unknowns. Adapting to change might turn out to be the defining feature of the human condition and the cultural landscape in the twenty-first century. I genuinely foresee a time in the coming decades when great events of Nature may cause us to have to put aside petty political differences and work together, valuing both the intellectual expertise and the physical competence that may save us and get us out of trouble. Climate scientists and removals lorry drivers may rule the roost in this quite easily imaginable future.

For example, suppose an ethical vegan lives in a house that is flooded out and declared uninhabitable, whether for a few months or forever, and finds themselves offered help with the physical moving of belongings out of the house by a helpful livestock farmer, I can see a time when it might be appropriate for the vegan to set aside their sincerely-held principles for a day or two over a weekend, allow the cattle-truck man and his lorry to help physically to move their 'stuff' to another house, and then on Monday return to the moral position of being an ethical vegan, without either party having compromised their philosophical view of life in the interim.

Similarly, I can imagine another flooding situation where a person who is normally a hunt saboteur might temporarily accept help from a fleet of horseboxes laid on by the hunt jungle telegraph (e.g. the hunt secretary and an associated email list of local practical people), and end up saying thank you very much hunt people, through graciously gritted teeth. This is exactly the kind of co-operation that already happens in rural areas, and which could potentially become more widespread and normal in the future. Whether climate-related or otherwise, there are many likely scenarios that might force us to temporarily abandon superficial differences, and make for the literal and metaphorical higher ground of helpful co-operation, amid dangers natural or man-made, known or as-yet unknown.

These scenarios seem not only realistic, but almost inevitable. In times of genuine crisis, such as being overwhelmed by unusual flooding, or something else unseen, we might suddenly realise that it is a modern luxury to be too fussy about who we accept help from, or what we choose to eat.

For instance, when I eventually moved out of London to return home to Suffolk, many years ago, I hired a white van and two men instead of a legitimate removals firm. These two were perfectly charming, and very amusing company, but it was only as we rattled home up the A12 that I realised they were both reformed burglars, recently released from several years of detention at Her Majesty's pleasure, the number of years suggesting it must have been quite a serious crime. It turned out that they had tried to pull off a not-very-great train robbery on the way to Devon, and had been caught. The fact that they were now reformed burglars operating a van-and-man service would probably be seen by a certain kind of vicar as proof of the power of redemption, but to me they were just two really strong and helpful removals blokes. I also learnt that they had a cousin who was the artist who shredded all his belongings in the C&A shop on Oxford Street.

Back to our coastal erosion predicament: at about the time of our formal demolition order, I met for the first time the Coastal Engineer, an almost mythical person who had haunted our time on the cliff, but who had not until now made his presence felt as a real human being. Bob, as it turned out, was a lovely, friendly and cheerful man. Clad in the ubiquitous hi-viz that ironically renders such people invisible in urban areas, Bob came to recce our cliff, again. This time he brought with him someone from Anglian Demolition. I recognised Anglian Demolition as being the firm which had demolished the previous house on the edge of the cliff in 2015, and who had genuinely left no trace at all, not even footprints. I hold Anglian Demolition in the highest regard.

The sight of the Anglian Demolition logo on a fleece was oddly chilling. *The demolition process is actually beginning, with this moment*, I thought, as I offered Bob and Mr Demolition a brew. We made convivial arrangements for when it would be convenient for Anglian Demolition to do an asbestos survey. This is the banal reality of the process. Just as 'saving lives' is usually just a sequence of wholly admirable but routinely rehearsed actions in an ambulance at the side of a road, so the wrecking ball is often less dramatic than it sounds. That is probably why crowds and TV crews gather when an MP is bidden to press the red button on the demolition of a distant power station cooling tower. There is actually 'a moment', and something to see.

While pondering the presence of asbestos, and the oddness of our tenancy agreement specifying that we should leave the chimneys swept and the windows clean, with no acknowledgement of the demolition, Fate came to the rescue in the form of Edward Vere Nicoll, who I now think of as the patron saint of housing, 'Saint Edward of Vere Nicollshire', from the Benacre estate office. They had a cottage empty, between tenants, and would I like to meet him there? I certainly would, and I did, and we very nearly moved into a village cottage on the edge of Wrentham. Plenty of space for all my mother-in-law's stuff. Outbuildings and big shed. Perfect. Keys were allowed on loan before the paperwork had been done.

We were saved.

Saint Edward followed me home to Easton Bavents to see the progress of our erosion as it would affect the erosion of land at Benacre, and he was appalled. He had been under the impression that the coastal erosion had been relatively stable up there recently. As it had been. But not any more.

We began to imagine life in this perfectly decent but nevertheless in-a-village cottage, and planned to make maximum use of the smaller bedroom at the back, from whose window we would still be able to see over the farmland and towards the open skies where the reedbeds meet the beach and the sea. From there we would no longer be able to see the sea, but we would still feel it. We would know it was all still out there, perhaps no more than a mile away, but seemingly a world away: the beach, the bitterns booming in the reedbeds, the sand martins nesting in the cliffs, the eerie cries of the oystercatchers and sandpipers, the larks 'ascending' over the arable, the seals, the sunrises, the sunsets.

Then another miracle happened, as in a passing conversation about when and how we might move in, another cottage was mentioned, Corner Cottage. Corner Cottage was apparently smaller, but right on the coast among the wild things, still vulnerable to coastal erosion but a whole field away from the edge, not nine metres. Corner Cottage is estimated to still be here until about 2055. All Benacre cottages seem to conform approximately to the old-fashioned definition of a cottage as a 'small dwelling with enough land to support the occupant', in that they have disproportionately large gardens, and brick outbuildings.

For miles around, the black and white heraldic Talbot dog 'passant' appears on various signs and gateposts, and the doors of all the Benacre estate buildings are painted what you might call Benacre Green. Some might see this as a bit feudal, in a bad way, but the general impression in real life on the ground is of mutually beneficial co-operation, of land being well managed and people being employed, to the visible advantage of the whole area, or at least the 7,000 acres of good farmland and important protected nature reserves that still form our collective local place.

We shuffled our paperwork and our keys, and pulled our fingers out with the packing and chaos, amid the unexpected interest of the press, so that on Friday 20th December, exactly two weeks from the day of our demolition notice, we moved in to Corner Cottage. That evening, on the way to a Christmas party, we stupidly got stuck in a flood in the dark and had to be rescued by the fire brigade. We had been warned by email that Water Lane was (unsurprisingly) flooded, but as we had spent the day loading boxes onto lorries in a high wind and some lashing rain, accidentally on telly while doing this, we hadn't read it and didn't know. This was a day greatly enhanced by helpful and competent men, and later an AA woman, with variously appropriate vehicles. These are the people whose jobs really matter, and who quietly get us all out of trouble.

On Christmas morning we went to church at Covehithe at 9am, and there were twenty-five people there, out on the cliff in a little church within an enormous ruin, in what many would see as the middle or edge of nowhere. We all agreed that we liked to 'get church out of the way early', before dispersing to our houses, great and small, and to the familiar comforts of Christmas and the Queen.

Meanwhile, unbeknown to us, somewhere in China, a bat caused a faint whiffling in the wind . . .

Demolition and dismantling

He who has once been happy is for aye
Out of destruction's reach . . .

W. SCAWEN BLUNT (1840–1922)

1

JANUARY

What happens when a house dies and gives up its soul? Who mourns it? What makes us love some houses to a degree disproportionate to the quality of their architecture? How can an inanimate pile of bricks or stones, arranged just so, inspire in us such affection? What is left behind?

The Easternmost House was a well-known if unspectacular local landmark. Visible from afar, stuck out there on the cliff, it was mourned by many people. In the process, it gave up not only its 'soul', but also some unexpected stories and little insights into its history and its occupants. People came out of the woodwork, as the local jungle telegraph rumbled and word spread that the life of the house on the edge had finally and inevitably come to an end.

The genuine affection shown to the house was much greater than you would ever imagine for such an architecturally unremarkable building, not even listed Grade II. Built of local red brick and 'blue' (black) pantiles, it was without any notable value as a 'heritage asset' (as planning and listed building officialdom puts it), and nor did it have any particular architectural merit apart from its admirable but ordinary original fireplaces, doors, stairs and cupboards. Its original windows had long been replaced by some weatherproof aberrations. But the cottage shrugged off such insults.

By an uncanny coincidence of timing, given that the house could reasonably have been expected to have had perhaps three more years, in the event its final summer was a kind of last hurrah. The cottage was oddly in the media spotlight for almost certainly the only time in its life. The wild yellow lupins burst forth in huge exuberant bushes, bigger than they had ever been before. The wild yellow lupins were descended from a single tiny bush I had rescued from the edge a few years earlier, and they operated on a strange three-year cycle, from being small green bushes, to vast flowering bushes then finally in the third year, a sad woody mess of hollow brittle death and dry kindling. Perhaps those unusually exuberant wild lupins that summer were trying to tell us something, a portent of what was to come, a glorious celebration of life and colour just before the whole scene turned to sand. But we didn't know that then.

Because of the book, there had been a surprising number of press articles, reviews, radio interviews etc., in national newspapers and magazines like *Country Life* as well as our local familiars like *The East Anglian Daily Times* and BBC Radio Suffolk. This meant that people near and far who had known the house from long ago instantly recognised it, felt emotionally invested in it, and wanted to revisit it for old time's sake, all through the summer. A few keen readers also wanted to see the house of their imaginations standing there in real life, and some came looking for it.

While the ongoing coastal erosion that characterised the house and its situation was in the zoomed out scale of *Easternmost Sky* thinking, the detail of the individuals who came to visit was very much 'zoomed in', like so many friends of the *Powers of Ten* picnic man. The first of the summer visitors was John Uden, the son of the head cowman who had been photographed with a calf in front of the cottage. John's father, Geoffrey Uden (actually Walter Geoffrey, Uden pronounced Yudon) had seen active service in the Arctic Convoys and had as a distraction daydreamed of working on a farm one day, preferably with cows, ideally in Suffolk.

When the war was over, he became the head cowman up on the cliff at Easton Bavents. A black and white photograph shows him standing proudly showing off a black and white Friesian calf in front of the cottage in which he and we had happily lived, and which was about to be demolished. He is dressed smartly in tweed with a collar and tie and a kind of baker-boy's hat. You can sense that the taking of the photograph is a bit of an occasion and a nod to a productive future, strong man and young calf smartly turned out and formally posed. Yet it is also utterly normal, a glimpse of an everyday moment in a time long gone, but in the place right in front of us in the here and the now.

I stood on the exact spot where the cowman stood, and it was so normal, and yet so oddly profound to be standing literally where his boots had stood perhaps seventy years before. He seems to have a compassionate kind of pride in his job and the calf in his care, and he was head cowman for twelve years. The cottage was then a tied cottage attached to the dairy job, and coincidentally his tenure there was the same length of time as ours turned out to be. Evidently he had good reason to be proud of the childhood he gave his son John, too.

A little later came Ivan Moore, a childhood friend of John's, the two reunited after 58 years by the magic of email and my little cardboard notebook of 'book visitors'. As the 'book visitors' amounted to only these two at that stage, it seemed hardly necessary to keep much of a record, but I am glad I did, as the memories and laughter that echoed around the house and garden in that summer were also the echoes of their everyday lives there in the 1940s and 1950s, edited highlights brought to us as if live on air, separated only by the distance of time, and made all the more fascinating for their ordinary workaday quality.

'We were never indoors.'

Being outside seemed to be the main theme of their childhood recollections, and in that alone, there is a significant distance in experience from many, if not most, modern children. There seemed to be several children at any one time at Easton Bavents, numbers and names vague and unspecified, but with various brothers and others having been born there, in the cottage where we had all lived. In the practicalities of the workings of the house, the children were put to work almost as a recreation.

'All we had to heat us was an open fire.'

'We were always dragging driftwood off the beach for the fire and getting the bow saw out.'

'Water was from a well pumped by a windmill on the farm.'

'The east wind was "the lazy wind". It doesn't go round the house, it goes through it.'

'That wind would cut you in two.'

'The Dutch Barn on Ferry Road was run by a Dutch

36

landlady, who interpreted a message in a bottle which landed on the beach at Easton Bavents. We replied and sent it back.'

To John and Ivan, who were still scallywag children and not cool pre-adult teenagers at the time, the beach at Covehithe was a tempting place to explore since it was well known to be bristling with live ordnance, unexploded bombs, unidentified metal objects and the general mess and paraphernalia of war, of unexpected attack and improvised defence. Even now, well into the twenty-first century, these items are still occasionally found exposed by the scouring tides. The beach is closed, the bomb or whatever-it-was detonated, and a short description of the specific type of missile or mine appears in the *East Anglian Daily Times* and on Twitter. There still remains a hint of genuine danger on this crumbling coast. Its deceptive calm seems as fragile as life itself.

Naturally, the Easton Bavents boys thought it great sport to scamper down the beach to Covehithe (a relatively dangerous venture even without a war, haunted as it was, and is, by caves, fissures, cliff-falls and bogs) to see what they could find. One day, they found what turned out to be a distress flare on the beach, and, boys being boys, pulled out the pin.

'It went off like a rocket!'

'Well it would, wouldn't it?'

'Then we ran away before they caught us.'

As John and Ivan told us this story they reflected, with the sober hindsight of those approaching the autumn of life, that at the time they had no idea what the 'rocket' was, or what it might do when they pulled out the pin.

'It's a miracle we stayed alive.'

Another 'book visitor' to the house in the summer of

2019 was John Barber, aged 93, who for forty years had been the Southwold Town Crier.

In 1943 John and his father had built a 'copper' in the brick outbuilding at Easton Bavents, and having seen an article about the house, he had come up to see if it was still there. And it was! In detail, the copper was an ingenious and practical design. A large iron bowl with copper pipes coiled around it was set above a fire, and the whole contraption was supported by a brick, concrete and render construction, the visible surfaces of which were unexpectedly painted in Hockney-esque bright turquoise. Its purpose was washing clothes, an ingenious if slightly primitive washing machine.

The time it must have taken to light the fire, heat the water, wash, rinse, and dry it all on the line, assuming it wasn't raining, would fizzle our twenty-first-century molly-coddled brains – and I speak as one who went to a boarding school at the age of ten, in a (then) remote country house known as 'NFL' and a Spartan establishment even by the notoriously eccentric standards of British boarding schools, where we had to wash our own clothes and wring them out through a Dickensian mangle in a cellar. Although, to be scrupulously fair, I vaguely remember that this unusually arcane character-building regime was gradually modernised after my first term.

John Barber's delight that the copper was still there was palpable, and with his visit came a mine of gentle wisdom and local history, quite at odds with his shouty Town Crier alter ego.

During the war (meaning WW2 but probably a comparable scene might apply to WW1 and even earlier conflicts), the farm at Easton Bavents was a restricted area, with a pass needed at the gate to the north from Southwold, out of bounds as the site of a radar station, with a listening station and watch room looking out to sea. No photographs were allowed, for secrecy. Oddly, given the rules, there is a black and white photograph of this scene, in which the Easternmost House sits quietly in the background, observing the observers, listening to the listeners, seeing it all and not telling its secrets. The bucolic farm scene now so familiar to us appears in the photo as a bleak and treeless clifftop landscape bristling with radio towers.

Along with the everyday industry of domestic life, and more than two hundred harvests, the little house has witnessed generations of human beings, stoically but seamlessly adapting to change, in whatever form it comes to their fatally ordained era.

'The meadow had an air show.'

'Henham Park was full of troops waiting for D-Day.'

The same kinds of unseen landscape memories will be lying dormant in the minds of older rural people all over the countryside of Britain, Europe and beyond. These memories lie unobtrusively and forever in the fields in front of us, unknown but not undone. No generation can know the precise form of change to which it will have to adapt, but we can be fairly certain that sooner or later, something big will come along, and that it will test us. And if it doesn't, we should understand in advance that it is overdue, and we should make ourselves ready to greet it, and to adapt.

After the war, John and Ivan enjoyed an idyllic rural childhood on the farm and the beach at Easton Bavents, in which they appeared to live in a perpetual real-life Ladybird Book, and in recalling these halcyon days, in the cottage and in the garden in the sunny summer of 2019, they revealed an improbable connection of the Easternmost House with what might be called Popular Culture.

Rural Suffolk in general, and Easton Bavents in particular, is not renowned for its connections to, or interest in, Popular Culture and associated celebrity credentials, but it turns out that in the 1950s a Jamaican artist called Joe James came to live at the Easternmost House (specifically No. 3, the end nearest the sea). According to John and Ivan, Joe James had 'about nine children', one of whom is David James, who used to be the England goalkeeper, and more recently appeared on Strictly Come Dancing. A bona fide celeb connected with Easton Bavents and the Easternmost House. Unheard of, but there it is. And there is more.

Joe James apparently came to Suffolk to paint, and at Easton Bavents he found the physical and mental distance from the general mass of humanity that he had been seeking.

'He was sort of a wise man.'

'He was looking for isolation, to paint in peace.'

'He was forever trying to capture the movement of the wind over the barley.'

'My mother used to bake him cakes.'

'He was almost the only black person in Suffolk.'

John and Ivan then showed us more black and white photos of the farm in the past, this time of Joe James and his family, and John and Ivan and their families, black and white, old and young, all living in harmony out in the sticks, at a time in the 1950s shortly after the arrival of HMT *Empire Windrush*, when in London and elsewhere, houses available to let were allegedly and infamously bedecked in signs saying something along the lines of: NO BLACKS, NO DOGS, NO IRISH. But not in Suffolk. Not at Easton Bavents. Not at the Easternmost House. Here, Joe James painted in peace.

There is still a sense of peace and isolation along much

of the east coast of England, and especially along the eerie coast of Suffolk between Easton Bavents and Covehithe. This makes it a safe haven for wildlife, in fur, feather, fin and sealskin. Yet there is no doubt that in the last fifty years or so, perhaps the post-war era, we have lost a great deal of our wildlife and our nature in general: wildflowers, bees, insects, and more.

John and Ivan, ever the founts of lost local knowledge, gave us an insight into the concept of what in modern eco-parlance is called Shifting Baseline Syndrome (meaning that current generations think we have plenty of wildlife because we are only comparing the numbers now with what we first knew, rather than with the greater numbers of longer ago) as applied to the Easternmost House, and specifically in relation to the breeding of storks.

'Storks used to nest on the chimney pots, only of these cottages, nowhere else on the farm.'

'Apparently they came from Belgium.'

'Whether the chimney pots were of the right specification . . .'

'We should stop making helium balloons. Helium is a finite resource and useful for other things.'

Sometimes John and Ivan's conversations went off on tangents, or they followed their own trains of thought without really seeming to listen or respond to the other, yet always within a sentence or three they were utterly harmonious, so that they became almost one being: John-and-Ivan.

The point about helium is valid, but more interesting is their insistence that storks nested on the chimney pots, specifically those of the Easternmost House. In the spring of 2020 there was a great hullaballoo in ecological and rewilding circles as introduced storks (or 'reintroduced

41

storks') were nesting and breeding on the Knepp estate in Sussex, home of the book *Wilding* by Isabella Tree. The Knepp storks were deemed to be the first to breed in the UK for six hundred years. *What about the Easton Bavents storks?* I thought. But then I realised there was no photographic evidence of our storks, and we were reliant only on the words and memories of John-and-Ivan. Besides, they never actually mentioned seeing stork chicks, they were only implied, not least by the annual return of the storks to the accidentally stork-specified chimneys of the Easternmost House.

It was against this backdrop that we received our notice of demolition on 6th December 2019. There were so many 'sleeping dogs' about the place, that time and nature had let lie, that it seemed like an intervention of Fate, or some unseen gods of the earth, that in the last ever summer of the existence of this little house and its place, something had happened, a book, that disturbed the sleeping soil of its memory, just in time to turn it over, and let the *genius loci* of the house, the place and the people, be preserved for posterity, in minds, in print and in the Bodleian Library.

Knowing a little more of the emotional context, it now seems absolutely natural that John and Ivan and others wanted to pay their last respects to the house in person, and say goodbye. Bearing in mind that this was an ordinary, albeit sturdy and attractive, row of three Victorian cottages, originally built by the Benacre estate for farm labourers, this outpouring of affection seems remarkable, if you only see what you could see in a photograph. But if you simultaneously 'see' all that there is to see, a tiny fragment of which is hinted at in the glimpses and memories above, then the local outpouring of love for the Easternmost House seems entirely rational. From the zoomed out perspective of Earth seen from even the relatively parochial orbit of 1 million kilometres (10^{+9} metres) in *Powers of Ten*, we are invisible, seemingly non-existent. Yet here we all are, living our deeply intricate lives and profound experiences.

What inspires affection in a building is not its architecture, or at least not *only* its architecture but an emotional combination of location, memory and association. This is what gives a house a 'soul', and once an entity has a soul, it has the capacity to die, to give up its soul, and to be mourned.

Because of the local press interest in the imminent demolition, which was picked up by the national press including a half-page story with a photograph in *The Sunday Times*, an unexpected following of the fate of the little house on the cliff developed among what might be called the Geographical Community, and in particular a subset, which might be called the Coastal Erosion Community. Although the life of the cottage was for two centuries 'an everyday story of country life', and an intensely local one at that, the coastal erosion aspect of its identity has been picked up on and is now followed by those with a global and scientific outlook, people studying climate change, archaeology and projected sea levels.

The little cottage seemed to be blowing a tiny warning whistle into the wind.

This series of events in the summer of 2019 has conspired to cast the cottage in the role of a forerunner or flag-bearer, drawing attention not only to the coastal erosion along the Suffolk coast, and the huge losses soon to come, but to the wider issues of climate change, rising sea levels and the fact that we are all at the mercy of the unpredictable forces of

Nature. Be cavalier in your relationship with Nature at your peril, the little cottage seemed to be saying.

The precise moment of any death is difficult to pin down, but for the cottage it was probably the moment when I tweeted a grey-skies photograph of the Easternmost House, taken from the usual spot on the cliff where I have taken many similar for comparison, just after receiving our written demolition notice and just before lowering the first pile of old copies of *Country Life* into the blue recycling wheelie-bin.

When that first copy of *Country Life* was moved from its usual place, that was the exact moment when the house was no longer being lived in normally: the beginning of the end.

The demolition of the Easternmost House began in early January 2020. We were giving a visiting friend a New Year mini-tour of Suffolk when we noticed, from afar, the first pantiles being taken off the roof to the front of the house, the part nearest the sea. The physical process had begun. The emotional experience of having to leave before we would naturally want to, and then seeing, demolished and broken, a house where we had known a happiness beyond contentment, I had rehearsed many times before, not least in imagining in detail the scenes of destruction, and writing them into a book, long before the demolition was actually happening in front of my eyes. I was used to it. It was other people who were upset by the scene and the loss of the house to the sea.

The financial loss of the cottages to the farm was considerable, in the loss of an asset and of three rental incomes (two of them ours, the third by then empty). However foreseeable this was, it was still a blow, especially as the farm also loses several acres of arable land every year, off the edge and onto the beach. *But* when articles pointed out that 'luckily' we only rented the house, I felt inclined to stand on my imaginary soapbox, climb the stairs to my little pulpit, and point out that luck had little to do with it, since when I had considered buying two houses since lost to the sea, I had taken account of the risks, the likely length of time we would have there, costs, benefits, and so on, and *I decided not to* buy the pair of houses on the edge, not even at one-tenth of their normal value. I had entertained thoughts of us living in one side, the landward side, and letting out the seaward side as a holiday let, thus making back my money and then eventually moving on when the sea claimed us. It would be fun, I thought. Better than working in an office anyway.

The point is, I didn't do it, because the erosion and potential loss were foreseeable, and too much.

I thought pragmatically that I couldn't risk losing sixteen metres in one tide, as had happened at Benacre a mile or two to the north, in case that perfect storm happened in my first year (and I also wisely left Giles out of these reckless financial calculations).

Many and various warnings, from reed-cutters and extra-sensory perception to ghosts of the past, may have helped me, but in the end it was a hard-nosed and realistic series of pragmatic business decisions which caused us to end up as tenants in the farm cottages with no financial loss. My savings had bought a more reliable cottage inland, with a tenant ensconced. In the event, if I had bought the pair of houses that I had considered buying on the cliff, we would have had twelve years, which was slightly more than I had allowed for. But it would have been anxiety-making and sad to have lived with that constant risk with no safety net, and then to have had to leave. So I didn't do it. It wasn't luck. It was judgement, of my own financial means, my emotional resilience, my desire for a lifestyle job and so on, weighed up against real and present danger, and obvious risk.

This, above all, I would pass on as a warning to anyone considering buying or renting any house in the twenty-first century, blighted by either flood or coastal erosion or any other adversity: PLAN AHEAD.

Heed the title of that book, *The Water Will Come*. Have an exit strategy.

What I had not quite taken into account was the degree to which I would have to relinquish access to the farm as soon as we had left the Easternmost House, while it was being demolished, and within our legal time of tenure, when normally we would have still been living out our two months' notice in the house (i.e. up to 4th February 2020). It is obvious that as I no longer lived there, there was no reason for me to be there. Therefore I shouldn't be there. At all. Not even to photographically record the demolition, for the benefit of the people of the future, as yet unknown.

At low tide and in normal circumstances, it is locally habitual and permissible to walk along the top of the cliff. The informal local fishing and parking arrangement would no doubt continue in due course, on the site of the ex-garden perhaps. But not when there is a construction site Heras fence across the track, with a sign saying clearly: DANGER. KEEP OUT. DEMOLITION IN PROGRESS. In the act of being there and photographing the demolition of the house and garden, I was probably now a trespasser. Having grown up in the country with land-dependent family and friends, and an understanding of what might be called traditional

46

rural values, this was no small sin. I was well aware that with rights come responsibilities and with privilege, duty. The land is not ours.

Nevertheless, as no one seemed to mind, and I didn't abuse the situation or visit very often (plus we would have still had several weeks of legal tenure to run if we hadn't already moved out), I did take a satisfyingly thorough sequence of demolition and dismantling photographs, mostly from the same habitual spot on the cliff, but also with some more haunting and ephemeral images. I'm glad I did.

The demolition photographs were not just for me, but for the people of the past and the future. People as yet unborn might one day be interested in the house and the place, this lost village, the UK's erstwhile easternmost parish. The situation was bigger than the farm and the present tense. Just as I had been fascinated so recently by the unearthing of the knowledge of John Barber, and the black and white memories and photos shown to me by John-and-Ivan, perhaps the people of the future might be interested in the Easternmost House and its last days. Its interiors, its inhabitants, its garden, its crops, its wild lupins may be seen as mere social history curios, but are nevertheless recorded for future scrutiny. More significant may be its place in the wider world, the world of coastal erosion and climate change, of *Easternmost Sky* thinking and *Powers of Ten*, of warning.

Who are we to know why the people of the future might be interested? As it happened, I was the only person to make any proper record of the situation at all. The same was true when the old radar station was demolished. I felt slightly vindicated for attempting to communicate with the people of the future.

47

The demolition of the Easternmost House was a careful exercise in dismantling and architectural salvage. Brick by cleaned brick, pantile by stacked pantile, rafter after rafter, room by room, the demolition days ticked by. D-days with no death or drama, just 'things' being moved from one place to another. Bead-and-butt doors were unhinged. Suffolk latches were saved. Mantelpieces were carefully propped against a wall. The little house gradually became less itself and more a stack of building materials, just as we and our sense of 'self' would be transformed by the process of death, from being a person, to being less of a person, to eventually becoming 'an assemblage of organic matter'. *I was not, I have been, I am not, I do not mind . . .* as the Epicurean epitaph puts it.

The last person from the past to visit the house before it was demolished was Brenda Moore. She had lived up on the cliff as a child in the 1950s and 1960s. Hers was another idyllic country childhood like John-and-Ivan's by the sounds of it, but a little later than theirs. Brenda told a little story about how her father had found a yellow sou'wester on the beach, of the sort worn by fishermen or lifeboat men (and they were always men in those days) in those dramatic stormy sea rescue pictures advertising the noble work of the RNLI. Brenda's father had brought the yellow sou'wester back from the beach (it still counting as beach litter, even if it was the noble litter of the genuine seafarer) and had hung it on a nail on the wall in the brick shed.

Every year, for years afterwards, a wren made its nest in the sou'wester on the wall. Whether it was the same wren, or several generations of wrens, we cannot know. But all hail the sou'wester wrens.

Earth to earth

All my possessions for a moment of time.

QUEEN ELIZABETH I (1533–1603), *last words*

2

FEBRUARY

If an inanimate stack of bricks and pantiles assembled in the form of a house can inspire affection, what of paintings, furniture and other 'things'? 'Things' are a mirror of our culture and collective histories, often the fruits of a supreme effort of human creativity, yet at some level they don't matter at all. Seen from afar, through the *Powers of Ten* lens zooming out, things of great beauty and cultural significance to us in the here and now, seem to cease to exist at all. Yet if we were to zoom *in*, to the *Powers of Ten* microscopic level, human genius would be revealed in every brush stroke, every molecule of pigment, every dust particle of carved stone.

Every object carries different meanings and powers depending on the pair of eyes through which it is viewed. A cathedral is a barn. The altar, a table. A wooden cross, firewood. Statues, rubble. Books can be bricks, insulation or fuel. Furniture and paintings, a boat with canvas sails. 'Culture' renders the human eye a kaleidoscope, distorting and colouring everything we view. What I see, you may not see. I see a noble depiction of a horse. You see a vehicle of historical oppression. I see an amusing pair of china dogs. You see kitsch tat. I see useful brown furniture. You see ugly old stuff. All of the above with the caveat, 'or vice versa', as to which of us sees what.

The demolition of the Easternmost House, and our hasty emergency evacuation, caused us to downsize from six bedrooms (albeit only two of decent size) to two bedrooms. We had a choice of two cottages on the Benacre estate, both of which by a miracle happened to be between tenants at the time. We sacrificed space in favour of beauty of location. 'Things' had to go.

To set the scene physically and culturally, imagine zooming out a bit from X, that lunch table in our former garden on the cliff. The Benacre estate is about 7,000 acres of productive farmland and assorted wildlife habitat, woodland, scrub, reedbed, beach etc., at more or less the easternmost edge of the UK, owned by the Gooch family in a direct line since 1746. Part of the estate is marked as Benacre National Nature Reserve. Benacre is perennially as dramatically affected by coastal erosion as the Easton Bavents farm and site of the Easternmost House are and were, if not more so. The estate has a number of tenanted farms, plus a home farm, and approximately a hundred cottages, farmhouses and so on, to rent to long-term tenants. The Benacre landscape is a pleasingly varied mosaic of land types and land uses, but from a zoomed out perspective it is a large enough acreage and productive enough land to be considered agriculturally important. Benacre land produces a significant amount of human food.

The attractive brick farm buildings and cowsheds at Easton Bavents, including the now-vanished Easternmost

House, are recognisably of the same architectural family as the cottage we live in now. It was wise to sell the most distant and most quickly disappearing part of the estate when death duties funds were needed in the 1920s. Much of that land was long ago lost to the sea.

A larger cottage on the edge of the village or a smaller cottage on the edge of everything, overlooking barley, beach and reedbeds, was to us a straightforward choice. The beach at Covehithe and Benacre is the wild and empty kind of beach, not a 'seaside-y' one, plus there is an array of ancient byways and footpaths across Benacre land, inland. Bigger landscape, smaller house, fewer people. This patchwork of different habitats is home to a diverse range of human animals alongside the many non-human kinds, each with their own varying degrees of domestication, boldness, timidity and wildness, yet together a coherent and co-operative flock.

The convivial families of free-range outdoor pigs who are our immediate neighbours in the wider landscape have been established here for long enough to have blocks and strips of woodland named after them: Hog Pen Belt, and so on. Stealthy populations of foxes leave their invisible scents about the place, clearly declaring their presence, and shriek at dusk. There is a healthy population of brown hares, sometimes openly lolloping over the crops, but more often crouching to the ground in a manner to which you adjust, to become good at spotting them. A white pheasant lives in the fields next to the cottage with a Spitfire weathervane. Roe deer and muntjac are ever-present, leaving neat footprints in the sandy farm tracks and footpaths or leaping across our path unexpectedly. Warren House, marked on the larger-scale Ordnance Survey maps, hints at a long-established population of rabbits and the historic job of 'warrener' in the past. The number of barn owls and other birds of prey regularly seen over the more open land suggests a healthy population of mice and field voles.

A bang on the back door revealed a cock pheasant being chased by a stoat. Weasels often skit across the roads and tracks, so the local mustelid population retains its reputation as the beady-eyed little boss of predation and survival. The famous photograph known on the Internet as #Weaselpecker and turned into a million memes was actually a brilliant photo of a weasel *attacking* a woodpecker, not 'taking a ride' on a woodpecker, and not 'cute'.

Everywhere, all year round, there are rooks, crows and pigeons, helping themselves to seeds and crops. You could write a kind of crop-predation Shipping Forecast about it. Rooks over the rapeseed oil. Crows over the carrots. Pigeons over the peas.

One for the rook, one for the crow, one to rot and one to grow, an old farming saying goes.

Our ancestors evidently allowed for three times as much seed to be lost as they might have expected to harvest, to cater for the thieving onslaughts of what used to be called vermin. The four-and-twenty blackbirds baked in the pie in *Sing a Song of Sixpence* may have been rooks, since country people used to routinely eat rook pie as part of their sustainable pest-control system. As corvids are scavengers, this sits slightly uneasily with the golden rule of unorthodox wild meat-eating: never eat a carnivore. But both rooks and the country people eating them seem to have survived.

There must be badgers in the woods, because we have found the skins and spines of 'empty' hedgehogs on a sandy track nearby, a modus operandi which is almost certainly the work of a badger. The sad sight of a roadkill badger, usually on the side of the A12 (Suffolk's nearest equivalent to a motorway), is noticeably more common than it used to be. This suggests that badger numbers are rising: hedgehog numbers commensurately falling, possibly partly due to predation by the badgers. This is not the fault of the Benacre badgers and their cousins, but it makes it all the more essential to help hedgehogs find safe havens, for instance by cutting hedgehog holes in all new-build housing fences, to allow hedgehogs to roam a wide territory of interconnected small gardens.

The Building Regulations should be amended to include architecture for animals: swift boxes and hedgehog holes etc. Some people blame farmers and the loss of hedges in the 1970s, not badgers, for the loss of hedgehogs, but here, there are still miles of ancient hedge. The Benacre hedge lines are punctuated with mature oak trees, managed and cut in this way for centuries, and a characteristic feature of the place. The country word for badger is 'brock', the root of many place names and surnames, like Brooke, and Brookeborough in Northern Ireland, whose family crest is a badger, and who collect 'badger things' in all their most kitsch and amusing forms.

People have asked why we have moved only a mile up the coast, to a place whose land interlocks with and adjoins the land we have just left; still choosing to live on the unstable edge of England. This three-mile stretch of privately owned coast is often reported as being more affected by coastal erosion than any in Europe, if not the world. From the zoomed out perspective of photographs taken from a small aeroplane, it becomes immediately clear that without doubt, within this century, starting c.2035, people here will have to heed that warning, *the water will come*. For us, the trivial thought of never again being under the path of the geese, flying over us in their ragged skeins and V-formations of convivial chatter, or coming in to land silhouetted against the setting sun, was enough to make us want to stay here on the edge. In fact the unconscious soundtrack of Covehithe and Benacre turns out to be the peep of oystercatchers, which is arguably even better. It was as if we had lived so long under the spell of this magical landscape of light and sky and water, that once we had found it, we could not leave. Perhaps we had been changed by the deep calm of this crumbling country and the ephemeral emptiness of the edge-lands, set free of mental clutter.

Life imitated one of those stories about a dog or pony that had once belonged to someone, but who somehow now lives wild in the local landscape. The dog or pony is spotted occasionally by locals, therefore definitely still alive (otherwise there would be no point to the story), and the narrative usually invokes some variation on a theme of, 'if you can catch him, he's yours'.

Of the many pony books I loved as a child, most of them handed down and noticeably old-fashioned even then, there was one quite memorable story of that genre, *A Pony To Catch*. In this book, a decent pony of Exmoor or similar noble stock, had somehow ended up living in the woods. Exactly whose woods was never stated, nor whether there were any pheasant pens and the like in those woods, and it did not matter in those days, or at least not for the purposes of the story.

The upshot was that some hapless pony-less child, who naturally longed for a pony but whose parents could not afford one, made it their lone quest to catch the pony, by means of patient day-by-day acclimatisation, trails of oats, amateurish horse psychology and so on. The happy ending charged inevitably towards the reader from a long way off, in that the much-longed-for pony was (spoiler alert!) eventually caught.

The logistics of where this fictional and metaphorical pony would live, and in what company, and what the parents thought of all this, were naturally left unsaid. Perhaps there was a kindly neighbouring farmer, whose own feral country children had loved the pony but the post-and-rails fence to its field had been broken by a tree crashing down in a storm . . . Perhaps someone had been riding bareback as we all used to, and had fallen off the pony and let go of the reins (unlikely since it wasn't wearing even a headcollar) . . . Anyway, in this kind of story, the kindly and well-equipped farmer would naturally be glad that the pony would have a good home. He would conveniently offer a small but well-fenced field, with a slightly tumbledown but sensibly placed stable or field shelter, a properly plumbed-in water trough, and the pony's original old complete set of tack that had seen better days, but would be perfectly safe and supple with a bit of saddle soap. And so on.

This book and many others in a similar vein, mostly written in the 1940s by the three Pullein-Thompson sisters, were charming and timeless, and they still are. In fact, *A Pony To Catch* was written by Elinore Havers and published in 1964, so was relatively modern for the classic pony-book genre. Yet now I rather yearn for the fictional metaphorical pony and his lost freedoms.

We had become like that pony, as if we had once been civilised, domesticated animals, but were now animals who, for reasons unspecified in our story, had been turned out into the wild for more than twelve years, who had now been profoundly changed by the experience, and who could now not be caught. We were that pony. So we chose to live at the convergence of two small country roads, lanes really, at a point which on the map literally looks like an arrow pointing out to sea. In this way, we are still to an extent in the woods, uncaught.

Coincidentally, there has been a real-life version of this 'domesticated animal living wild in the woods' scenario playing out all around us for several years. There is reputed to be a white terrier living wild in the woods at Benacre. This dog is allegedly similar to Snowy from *Tintin*, possibly a Fox Terrier, and was apparently rescued from (or given by) the gypsies, or a terrierman, or some other rural character of slightly roguish repute, depending on who tells you the story. Anyway, the upshot is that this mythical white terrier is occasionally sighted, adding to the authenticity of the tale. The precise age of the story, and therefore the terrier, is slightly lost in the mists of time. There is probably an element of truth in this story, just as there is an element of truth in the stories of big cats living wild in the Suffolk countryside, escapees from the Africa Alive Wildlife Park a few miles up the road.

More recently, we have lived locally with a sadly true version of the 'dog living wild in the woods', in the form of a Great Dane. A rural neighbour had a dear old much-loved Great Dane who died, and she found a new friend in the form of another Great Dane in a rescue place of some kind. Unfortunately, the dog seems to have been let off the lead too early in its rehabilitation, and has since been roaming around the extensive acres of Benacre, being occasionally spotted by the search parties, including us, but always loping off towards a far-off hedge line at any attempt to catch it.

This attractive but enormous dog now seems to live in a wood marked 'Nature Reserve', one of several areas of woodland around here, great and small, with this designation. He or she has been fed at a particular spot, mostly on locally shot muntjac, the idea being that it can a) be kept alive without it having to help itself to some of the smaller farm animals, and b) eventually be caught. Muntjac are the small tusked deer we have in East Anglia, all descended from escapees from Woburn Abbey, and considered by most rural people to be a pest worth shooting and eating. Wild venison is carbon negative, as well as being lean, healthy, ethical and delicious. At the very least, the muntjac fed to the Great Dane living wild in the woods would have benefited the local nightingale population, since muntjac are known to browse low scrub at exactly the level that nightingales choose for their nesting sites. Nature always provides pros with its cons.

This cottage is probably one of the smallest houses on the estate, and we love it. The quietly honking geese in their V-formations do fly over us, over the reedbeds and 'broads' (Benacre Broad, Covehithe Broad and Easton Broad). The broads are shallow saltwater lakes on the landward side of the beach along this part of the ever-shifting coast, a wetland home to many animals and birds who live relatively undisturbed by human intrusion. We can still see land, sea, sky and sunrise.

But there was a small problem. Space. Things. Stuff.

Obviously we all have to 'let go' from time to time. I am a habitual 'letter-go', of material as well as mental clutter. Few things truly 'spark joy', even if they genuinely pass the useful or beautiful test. I have an efficient system with a charity shop in Southwold. I thin out things, books and clothes on a regular basis. Decluttering and what might be called the 'vintage circular economy' is conveniently eco-friendly, creating less material 'stuff', reducing our carbon footprints. It can also quite easily become borderline self-righteous, and even priggish.

I am not by nature a hoarder, except perhaps of books. Especially old books. And pictures, especially of horses and/or dogs. And things that I 'know to be useful or believe to be beautiful'. And elegant old things I have inherited from elegant old people who were the making of my childhood: Granny, Mrs Hamilton, Lady Biddy . . . This is the problem. It is not just sentimental value. It is that there is a sense of custodianship verging on *duty* in some of these possessions. They are invested not only with love, but with the desire for these real people not to be forgotten, either by us personally or by the world at large. So we keep them. This is not a materialistic instinct but a cultural one, connecting in some way to our ancestors in the loosest sense.

Through these objects, there is a sense that when some unspecified hypothetical hard times might come, we would personally still have the recent memory of ancestral traditions, like riding horses and plucking pheasants, which might save us. My hands still know what to do with a bridle or a butcher's knife, and I could hand on this knowledge in less than an hour. I remember Granny telling us how she drank the vegetable water during the war, for the vitamins, and this odd little detail is literally brought home to us in the everyday use of old things.

Despite the much greater losses to my extended family in the war, not least the eventual demolition of family HQ, a country house requisitioned and subsequently ruined as many like it were, and the death of my mother's father, it is the small detail of Granny drinking the vegetable water which has somehow trickled down the generations, to me. I still cook with this particular worn wooden spoon, or that particular stained cast-iron pot, or we eat off these oddly grand-looking old plates, ordinary enough objects much older than I am, which somehow seem to have been ennobled by their shared characteristic of having been 'handed down'. Whatever trials we may face, there is a sense that these 'old things' are genuinely old enough to have witnessed much worse.

There is a strand of anthropology and anthropologist that is interested in 'material culture'. These people might be interested in the way county people save binder-twine (baler-twine), the ubiquitous and indestructible orange string that holds rural life together, in case it might be useful. Which it always, eventually, is. As I write from our kitchen table, less than a metre away from me is a loop of binder-twine hanging off a dresser drawer handle. I know that this particular loop is the one from which hung a brace of pheasants 'in the feather', given to us on the last day of the Benacre shooting season. This practical gesture could be seen as a contemporary expression of tribal bonding, but one that might now seem alien if not immoral to a considerable percentage of the UK population, in our increasingly urban age. It so happens that my hands knew what to do with those pheasants, and the familiar orange string might yet save a life in some hideously unforeseeable circumstances.

This is where the 'material culture' of things crosses over into culture and survival. If our lives depended on doing a PhD about some physical object or material, and its significance to human culture and history, there could be (and probably are) many lesser PhDs than my chosen subject: *Binder-Twine: The Cultural History and Multiple Uses of Agricultural String in the Twentieth and Twenty-first Centuries*. The multiple rural uses of binder-twine hint at human ingenuity, and our remarkable ability to improvise and to adapt.

We absorbed my mother-in-law, and her houseful, into the Easternmost House. Although not literally living with us under our roof, my mother-in-law was only a few miles away for the last four years of her life. She was alongside me for much of the day during the working week, until frailty finally overcame her. Every day was 'Take Your Mother-in-Law To Work Day'. Every Saturday and every Sunday for those last four years, she came to lunch with us, seeing old friends, children and dogs, often outside at the shipwreck table in the garden at X, our original *Powers of Ten* 'picnic man' reference point. She began to sleep more in the afternoons. One day, at about 5pm, she didn't wake up. Watched over by a portrait of two of her dogs – a black Labrador and a Beagle, painted in the 1960s – at the age of ninety-three, she died.

This must be a pattern of family life all over the world. People are quietly living and dying among their families, at home. Someone in each family is probably sacrificing normal working life (and therefore normal earnings) to fulfil these familial duties of care. And yet it is increasingly unusual in the modern West, where everyone is so 'busy' that these simple pleasures and duties are typically 'outsourced' to carers. Sometimes professional help becomes necessary. Often our own work makes it difficult or impossible to be a part-time carer as well. But routinely, understandably, many people who could in fact adjust their work prefer to earn the money to pay someone else to do chores like cooking and cleaning, rather than do these things for their mothers-in-law themselves. This loses crucial social connections: chat, gossip, criticism, reminiscence. This disconnection from the processes of death, and therefore from Nature, may come back and bite us, in ways we have forgotten, or in scenarios we have not anticipated.

At about the same time as my mother-in-law died, Chuffy, our brindle ex-racing greyhound, visibly began to age. His back legs occasionally buckled and his magnificent muscular body became less strong. His demeanour was cheerful, but gradually, as his beautiful pointy-nosed greyhound-face faded literally to grey, he too began to fade. If one year is seven years in dog-years, logically one day is a week in dog-years. That puts the apparent speed of the process into perspective. The inevitable day came. Chuffy was snoozing in his bed when the vet (and trainee vet) called to say they were just setting off from the surgery. Never have the words 'We're on our way' been less welcome. Every fibre of my being wanted to bundle Chuffy into the Mighty Jimny (the rural vehicle of choice) and head for the hills, or rather the flatlands, of the Old Rec. But I didn't.

I did the right and kind thing, and I stayed with Chuffy until he breathed his last breath in his bed. The vet listened until his heart stopped beating, and then they took his body away. He was so big that I had decided he would not physically be buried with the others in the dogs' graveyard at the Old Rec. Like Speedy before him, his DNA in the form of fur, and a time capsule capturing his spirit, would be buried in the dogs' graveyard. His soul would remain with us and in us. And his body would be scattered in the garden around the pet crematorium on the road from Royston to

Cambridge. *Of course it would* ... I thought. *Not.* If any ashes (of dogs or people) were returned to me, I would personally struggle to believe that they were actually the ashes of 'the loved one'.

Memorial to a dog in a Kentish churchyard:

PAT, 1924–1934.
BE COMFORTED, FOR THOU TOO, O LITTLE DOG,
SHALL AT THE RESURRECTION
WEAR A SHINING TAIL.

The book *The Loved One*, by Evelyn Waugh, has to me rendered the phrase, and everything associated with it, comical and absurd. My first true (human) love died of cancer aged forty-four, in the prime of life, so I am immune from excess grief, as it can only ever now be revisiting a place I have been to before, nothing new. I will never understand why that particular tragedy had to happen to him, to them, to all of us who were close to it and affected by it, but it did. Such a past tragedy remains with us quietly all the time, and softens the loss of a much loved mother-in-law, or a grumpy old greyhound, or a cottage on a crumbling cliff. It becomes easier just briefly to give thanks for what was, and has been, and let go.

That Epicurean epitaph echoes my own attitude: *I was not, I have been, I am not, I do not mind.*

When it came to our 'material culture' and inherited things, some of them had to go to the auction rooms. We had to reduce the physical symbols and paraphernalia of lives which had now ended. After a brief effort of decluttering on an epic scale, trips to the charity shop, the clothes bank, the recycling depot, we were left with only the beautiful, useful or old things. Most of these 'things' had all three of these qualities. Some, we kept and use every day. Some are stored in the Old Rec barn. The rest, sold. We just let it go. This is the practical reality of environmental evacuation that many people may have to embrace, and soon. A predictable amount of time, and a carefully planned decommissioning and retreat, is not always what nature allows in real life.

Looking to the physical future of this coast, there is great loss to come in the next century, beginning today, and every day, with the gradual loss of land. According to Wikipedia, Covehithe has a population of 'about 20'. The Benacre to Easton Bavents coastline is often described in articles as the location with the most active coastal erosion in the UK, if not the whole of Europe, but even this dubious honour is changeable, imprecise and unreliable. It is enough to know that the whole of the east coast of the UK is physically crumbling into the sea, and the sea level will rise.

My personal observations of twelve years of coastal erosion at Easton Bavents, and the related erosion along the coast between Covehithe and Benacre that we live with now, lead me to conclude that the erosion here is even more dangerous and dramatic than that a mile south where we were before, specifically in the fact that here there are 'fissures', I think you would correctly call them. There are great cracks running from the edge of the cliff and into the crops, each crack running for perhaps twenty metres or so into the farmland, and then suddenly opening up into V-shaped chasms at the edge of the cliff. The chasms naturally open up into wider U shapes, with significant chunks of land crashing onto the beach. The whole spectacle is amply illustrated in terms of agricultural loss to the Benacre estate when crops of various kinds end up on the beach, such as the hundreds of parsnips and onions recently scattered all over the beach at Covehithe.

This landscape is alive with harvests all year round, seen and unseen, and some perhaps unknown or disapproved of. There is the harvest of pheasants and partridges in winter, shooting paradoxically partially funding the services of the hedgelayer that will later in the spring and autumn benefit the songbirds. At least one local hedgelayer, Richard Negus, also shoots and writes for *Shooting Times*. You can hear him talking about hedgelaying, wildfowling, shooting and conservation in a monthly *Country Diary* feature on BBC Radio Suffolk. Richard used to be in the Household Cavalry, which is why he calls himself @TrooperSnooks on Twitter. No one fits easily into pigeonholes or lazy stereotypes these days, if they ever did. We all seem to do many and varied jobs. Gamekeepers are also 'security', which on special occasions, such as the summer solstice roughly coinciding with the unlocking of the Covid-19 lockdown, also might mean picking litter off the beach or fencing off the crumbling caves.

There is great activity in the harvesting of sugar beet, bright lights and dark outlines of machinery rumbling about on the fields until well after dusk. Mountains of sugar beet are piled up near the entrances to the fields, waiting to be lifted by conveyor belts onto the convoys of lorries that will rumble off to the sugar-beet factories the other side of the county, at Bury St Edmunds and elsewhere. Sheep will be turned out to eat the beet tops after the harvest, and the by-product of sugar-beet pulp will be turned into animal-feed, as the circle of life churns on and spring is palpably in the air. This is British sugar without the associations of sugar cane, without the history of slavery, and without the general public seeming to be much aware of its existence at all, at least if Twitter is to be believed (which arguably it isn't).

Along the cliff edge, pussy willow bushes with their fluffy grey buds are incongruously placed against a backdrop of grey North Sea and sky, because the land has been eaten away. These errant pussy willows now look lost in the wrong habitat, teetering on the edge. Next year, the same pussy willows will no doubt be on the beach below, or somewhere far out to sea, eaten, pulped or pounded by the waves. Gone.

As well as the considerable loss of good farmland and woodland to coastal erosion, there is also the loss of buildings, with much of great cultural, emotional and financial value already lost, but much more yet to come, soon, here. Several churches have already been lost at Dunwich and Easton Bavents, and Covehithe church will be next, unsaveable. Listed buildings have no more protection from the sea than any other building on the edge.

The demolition and dismantling of the Easternmost House continued throughout that first February after we left. The walls were gradually lowered and the whole edifice became nearer the ground, until eventually it took on the appearance of a ruin. I walked around the half-demolished house, and was barely able to recognise the individual spaces, or where they began and ended. Here was our cosy sitting room with the fireplace where the Household Cavalry trumpet banner used to hang, the room with the telly and e-comms. Here was the kitchen where I wrote *The Easternmost House* ... barely there at all now, just a few jagged dusty low brick walls, but still as poignant an X in space for me as the once-sociable shipwreck table outside.

Here was the other sitting room, which had housed my late father-in-law's rather scholarly library, a mini version of what had once been my mother-in-law's elegant drawing room in another house. Even when condensed into a clifftop cottage with the waves crashing outside, it retained that more formal air.

Many hours' worth of tapestry remain in our cottage today, as a useful and usable living tribute to my late mother-in-law and her skills. Several of her friends have since died, so these time-laden cushions, chair seats, footstools and whatnot, embellished with emblems of ritual and regiment, architecture and animals, serve as a memorial to them all, to their friendship, and to their era.

The mantelpiece of my mother-in-law's miniaturised drawing room was loosely propped up against the wall where it had stood firm for two-hundred-odd years, framing the hearth and heart of the home, while the back of the house genuinely looked like a scene from the Blitz, all broken bricks and walls open to the elements. The scene served us well as a sharp reminder of how lucky our generation, several generations, had been, never having faced real dangers or deprivations, or at least, not life-ending dangers which literally fell from a clear blue sky. The effect of the Blitz was heightened by the constant burning of bonfires in what had so recently been our garden, populated by sociable visitors and convivial lunches al fresco for all those summers.

Eventually, the end came, the final few fragments of the 'ruin' vanished and the house was no more. That was it. All gone. People often asked us if we minded, and said wasn't it sad, and so on. There is a useful line uttered by Lawrence of Arabia, or at least Peter O'Toole: 'The trick is not to mind'.

I have used this trick many times in different situations, and I recommend it. The odd thing was, by the time the house was no longer there, I had personally left that episode well-recorded, but in the past. I had already let it go, long ago. We recently walked up the beach at low tide to see what, if anything, of us was left, and what was there now. The site fencing told us that the farm knew they hadn't quite finished the job, which was lucky, because they hadn't, and I really wouldn't want them to think they had. There were still a few remnants of a working demolition site scattered around.

The shape of the house and the brick outbuilding was legible on the ground, as hard flat surfaces where the floors had been, the 'footprint' of the buildings now reading like an architect's site plan drawing, at 1:1 scale. A rusty wire bird feeder hung in the now handsome little tree I had allowed to grow from a self-seeded sapling, nurturing its shape over the years. I removed the bird feeder, as without us it would now count as litter. Otherwise, there was nothing left of us, and very little left of the house. For old time's sake I took a few photos, including one from my usual spot on the cliff.

Then we took a last look and marched briskly up the beach towards home.

Skylines

Some trust in chariots and some in horses.

Psalm 20:7

3

MARCH

It must have been dreadful in many ways to have lived through the adaptation from horses to the motor car and tractor. Change is not made without inconvenience, even from worse to better. It must have taken an enormous effort of cultural upheaval to make the change and embrace the new technology, with the car bearing no resemblance to the horse, only to the carriage. The horseless carriage would have been such a threat to many jobs, and a whole way of life must have vanished in a generation. Many traditional hay meadows were lost. The Suffolk horse is now a rare breed, on the Rare Breeds Survival Trust's critical list. People would have had to adapt, adjust, retrain and reskill: farriers to mechanics, saddlers to upholsterers, grooms to chauffeurs, wainwrights off to the car production lines. Who knows what became of the ostlers. Yet it all now seems to us almost irrelevant. We have bigger fish to fry.

If the most successful animals are not the biggest or the fastest or the strongest, but the most adaptable to change, humans are evidently super-adaptors. The greatest changes to human life are relatively recent, specifically the Industrial Revolution, two World Wars and the arrival of the Internet, although seeing these as among the greatest changes may be more a reflection of a modern narrow-minded perspective than provable fact. Perhaps the taming of the horse, the invention of the wheel and the printing press were actually greater changes at the time. However, all these pivotal moments in human evolution and progress are in the past, and it is change in the present and the immediate future that we are naturally most interested in.

In the twenty-first century, we will have to go on adapting, and probably at greater speed than ever before. Whether because of climate change, rising sea levels, coastal erosion, flooding, or that perhaps more frightening threat, the unseen, the unknown unknown, we have been overdue a Big Test, by two or three generations, if history is our guide. Pampered post-war generations in the Western world have generally avoided the four horsemen of war, famine, pestilence and untimely death, so survival skills like butchery have been lost. This may yet prove to be unwise.

I don't truly believe that horses will routinely 'strain once again to the sound of the gulls in the wake of the deep plough', when the oil runs out, or something unforeseen happens. From the perspective of 2020 and beyond, a time which is likely to be characterised by future historians as a time of increasing first-hand experience of the long-anticipated but vaguely defined climate crisis, coupled with an unexpected coronavirus pandemic, it turns out that we may soon need to do quite a bit more sharing of all our resources. In the practicalities of adapting to change, a climate crisis and a pandemic have a good deal in common, both situations having much to teach us about how to organise ourselves, which past mistakes to correct, and what to do in the future to survive and thrive.

Just as the Household Cavalry and all relevant others regularly rehearse and update the plans for 'Operation London Bridge', and other 'bridge events', Forth, Severn etc., concerning senior members of the royal family (deaths of and funeral plans for, to save you googling it if you're not already familiar with the code words), so we are led to believe that from time to time the Government also tests what might be called 'civilian resilience planning'.

Civilian resilience planning involves rehearsing which buildings will become what, and what roles the Army will play, for instance in the case of a biological attack, a virulent global pandemic or catastrophic flooding of London. These clandestine rehearsals are reputed to highlight an alarming array of fatal flaws in things like crowd management, security, policing, medical supply chains, food availability, and so on, so that when 'the event' happens in real life, all will be well.

At least, that is the idea.

Contingency planning for climate-change-related adaptations is also already on the radar. Transport is planned and evacuation routes already subtly marked in case of the need for sudden mass evacuations caused by coastal erosion or flooding 'events'. The setting up of camping-style temporary accommodation in village halls and school gyms, the speedy construction of Army-engineered temporary flood defences, supply chains of food and water, and the provision of emergency tea bags and kettles and so on, all comes under the general heading of 'civilian resilience planning'. The mood seems quite *Dad's Army*, but the contingencies are deadly serious. The bleeps on the meteorological and metaphorical radar are becoming ever louder and closer. We may need to up our game.

In 2020, as the world was suddenly entrenched in the unfamiliar state of the Covid-19 pandemic lockdown, we all had a living dress-rehearsal for adapting to radical change. From a *Powers of Ten* perspective, as that tiny bat whiffling in the wind caused a cocktail of inconvenience and tragedy affecting every individual person, in London or Los Angeles, Little Snoring or Lochinver, it also proved that humankind across the globe was capable of adapting at great speed, and on the whole, is kind and co-operative as a species, with a small percentage being completely ruthless.

We can therefore see what a climate change emergency scenario might look like on the ground. First the schools closed down. Then the pubs. Then normal life itself. We have proved that change that might usually take months or years, can be made in days or hours. And we have also proved that the majority of people comply, at least at the beginning. When the climate emergency eventually forces us into comparably dramatic change, we now have a useful collective reference point for the future, a globally shared experience, a lived model.

The UK Prime Minister's Covid-19 slogan was: 'Stay at home. Protect the NHS. Save lives.'

In a climate emergency it might be: 'Leave home. Listen to the BBC. Save lives.'

When the Queen addressed the nation, it was reported that twenty-four million people watched the broadcast at 8pm on a Sunday, all watching together at the same time, in a rare moment of national unity. That alone was proof that we were living through unusual times. Then came the news, 'The Prime Minister is in intensive care'.

It does not take a great leap of imagination to conjure in the mind a comparable scene in which His Majesty King Charles (or William or George) similarly takes to the television screen from some intimate drawing room in Windsor Castle, safely above the Eton floods, to address the nation about the Coastal Evacuations Crisis, or the East Anglian Abandonment Scheme. Instead of 'The Prime Minister is in intensive care', the climate emergency news might be, 'The Houses of Parliament are extensively flooded'. Instead of 'The Queen and the Duke of Edinburgh are in lockdown at Windsor Castle', the news might be, 'Sandringham House has been decommissioned and was today formally abandoned to the sea'.

As would happen in a climate emergency, Covid-19 spawned a new lexicon of previously unheard-of words and phrases which became commonplace within only a week or two, 'covidiots' being an early and necessary invention. New words evolve easily and naturally. We invent words all the time.

If ever there was a good time to be part of a real community able to co-operate and help each other in practical ways, an 'unprecedented' global emergency is it. For all its multiple faults, humankind seems to have a tendency to gravitate towards kindness in times of crisis. In formal and informal groups, we seem to have a default factory setting to help the isolated or vulnerable. In any disaster on the news, there are always people instantly helping, even when they are themselves still in shock from the bomb or the tsunami or the fire. As with our relationship with horses and dogs, this apparently selfless kindness may not be wholly altruistic, but the hard-wired key to our mutual survival. Perhaps we needed the wisdom of the elders in our caves, or at least their practical cooking skills, or their humour, so we had a vested interest in looking after them kindly just to keep them cooking and making us laugh, thus bonding the whole tribe across the generations. I like to think we just enjoyed their wise old company and were (are) inherently kind.

The coronavirus pandemic showed us patterns of human behaviour which might also apply in a climate emergency of some kind. City streets were deserted. Second-homers driving out of London to escape to rural areas, where there are vastly fewer facilities of every kind, were suddenly portrayed in the media as the new social pariahs. The idea of being able to buy your way out of the situation seemed instantly unsavoury, which is a salient lesson for the future. In a climate crisis even more than in a pandemic, you would be unwise to behave in such a way as to make yourself into an outcast. We know from Sir David Attenborough's films that outcasts tend to be killed by predators or turned on by the flock, the herd, the pack, the mob.

Southwold Town Hall briefly sported a yellow banner which was mentioned on the national news:

A day at the seaside or a week in your holiday home
are NOT essential travel.

PLEASE RESPECT US. DON'T INFECT US.

This might all seem a bit 'pitchforks at dawn', but in a life-or-death situation, who really knows how far people would go, to survive? Coastal people are more likely to be the ones escaping in the future, when the sea comes in over the land, or the storms become more unpredictable. Whether in New Orleans or Norfolk, Bangladesh or Benacre, it's all the same experience when the sea overtops the sea walls or rushes in over the fields, as it surely will, the only questions being when and exactly where.

For the first two weeks in lockdown, most people did not use their cars at all. There was a 70 per cent decrease in petrol consumption and a 140 per cent increase in the amount of money spent on bicycle repairs in the UK (according to the Petrol Retailers Association and Halfords). We tramped the most isolated footpaths and byways and did not leave Benacre land. By the third week of our lockdown walks, we seemed to be living in a rural idyll of blossoming hedges and roads with no tarmac. As an unexpected bonus, we discovered a remote old farm building on what might be called a hill in Suffolk, at the junction of three byways (some of which are also marked on the map as an ancient 'green lane'), the whole scene reminiscent of the Rubbing-Down House on Newmarket Heath, as immortalised in paintings by George Stubbs (1724–1806).

From a point near the building we now routinely refer to as the 'Rubbing-Down House', there is a view that takes in the woods of Easton Home Covert, the same block of woodland which we overlooked when we lived at Easton Bavents, but from the opposite direction. The view from the Rubbing-Down House takes in the entire territory of *The Easternmost House* (house and book) in a single panorama of land and water and sky, stretching out over the farmland and onwards to the reedbeds and the sea, a little world of its own. From this vantage point, it is easy to imagine where the water will come, and how it will cut off the useful road through the reedbeds as one of the first of its inconvenient impacts. We can look out over this view and think, *I've been here before*, as Charles Ryder does at the beginning of *Brideshead Revisited*, an innocuous phrase which can't begin to convey our familiarity with and the depth of our involvement in the place, or the grand sweep of Charles Ryder's involvement with Brideshead.

Our extensive expeditions and the discovery of new views and old buildings 'hidden in plain sight' were among many unexpected benefits of rural lockdown. Seeing the same farm buildings, tracks, fields, woods, reedbeds and so on, from a slightly different viewpoint, opens up a whole new depth of understanding of this already familiar landscape, and of how the different habitats and land uses all fit together. Exactly the same principle applies to exploring urban landscapes. In the country (at least in England), there are about 150,000 miles of footpaths and byways. In cities, there are all manner of alleyways and back streets to investigate freely. The simple act of *walking* or *exploring* may be the key to a sense of belonging, anywhere.

When we eventually broke out and ventured forth to the village shop a few miles away, the new buzzword around shopping was 'essential', as in is it or isn't it? It turns out that in any kind of Crisis, much depends on what is considered 'essential'. One rebel told of how when buying 'essential' petrol he had also bought some chewy snakes, *wantonly not* essential items, and it had felt like a tiny victory. Heaven knows what would be considered essential in a climate emergency. Petrol might be limited, with supply chains disrupted.

Electricity substations might be damaged and flooded, preventing the pumps from working. Electricity substations must be a top defence and civilian priority, if you think what would happen if the freezers and tills in the supermarkets went down. Hand tools, matches and alcohol are always popular. Horses and the skills to go with them might be at a premium too. I favour stocking up with scissors and horse-clippers, because in the land of lockdown, the hairdresser is king.

Queueing obediently two metres apart, people chatted convivially about when and why they had last been out. There was a slight sense of one-upmanship (or one-down-manship) about who had managed to literally *stay at home* for the longest. Not since Tuesday was clearly trumped by not since last Sunday morning. One person at a time was allowed in the shop. Three or four people patiently 'self-distanced' in the sunshine, with a placid calm that invested them with an almost bovine serenity. What is this life if, full of care, we have no time to stand and stare... at our iPhones, while we wait to buy the same staple foods as our ancestors, bread, milk, eggs? Five minutes later, there was a hail storm. Perhaps this is the nature of Nature in the twenty-first century. The climate crisis seems already to be happening, yet outside the village shop, hardly anyone seems to have noticed.

The coronavirus pandemic has taught us that we can do things that we thought we couldn't do, globally. Not only can we make sweeping changes to our daily routines and freedoms, but we can adjust to this new regime as seeming normal in a matter of days. It plants the seed of thoughts along the lines of, *one day, maybe we could*... followed by a string of ideas to permanently reduce our impact on the natural world.

Maybe we could... limit our flying, ration our air miles

to 10,000 miles per person per year, or maybe 5,000. *Maybe we could* ... introduce carbon trading between those saving excess air miles and those wanting to fly long haul. It is easy to imagine the evolution of carbon trading abbreviations, *am* (air miles), *pppy* (per person per year), and so on, becoming as everyday as *ur*, *lol*, *ftw* or *omg* did with the spread of texting. *Maybe we could* ... no longer allow people to own second homes, or at least not leave them empty for much of the year. Think of the millions of homes that would be released for people to live in, and the vast tracts of land set free from development for at least a century. But as soon as they are formed, let alone articulated, these *Maybe we could* ... thoughts immediately have to be suppressed, because people will say this is not the right time, this is draconian, this is anti-libertarian, this is *wrongthink*. But it is never the right time. We don't even seem able to stop people dropping litter. Millions of us are evidently not *that* bothered about the environment. If we were, we'd look after it better. It is never going to be the right time to get a grip on ourselves, so why not now?

This is precisely why *this is the right time*, to grasp this moment of enormous change, for the greater benefit of the natural world, its plants, its animals, its water, its air and its *beauty*, and change our ways for the better, for the environment, forever. *Zoom out! Think bigger!* If not now, when?

Modern media channels have proved that important current affairs and twenty-four-hour news broadcasting can be beamed to us at our kitchen table office, directly from the homes of television presenters. Ditto global networks worldwide. Ditto entertainment, to keep us quietly sane. The concept that we can zoom in and out at will is not only useful for the purposes of a *Powers of Ten* perspective and

Easternmost Sky thinking. Zooming in and out in the split-screen Zoom meetings sense now also allows us to scrutinise other people's bookcases. It has all gone a bit Pathé News and Ealing Comedy, back in time for a glimpse of the future. Even Radio 4 seems to be broadcast from anywhere but Broadcasting House.

Here is *Any Questions*, live from an attic in Hackney. Here is *PM* at 5pm from a flat in Finsbury. Here is the *Today* programme live from a terraced house in Tooting. Here is *Farming Today*, live from a farm, producing your food. This is a convincing portrayal of how information might be broadcast to us in a peculiarly parochial but stirringly British climate emergency disaster film. Or in real life. The British climate emergency disaster scenario seems destined to revolve around village halls, trestle tables and tea bags.

Everyone who can work from home, is . . . possibly forever, surrounded by children, dogs, projects, hand-drawn posters, hand-written recipes, bread. People suddenly appreciate the skills of the artisanal trades and hand skills. With cars and aeroplanes silent, even if only temporarily, people noticed they could hear the birds sing. There may in the future be a very specific kind of lockdown nostalgia, not just for the quietness, but for the lack of freneticism, the absence of social obligations, not having to look at the diary, to see where to go, what to wear.

It seems a shame to go back to normal after this brief, beautiful intermission, this pause. Lockdown is like an environmental version of the book (and film) *Awakenings*, as if a veil has briefly been lifted from our collective eyes and revealed to us a better way. It reminds me of an old project I once did as an idealistic architecture student, in a world of imagination where with a few deft marks on paper, or an assembly of three-dimensional bits and pieces stuck together as a 3D model, you could suggest not only the architecture but the way of life that might happen in and around it. I was a bit of an eco-warrior then, with an unusually rural outlook for an architecture student at the time (then as now), so green architecture seemed a natural choice of preoccupation, especially as it neatly side-stepped the style wars that were going on at the time, goaded by Prince Charles.

Lockdown was as if my student project was suddenly happening in real life, or at least parts of it. A long time ago, I designed a project which I called *The Extended Household*, in which I imagined a more eco-friendly future, involving rammed earth architecture, green roofs and happy people living harmoniously and co-operatively, free from the tyranny of the office. The people in my drawings all seemed to be blacksmiths, saddlers and stone-carvers, as one of my remits at the time was the promotion of skilled manual trades as the most satisfying of all work. There was a workshop building inspired by the anatomy of an animal, with spine and ribs, and an articulated wiggly tail-bridge which led down to a lake. The entire thing was a fantasy, but quite a fun one. Materials were natural, and local, although *all* materials must originate from nature and be local to somewhere, so it was more a woolly intention than a specification. I gave no serious thought to budget, although I mashed up some £ signs to fulfil that part of the brief.

The Extended Household included architecture for animals, a perennial preoccupation of mine (see #ArchitectureForAnimals on Twitter). Farm animals and wild creatures roamed around the place and birds flitted here and there. Grass was left long. Bees buzzed around the wild flowers, which were native weeds deliberately spread about, artfully labelled Farmers' Nightmare on the drawings. This was rewilding on a small scale, though rewilding hadn't yet been invented, or at least not called that then, and it wasn't a fashionable idea, it was an *original* one, mine. I felt quite annoyed when more recently rewilding became a fashionable cause, mostly among urban people. It felt as if they had stolen my idea, but of course they hadn't really. Nature was there all along, we had just got into the habit of over-tidying it, and routinely beheading it with a lawnmower.

The imaginary people of my imaginary project also grew their own food in a small-scale farming manner, not as back-garden chicken-keepers, but as proper food producers, selling locally, and doing 'skilled manual' things to various ingredients. There were pigs and sheep, and an indication of a few cool agricultural structures and interventions whacked on at the last minute to add interest to the drawings. Solar-powered vertical urban farms were alluded to in notes and sketches, as a loose suggestion of 'the future'. *The Extended Household* slightly baffled the RIBA 'crit' system at the time, so it was awarded Distinction, just to be on the safe side, in case its ideas ever turned out to be even remotely prescient. It was then snatched off the wall for the launch of the Ecological Design Association in Covent Garden, never to be seen again. Until now . . . in real life.

Within five miles of here, the Adnams warehouse and a new house nestle discreetly under sweeping curves of green roof, almost invisible in the landscape, just as I had once imagined real buildings could be. The largest urban farm in the world is now literally bearing fruit in Paris. Sales of seeds for growing vegetables soared during the 2020 lock-down. People baked bread, even though there was never a shortage of shop-bought bread. Our future king and his family were photographed delivering homemade pasta to isolating neighbours around Anmer in Norfolk. It was as if we needed to reconnect to the sources of our food, tapping into an instinct stored somewhere deep in our genetic memory, to be sure of security of supply.

The world was momentarily transformed during the coronavirus global lockdown. In the future we must not forget how it was, how we were. People in Italy sang from their balconies. The streets of Siena and Assisi echoed with arias. The villages of rural Britain are already habitually geared up to help the vulnerable and the isolated of the parish, but there was also a kind of village-ification of towns and cities, in places where such neighbourly connections and mannerisms might be rarer. A modern Land Army of crop-pickers volunteered to be on standby to harvest crops which might otherwise rot, because of travel bans causing labour shortages. Pickers, packers, carers, bus drivers, cleaners, the people who collect our rubbish, and so on, are likely to be appreciated more than they were before the pandemic. Aeroplanes left the sky clear of vapour trails. Pollution diminished. Noise quietened. Cars switched off. The Himalayas were visible in India, free of smog. A seahorse was filmed in the Grand Canal in Venice. Goats took over the streets of Llandudno. *Nature is healing*, was the happy collective mood. For a brief moment, it was true.

People seemed to be discreetly rethinking everything... What is important? What are our priorities? It was as if we pressed the Reset button, and found we liked it. It is tempting to suggest that we should return to the deep peace of lockdown, all of us, the whole world, for perhaps a month a year, every year, to let nature recover.

Nothing like this has happened for the climate, to curb our CO_2 emissions, but it clearly could.

My own past agricultural experience working long days for several seasons in the strawberry fields, vineyards and orchards of Suffolk, mostly skilled work, and physically tiring, is suddenly seen as valuable. Priorities have changed almost overnight. Not one person in architecture ever asked me about my agricultural labour experience, even though it was always on my old CVs. Along with everything else rural, dykes and ditches, horses and hedges, pigs and parishes, country life in general, and agricultural labour in particular, had for many years been seen by a significant section of the population as unskilled, quaint, old-fashioned, irrelevant. But perhaps not any more. Not now that global food-chain deliveries to supermarkets can no longer be taken for granted.

This is where long-term loyalty to the local Spar, the farm shop or the roadside honesty box pays off. The remote farm shop and roadside honesty box network is a whole subculture of food-shopping, entirely invisible to many, and certainly considered the poor relation of sophisticated Waitrose and Ocado deliveries, with their extraordinary interpretations of the word 'essential' when applied to the packaging of ingredients. Obviously the farm shop and rural roadside honesty box network is not going to feed the world, but it wouldn't take too much disruption to Ocado deliveries for this anarchic local food subculture to become a life-saver.

The collective memory of our ancestral skills and the anachronistic idea that 'my hands knew what to do' when

85

faced with a pheasant or a field, might yet prove useful, even in the modern world. It is not so much that *even* in a digital age it might be wise to relearn and hone these old-fashioned skills, but *especially* in a digital age that it might be wise, when so many people may have lost these practical skills or hold them in some kind of contempt. 'Local' suddenly seems less left-behind. 'Global' suddenly seems less glossy. You can't eat a warehouse distribution centre. A cargo of avocados, almond milk and quinoa is no good to the people of the UK if the chilled containers are stuck in Mexico. And if the electricity substations are damaged, the chillers won't even be chilled.

The memory of plague is never far from human culture. The plague is visible today in the architecture of the Salute church in Venice where people gave thanks for being saved, or in the plague stones on the parish boundaries of remote farms around the British uplands, where people paid for food by leaving coins in a pool of germ-killing vinegar. The plague is visible in the ruined Suffolk churches of Walberswick and Covehithe, where the vast original churches are now supplanted by much smaller churches, built within the eerie ruins that still hold these ancient memories in their air. We never really forgot. We were just let off the hook for a century, or four.

All things rural, once seen as eccentric, now seem desirable. Remoteness, isolation, unruly kitchen gardens, larders, old-fashioned cooking ranges that lose heat when the tops are left open, shooting and fishing for food, or hoarding jam jars, all now seem more understandable and acceptable, even wise, in this strange survivalist era.

The common-sense design of 'the architecture of food' has become apparent for the first time since the war: the stone slabs and brick arches of the larder, the mesh-doored timber game larder on the north-facing side of the kitchen garden wall, the pear tree and peaches on the south side of the same wall, the greenhouse, the cellar. It is all so sensible. The Old Rec is as fine a case study as any, when it comes to 'the architecture of food'. With the right tools and animals, and a fit body, you could in theory live there away from the world, producing your own meat, fruit, veg, milk, cheese, cider etc., in perpetuity. Yet you could never be properly self-sufficient in the twenty-first century, even if you decided to go the whole hog, because who would mine the cobalt for your iPhone batteries, who would fix your Internet, your laptop, or the mutiny of our artificially intelligent 'Internet of things' when it disobeys your collective bossy instructions?

The mainstream media over the past few years has sketched out many opinion pieces about the pros and cons of being an Anywhere versus a Somewhere. This concept probably originated with *Anywheres Versus Somewheres: Britain's Hidden Divide* by David Goodhart. The 'versus' is quite telling. These two types are being set up from the outset as rival tribes with rival sets of values, meaning that one must be better than the other. As the mainstream media has a predominantly metropolitan outlook, with articles often written by metropolitan journalists, the accepted concluding consensus was that Anywheres were on the whole the more right, as in the more correct, of the two tribes. But that was in the 'before' world.

Somewheres are apparently rooted in a particular place, and tend to be less educated, perhaps a bit backwards and backwoods, valuing the traditional, local and familiar, including in domestic and family life. Anywheres (or 'we Anywheres' as David Goodhart put it) tend to be more educated and with a global outlook, valuing university degrees and the knowledge economy, from which Anywheres apparently derive status, while also favouring an 'anti-domesticity family unit', meaning that they are more likely to neither aspire nor conform to the traditional nuclear family model of a married Mummy and Daddy living in a mortgaged house with their two wholesomely gender-conforming children and a dog.

Somewheres might live in Derbyshire with a wife who cooks roast beef. Anywheres might live in Dubai with a partner who assembles Ottolenghi salads. The favourite foods of British Gen Z Anywheres teenagers would probably be something like ramen or seitan katsu. Somewheres had somehow become 'left behind'. At least, that seemed to be the gist of the *Britain's Hidden Divide* thesis.

Yet when it came to adapting almost overnight to a changed world, it was suddenly the Somewheres who had an unexpected advantage. It was the Anywheres who had just been skiing who turned out to be the early 'super-spreaders', more likely to be exposed to the virus and to spread it, especially among dense, urban populations, including key workers who could not work from home. What was true for the coronavirus pandemic could teach us lessons for a climate emergency. Somewheres travelled less, and often worked outdoors and/or in isolation, at home, on tractors, up hills or laying hedges, so were less exposed to the virus in the first place, and were unlikely to catch it, carry it or infect others. At this most basic level, Somewheres were more likely to survive. Somewheres also had reliable food security, in the form of access to local supply chains, farms, farm shops, wild game and crops growing in the fields around them. Somewheres had space and distance, in the form of remote villages, cottages and farms. Considerable rural inconveniences were suddenly treated not with habitual disdain, but as desirable.

As usual, the truth is more nuanced, and we probably all need to be partly Somewheres and partly Anywheres, not either/or. Imported avocados, almond milk and quinoa have an established place in the modern diet, just as pomegranate seeds are an attractive decoration in an urban salad. But the just-enough, just-in-time supermarket delivery system was suddenly showing its potentially fatal flaws and vulnerabilities. London streets went silent, loo-paper hoarders hunkered down, and a siege mentality haunted the now-unpolluted air. But you can't eat loo paper. Global food supply chains have been exposed as vulnerable. It is all very well having 'warehouses of tinned food', but if it can't be moved around in time, the nine meals to anarchy scenario will play out. The edict that at any time we are all only nine meals from anarchy is a shrewd observation first articulated by Alfred Henry Lewis in 1906. Among predictions of what might happen in a climate emergency, fighting over food seems likely, especially in cities.

Most cities are entirely reliant now on just-enough, just-in-time deliveries, which should give us a clue to the behaviour to expect if the supply chain goes wrong. Urban riots, and then some... Wherever there is a high density of population relative to the amount of food available on any day, there is vulnerability and dependency. With just-enough, just-in-time delivery systems, the obvious question is what happens if there isn't enough, and if it doesn't arrive in time? We saw a glimpse of it with the empty shelves at the beginning of the coronavirus pandemic, and it wasn't just a falsely perceived shortage of loo paper because of hoarders.

There was a run on dried pasta and tinned tomatoes. People fought over random tins in the supermarket aisles. Flour during lockdown was like gold dust. In the absence of football grounds, pubs, music festivals and clubs, people apparently unused to open spaces ventured into unfamiliar territory for their daily exercise, and as the sun came out *a few* trashed beaches and rural beauty spots with disposable BBQs and litter. We should learn from these warnings about global food supply chains and human behavioural psychology. It is like being given a second chance, for next time, the big one, climate.

We could eat the fruits of incompetent food shopping and the contents of the store cupboard, and survive perfectly adequately. But my hunch is that good manners would not last long if we took that route. People would fight over the curry powder that might make sense of random ingredients. When asked by a food writer on Twitter what ingredients would be most useful to stock up on *in extremis*, long-life flavourful things like olive oil, salt, garlic and cheap bottled lemon juice scored highly, as with these it was reckoned we could make anything taste good. This is the kind of thinking we may need in the future, but with local British rapeseed oil and sea salt, since everything else may be stuck in the global just-in-time supply chains.

Millions of people may face coronavirus-related financial ruin, as well as bereavement and other long-term trauma which may present itself years or decades later. Yet in city, town, suburb and country alike, there has been a revelation of latent community spirit and an epidemic of kindness. The importance of access to outdoor space in the inner city has never seemed so essential to human well-being. A nightingale may yet sing in Berkeley Square.

In the three months or so leading up to the peak of the 2020 pandemic, the world had seen wildfires in Australia, a plague of locusts over several countries of Africa, and serious flooding in the UK. Reporting of these events often included the words 'biblical' and 'unprecedented'. For once, 'biblical' seemed apt. People directly affected by these *other global events caused by Nature* will be adapting and rebuilding for many years, yet are already largely forgotten, superseded by a pandemic which has affected more people more personally. But these other global events caused by nature have not gone away. They do not know about the pandemic so they will not hold off out of good manners. They will be back. Farms, houses, animals, crops, vineyards, orchards, woodland and thousands of acres of British farmland were lost or damaged beyond immediate use. In some places, the question of feasibility, of long-term viability, raised its head. Uncomfortable realities will need to be faced. Climate change is not coming soon. It is happening to us now.

The early days of the coronavirus pandemic gave a glimpse of just how adaptable humans can be, and how quickly adjustable we are in real life when we need to be. This is encouraging. The adaptability trait may be our salvation, whether relating to a pandemic or to climate change. Both of these problems are global, natural and a crisis, and both are here, now.

In any unusual scenario, we can expect innovation, and innovation generally flourishes in freedom. This is why *The Extended Household* was possible as a student project, but not in an office. In pandemic conditions, the Army helped fit out a pragmatic design layout for the 4,000-bed Nightingale hospital in what is normally an exhibition space in London. Eton provided free accommodation and schooling to key workers and their children. Deep-sea divers provided expertise in administering oxygen to Covid-19 patients. The Adnams Brewery down the road from us in Southwold produced alcohol to make hand sanitiser. Barbour, normally associated with old-school country coats, made scrubs. So did the Queen's dressmaker. Weatherby's Bloodstock printed patterns for NHS kit instead of race cards. And so it goes on. If these old, traditional and essentially rural companies can jump to it and become highly innovative and adaptable in the blink of an eye, anyone can. For urban creative industries armed with 3D printers, such innovation should be second nature.

There is so much almost instant invention, adaptation, genius and kindness on offer, it is hard to see how and where all this creative energy is normally expended, in everyday office life. Some business are questioning the value of office life and whether they should continue to rent extensive – and expensive – inner city buildings. Why are all the lights left on in all those London office buildings, long after office hours? Why couldn't many of us permanently reduce our travel time, fuel consumption and pollution, and work from home all the time?

There is an illustrated children's book called *What Do People Do All Day?* by Richard Scarry (1968), in which people (animals) are shown busily doing interesting jobs of all sorts, with everyone apparently completely engaged and fulfilled by their work. All kinds of jobs are shown, with no sense that one kind of work is preferable to another. The book seems to be quietly saying to children, you too could be a bricklayer, a taxi driver, a doctor, a ballet dancer, a farmer. 'Skilled manual work' seems to be the subtle bias in *What Do People Do All Day?* All jobs seemed fun and worthwhile in that book. While the coronavirus era has focused our attention on ingenuity and invention, it has also made us appreciate anew the skills, necessity and quiet bravery of those most exposed to the virus when going about their normal daily jobs, the unsung non-medical frontline workers, bus drivers, train drivers, ambulance drivers, delivery people, shop workers, rubbish collectors, cleaners, warehouse workers, factory workers… exactly the kinds of jobs held in such esteem and respect in *What Do People Do All Day?*

Surely all this latent ingenuity could later be marshalled in the cause of mitigating climate change?

Spring in the countryside is still associated with ancient customs like lambing, Lent and Lady Day, and it is not difficult to imagine a scenario in contemporary life in which knowledge from days gone by might still be useful. Some of this lore is remembered and alive. Which wild berries can we eat with pleasure? Which leaves will cool a sting? Red sky at night, shepherds' delight. Rain before seven, fine before eleven. These sayings contain genuinely useful observations and forecasts of weather, handed down, but much of this knowledge has been lost. The day may come when we need to tap into the retained collective knowledge of the past, and acknowledge once again that it might be wise for us all to be able to say, 'my hands knew what to do' with a bridle, a butcher's knife, a pheasant or a field.

It may yet turn out to be counter-intuitively more progressive than regressive to decide to be able still to feed ourselves, locally and seasonally, not letting ourselves become entirely reliant on global food supply chains. We can still enjoy coffee and lemons and food from across the globe, but it may be wise not to forget *all* our ancestral survival skills too soon.

It may be wise, when in thrall to the glamorous and global, not to simultaneously mock the local. It may pay to retain in our genetic memory a collective respect for the gentle power of working horses, with their noble bearing, and a place for the gulls following the plough, against those empty skylines where the lost villages used to be. It is unlikely that we will need to plough with a horse again, but we might need to retain knowledge of our own crops. Soil will outlive sand. People will always need food.

Spring gaiety

Do remember, they can't cancel the spring.

Why are my iPad drawings seen as a respite from the news? Well, they are obviously made by the hand, depicting the renewal that is the spring in this part of the world.

We have lost touch with nature, rather foolishly as we are part of it not outside it. This will in time be over and then what? What have we learned? I am 83 years old. I will die. The cause of death is birth. The only real things are food and love in that order, just like our little dog Ruby.

I really believe this, and the source of art is love. I love life.

DAVID HOCKNEY, Normandy lockdown,

Spring 2020

4

APRIL

Zooming in and out, in the manner of the *Powers of Ten* flipbook, including in the fourth dimension of time, makes it easier to take the long view of any contemporary situation or problem. There is a BBC Radio 4 programme called *The Long View*, which does exactly that, and which is almost worth the licence fee on its own. Going back in time by a few decades is the 4D equivalent of zooming *in* from the original *Powers of Ten* picnic scene, but by only one or two x10s. Going back by centuries or millennia is the equivalent of zooming in by many x10s. Zooming forward in time seems more the equivalent of zooming *out*, as it goes with implications of space exploration and being further afield, further from home, literally and metaphorically. Zooming out to a relatable but slightly dystopian scenario is the source of most sci-fi and disaster films. How far would we go? Could we kill *this*? Could we eat *that*? For the avoidance of doubt, (spoiler alert!) the answer to these questions needs to be Far, Yes and Yes if you are to have a realistic chance of surviving the film. True stories tend to be the most haunting. Zooming in or out to a relatable, recognisable but significantly different past or future tends to be of most interest to us.

In the 'nursery' of my childhood at the Old Rec, there was (and still is) a little picture with the title *Spring Gaiety*, by Molly Brett, dated 1959. This picture, and its title, seemed old-fashioned at the time (the 1970s), but it was enchanting to me then, and it still is. *Spring Gaiety* depicts two ideal-ised children 'frolicking' among a troupe of idealised baby animals, wild and domesticated, in an idealised version of the English countryside, in spring.

In the landscape of *Spring Gaiety*, lambs and fox cubs are 'gambolling' together in the same frame, surrounded by an array of British seasonal flora and fauna, deer, rabbits, squirrels, birds, catkins, pussy willow, daffodils, cowslips and so on, the whole scene imbued with an almost religious aura of heavenliness. *Spring Gaiety* is similar to comparable pictures from the same era, depicting country life in what might be called the 'children's prayer book style', St Francis of Assisi surrounded by tame wild animals, Gentle Jesus suffering the little children to come unto him. That sort of thing.

Nothing bad ever happens in pictures of these creatures, in this era, in this style. In such a scene, 'frolicking' and 'gambolling' are exactly the right words to describe the action, yet these words seem too absurd and tainted by saccharine cliché to use with a straight face, even if they are pragmatically entirely descriptive and correct.

With hindsight, and bearing in mind the date, 1959, I think this picture might have been a manifestation of my mother's as-yet unfulfilled desire (possibly longing) to have children. Even my elder sister was still several years away at the time. Perhaps my mother bought the little picture in the hope of one day putting it in her first child's bedroom, blessing the child (and the room) with a little vision of the world as a place of beauty and peace, and plentiful baby animals. Perhaps it was given to her. Either way, as it happened, our real-life world at the Old Rec in the 1970s really was a place of beauty and peace, and plentiful baby animals. Perhaps that is why I like the picture. It harks back to my age of innocence, as a child, running freely in the wider territory of the fields, orchards and separate areas of the garden at the Old Rec, before anything bad had happened. The room we still call the 'nursery' at the Old Rec is hung with the same old hunting scenes and pictures of racehorses that were there when we were children, to give you an idea of context. These pictures are familiar to me in every detail. The long neck of the grey horse in *After The Race*. The pencil signature of A. J. Munnings on the border of the print. The watercolours of hunting scenes. The hunting scenes actually include my mother's parents in the action, just before the war, Granny easily recognisable on her flashy-faced chestnut horse, just before she became a war widow with three young children. This was the background against which *Spring Gaiety* seemed so sweet.

Many people would sneer at *Spring Gaiety* and pictures like it, both on the grounds of its sentimentality and lack of realism about the behaviour of rural animals, and on the grounds of its idealistic, overtly figurative artistic style. I think these sophisticatedly urbane critics are missing something. I see their point on both counts, and have a few of my own to add if I was so inclined, but there is much to be said for having both an eye for beauty and a spirit of optimism, and in *Spring Gaiety*, Molly Brett demonstrates both. We need beauty and optimism, in any century, and there is much to be said for innocent art with no desire or intention to be 'challenging'.

In the future, people may secretly wish to 'zoom back in time' to that brief moment one spring when animals innocently wandered the cities of the world and breathed amusing and unexpected life into deserted streets and familiar views. As the coronavirus pandemic spread and human populations across the globe retreated into lockdown, animals stealthily seemed to be reclaiming their lost territory. Against a background of individual human tragedy, it was a collective joy to behold all these 'animals in the wrong place', very much in the overtly anthropomorphic, sentimental and slightly surreal spirit of *Spring Gaiety*.

At some level, the animals in the cities could be seen as a warning. *We are here. You have taken our land and our forests to build your civilisations, but don't forget us. Don't forget that we have the power to make your lives uncomfortable. Don't forget that all nature is intertwined. Nothing you can do can usurp us, at least not permanently. We are here. Pitter patter. Clip clop. Etc.*

While some reports about animals reclaiming the cities were clearly made up and/or photoshopped, such as the Doge's dolphins apparently swimming in the Grand Canal in Venice, there was and is an uplifting grain of truth in the often repeated mantra, *nature is healing*. There really were fish and swans swimming in clear water in the canals of Venice, just not in the Grand Canal but across the lagoon in Burano. In Florence, a badger trotted along a deserted street. In Bergamo, a wild boar sow trotted along with her little troop of wild boar piglets, tidily truffling along the deserted pavement, instinctively avoiding the road, her demeanour still watchful and wary of the human being who must have been there, filming.

The spirit of *Spring Gaiety* also extended to the British urban lockdown landscape. If only we could hold onto these scenes and forever share our spaces more freely with other animals. It would surely be good for our mental health to permanently live alongside animals in the wrong place, like the wild goats of the Great Orme who reclaimed the streets and gardens of Llandudno. It was enchanting to see goats running amok, delightfully climbing on hedges and leaping onto roofs, trotting about in little gangs of mischief, and generally being amusing in the arrogantly careless manner that goats are so good at. Goats routinely climb trees in Morocco and lick minerals out of the near-vertical surface of a dam in Italy, so Llandudno was a doddle. With their thick mops of cashmere hair and their enormously long and noble horns, surely anyone but a misery-guts would say that the urban streetscape of Llandudno was *greatly enhanced* by the presence of goats. It was like a real-life Saki story. Farm animals running amok in the wrong place, the more formal the better, ideally a grand drawing room or similar, is a recurring theme of the stories of H. H. Munro, known as Saki.

Elsewhere in Wales, wild ponies gathered outside a surfing shop. It seemed the most natural thing in the world, and no one seemed to mind. In fact, these stories of animals in the wrong place seemed to make people (and the animals) happier. Perhaps we could retain something of this magical blurring of our boundaries, and the brief cessation of our endlessly revving engines.

Even in London the deserted streets presented wild and

semi-wild animals with opportunity. The usual urban foxes and grey squirrels were joined by deer. In and around Harold Street in East London, a herd of roe deer took to lying languidly about on lawns and occupying with intent those triangular patches of grass which I believe are known as SLOAPs, 'spaces left over after [bad] planning'. *Spring Gaiety*, the scene and the spirit of it, was everywhere.

The reclaiming of human spaces by wild animals will be more permanent on the Suffolk coast once we have gone. Our farms, houses, churches and landscapes will be taken by the sea, to become empty sky again, literally leaving the coast clear for the animals and birds.

To understand the nature and detail of what will soon be lost to coastal erosion in Suffolk, with some serious losses of farmland and listed buildings due to begin within about fifteen years, *c.*2035, it is perhaps worth doing a kind of inventory of what is currently there. Without any record, the people of the future will not know what was lost.

The people of the present might also be interested, not only in seeing what will soon be lost, but also to see a version of everyday country life in the twenty-first century, a slice of working landscape that may on its own seem insignificant, but which is nevertheless part of the mosaic of cities, home counties, suburbs, market towns, uplands, moorlands, lowlands and fens, highlands and islands, and so on, that is our home and habitat, wherever we are in the UK and the world beyond. This is a productive working farmed landscape that significantly contributes to feeding people, so it matters for that fact alone.

The East Anglian coast in general, and the Benacre estate in particular, is a mixture of farmland and woodland that melts away from the higher ground towards the lower and wetter landscape of what might be called the edge-lands, of marsh and estuary, or cliff and dune, reedbed and beach. The erosion means that one type of landscape tumbles into the other in a way that normally it shouldn't. For example, the woodland falls onto the beach, so that tree trunks become bleached and beached in the sun, giving the air of ancient fossil-woods.

On a typical evening walk, you can often see all of these different landscapes at the same time. Even where the localised landscape is more enclosed or specific, for instance alongside certain of the larger blocks of woodland, it soon opens up to offer a varied panorama typically including some combination of crops, pigs, reedbeds, sky and sea. Sheep graze on the parkland surrounding Benacre Hall, formerly Gooch family HQ, rebuilt after a fire and now converted into several apartments, but still retaining its presence, with all the usual lovely old country-house paraphernalia: classical lodges like miniature versions of the house at the gates, a proper kitchen garden, larders, pantries, sculleries, boot rooms, and so on, still in existence within the house and the grounds.

Living on the same patch all the time, albeit quite a large and varied patch, offers the chance to get to know the locations and behaviours of some of the local wild animals and birds. I am sure there are plenty of animals we never see, carefully tracking us and avoiding crossing our paths as we all go separately about our business, but inevitably the observant will notice who lives where, and who comes out when, and does what, with whom, for how long, and so on. Here I am really talking about the routines and behaviours of our local non-human animals and birds, wild and domesticated, but similar observations, about habits and habitats, comings and goings, could equally apply to the local human animal populations, wild and domesticated.

Among the human neighbours, we all tend to have an easy, familiar but often physically distant relationship, perhaps passing each other on the little roads, raising a finger in thanks to the one who stopped in the passing place, perhaps a wave to the tractor driver as we scrape past each other, occasionally congregating in church, perhaps going to lunch or dinner in each other's houses, occasionally rumbling on about some particular parish problem or event. These manners and mannerisms, and similarly seasonal patterns and rhythms of life, are probably repeated in rural areas across the country, and across the world.

In this way, we all seem to feel connected to other people all the time, even when, in all conventionally measurable ways, often we are not. If I plan to light a huge bonfire of prunings in the kitchen garden at the Old Rec, I might warn Phillip, our farmer neighbour, so that he is expecting to see the smoke, but might notice from his tractor cab if I set fire to the trees. When we are walking around the byways of Benacre, we will keep an eye out for that lost dog. Probably, people are also invisibly noticing what we are doing and where, just as I might know from afar whose is which Land Rover, Jimny or Hilux, whose pick-up is rattling along towing a trailer, whose horse or dog or donkey, or who is in that distant tractor cab. I freely admit to not being wholly dependent on the land for my income, but I have for years been at least partially dependent on outdoor earnings. I am fairly typical of the modern rural scene, in which many of us multitask and are paid jacks of several marketable trades, no single skill being considered more important than another, when all of them are needed at different times of the day or year: feeding sheep, checking water, pruning vines, drawing buildings for planning applications, writing heritage statements for listed building applications, mucking out, riding horses, plaiting manes, writing books . . . and so on.

The hedges seem to have ears. Some time ago, a large number of us, separately, drove the considerable distance from our easternmost territory to our nearest point-to-point course, for 'our' point-to-point. Annoyingly, in order to arrive at the right time to sell racecards or whatever our job that day might be, we always have to set off before the official course inspection has taken place. It so happens that the course at Higham often has a frost pocket on the far side, preventing racing, and that was the case on this particular occasion. The point-to-point was cancelled, 'frosted off', so a lot of annoyed P2Ped-off people went to have their picnics together in someone's garden. The following day, I happened to go to the greengrocer's shop in Halesworth, and the man greeted me with a cheery, 'You all had a wasted journey yesterday, didn't you?'

It was reasonable for him to know about the abandoned point-to-point, but how on earth did he know that I personally had been among the point-to-point traffic, and so soon after the non-event? Even by Suffolk standards, this seemed an extraordinarily accurate level of surveillance from the hedge. Yet rather than seeming intrusive or nosy, it actually has the effect of seeming quite caring, as if people are looking out for each other.

There are rhythms to the day in the natural world that can be as predictable as the cockcrow or church bells. At dusk, there is a murmuration of starlings which swoops about every evening, over the reedbeds and Covehithe Broad, regular as clockwork. This huge flock sweeps in over the farmland to the west, near the building we call the Rubbing-Down House, and then proceeds in swirling circles towards the sea. For about an hour every evening just before sunset, this crowd of tiny birds swoops about in the sky, sometimes in what appears to be a faint and faraway wisp of white, then condensing to become a dark grey cloud, like those heralding an incoming storm. This density of birds in such close proximity finds no cause to fight or fall out of the sky from bumping into each other. There is a silent, mysterious communication.

For a long time I thought the murmurations were remarkable in their ease of fast movement without ever seeming to make mistakes, and with a noticeable lack of collisions. It seemed an almost supernatural natural event, every evening. Then I began to think of comparable movements that humans make, also without apparent conflict or collision, and the most obvious of these is the way humans scamper about city streets without bumping into each other. The effect is exaggerated when film footage from above is speeded up and accompanied by the frenetically repetitive music of Philip Glass. We too are ants, or starlings, or migrating anchovies swooping about the seas in an enormous shoal. Where once I might have marvelled at the way (some) humans and other animals seem to thrive in dense communities, in the coronavirus era it now seems instinctively sinister, as if there is a natural density of population above which perhaps we should spread out a bit, self-distance.

The movement of animals, birds, insects, fluids and gases, and even traffic, all seem comparable and related, as if defined and differentiated only by scale. A flock of sheep herding through a narrow farm gateway moves in much the same way as grains of sand pouring through the narrow 'farm gateway' of an old-fashioned egg-timer. An ant colony resembles the frenzy of rush hour.

If a bird or an alien were to look down on Trooping of the Colour without understanding what was going on, not understanding that it was rehearsed and there is someone barking out orders, they too would probably marvel at the peculiar spectacle, at the complex movements of the Household Division in full fig, shape-shifting their formal squares into different formal squares, whirling into the mysterious Spin Wheel movement without bumping into each other. Even if it is rehearsed, and with someone barking out orders, it is still a bit of a feat of people (and horses) not bumping into each other.

The same would be true of any large sporting event: Cheltenham Festival, the Grand National, Royal Ascot, the FA Cup Final, Wimbledon. Huge crowds of people automatically and seamlessly move from paddock to stands to winners' enclosure, or from Tube station to stadium, without any instruction other than the natural course of actions, coupled with their own prior knowledge of the conventionally most advantageous 'form', vantage points, routes etc., for each event.

It is easy to wonder how penguins ever find their own family in those enormous flocks which gather in Antarctica, and then we remember that if we can find our own car at the point-to-point or the Game Fair, or our own tent at Glastonbury, then surely the same inbuilt mechanisms of navigation, memory and instinct must be at work for the penguins. Nevertheless, our nightly murmuration is remarkable, and like the sunset which follows it, surely no one ever tires of seeing such natural wonders.

An odd thing about these natural wonders is that they are just nature doing what it does, indifferently, unaware, and probably it is only when witnessed from a human point of view that these events come to be seen as *wonders*, or *spectacles*. Does the fox stop to appreciate the colours of the sunset, his eye tracing the nervous-system lines of the trees, outlined in silhouette for centuries against these fiery skies, or does he just see the red sky as a daily reminder marking the start of his hunting jaunts?

Does the mouse or the muntjac pause to admire the murmuration? Does the owl in the oak tree like to see the sea? Is the hare aware?

Although supposedly rarer than rabbits, hares are plentiful in East Anglia, and we see more of the hares than the rabbits, as they live above ground on the arable, rather than over yonder out of sight among the gorse bushes on the way to the Rubbing-Down House. Rabbits are still plentiful in the sandy edge-lands and heaths along this coast, with their historic warrens marked on the map in the names of places and buildings: Warren House, the Warren, Warren Covert, and so on. And the famous Warren Hill in Newmarket, obviously.

Warren Hill is central to the racing operations at 'HQ', as Newmarket is referred to around here. Warren Hill is 'gallops central' in the early mornings, with strings of horses swirling around in the early dawn light, the lads (including female lads) riding out in hi-viz on the earliest of the first lots, and the whole magical operation having something of the mysteries of the murmuration about it, this time with valuable racehorses instead of starlings, but still with the elegant choreography of multiple simultaneous movements, and still apparently with no one bumping into each other. A minor miracle, every morning.

The fallow deer in *Spring Gaiety* could represent the herds of Benacre roe deer we see around us almost daily, perhaps six or seven at a time, suddenly appearing and skipping across the crops in places they probably shouldn't be, agile and elegant, a pleasure to see. The deer in the picture could also represent the muntjac munching away at the nightingale habitat scrub, although they can't help it, and there's surely room in the world for both muntjac and nightingales. Part of the appeal of the slightly ridiculous scene in *Spring Gaiety* is the way all of the creatures coexist in the same place at the same time, without malice or murder among them, or towards them.

The lambs gambolling so artfully in *Spring Gaiety* obviously abound in the English countryside in spring, albeit in Suffolk nowhere nearly as ubiquitously as in the upland areas of Britain. Here, our pampered lowland sheep live on flat land, decorating enclosed areas of parkland or managing the meadows by nibbling away at the tiny shoots of the thistles and docks. Sheep are also turned out temporarily in a rotational mob-grazing manner, to eat the sugar-beet tops after the sugar-beet harvest, while also naturally fertilising the land for next year's wheat or barley or oilseed rape. Suffolk sheep (meaning those living in Suffolk, including but not necessarily Suffolk sheep, as in the breed) are not expected to put up with the snows and winds of Swaledale, and they would be alarmed by the precarious and precipitous peaks of the Brecon Beacons and beyond.

George Monbiot, who writes on environmental matters, refers to sheep as 'woolly Mesopotamian maggots', and refers to the places they graze as 'sheep-wrecked'. This seems a little unfair, although he has a point, since sheep have apparently nibbled the ancient British forests to a green baize over the centuries. The Jacob sheep at the Old Rec are mentioned in *The Bible* (Genesis 30:31–43, 'Jacob took the speckled and spotted sheep from his father-in-law's flock and bred from them.') Jacob sheep used to be considered a rare breed, but now are not. If you want to save a breed, of sheep or any other herbivorous animal, 'eat it' seems to be the counter-intuitive moral of the story.

As well as wild game in the woods, including pheasants, partridges, roe deer and muntjac, there is also the wild larder of the wildfowler over the reedbeds and marshes, mallard, teal, greylag goose and so on, all seasonally available according to their respective shooting seasons and permissions.

There are also plentiful pastoral free-range pigs. Roaming freely in family groups within what can only be called 'pig communities', the Benacre pigs truly live a life that if applied to humans, might be described as on the pig's back. Clustering around the ancient ruins of Covehithe, these pigs complement the architecture, and the architecture complements the pigs. If you wanted to build a cottage using the local vernacular architecture and building materials, or a pigsty fit for a Benacre pig, the reedbeds and reed-cutters could supply you with Benacre thatch.

It was the reed-cutters at Easton Bavents who originally warned me that Benacre had lost sixteen metres of land to erosion in one tide, and who therefore dissuaded me from buying 'the house on the edge' of the cliff at the time, an act of Fate which resulted in us living at the Easternmost House for twelve years as tenants, and ultimately led us back here, to Benacre. The reed-cutters' job has barely altered since medieval times. The scenes from the twenty-first century reed harvest, the reed-cutters themselves, the diameters of their bundles, the measuring rods they use, and the stooks they stack, could be scenes from any year, from 1220 or 2020, it makes no difference.

In the early evenings in spring, the boom of the bittern can be heard from these reedbeds, a haunting *whhoooff* sound, like the wind blowing over the neck of a bottle. The bittern has brindle feathers and blue feet to match the reeds and the water in its watery reedbed habitat, and allegedly sticks its beak up in the air to mimic the reeds when it is alarmed, as complete and unlikely a lifestyle-and-camouflage story as anything found in those most improbable stories of evolution, the *Just-So Stories* by Rudyard Kipling.

Away from the unseen mysteries of the reedbeds, the timber for the structural elements of this hypothetical cottage or pigsty could easily be sourced from the woods around this cottage. Central heating would be in the form of the Benacre biomass crop, sorghum. If, or when, it becomes necessary to live and build in a genuinely sustainable manner once again, Benacre could quietly help us remember what our ancestors knew all along. In the long term, the loss of this land to coastal erosion and rising sea levels will be of a great enough acreage to appreciably affect the supply and security of British food. Here, you could genuinely live off the land and eat normally.

Supposing you were to zoom back to that lunch table, our *Powers of Ten* 'picnic': regardless of the time of year, it would in theory be entirely possible to eat only crops and animals from Benacre land, as a true 'locavore'. The principle of being predominantly a locavore, eating mainly food from a reasonably local radius around wherever is home, could apply wherever you live in the world.

Locavore menus could be contrived in a regional culinary

style which for this example we might call *Cucina Tipica Benacre (Bene Ca')*, for instance:

CUCINA TIPICA BENE CA'

(Ca' is Venetian dialect for a big house or palace, therefore Bene Ca' approximates to 'good big house'.)

Regional cooking from the Benacre estate.

All dishes may be accompanied by a choice of Adnams beers made with Benacre barley. Benacre elderflower cordial is made with Benacre elderflowers from the edges and hedges. All bread and biscuits are made with Benacre wheat or rye, and all crisps from Benacre potatoes. All vegetables and roast ingredients are basted and/or roasted in Benacre rapeseed oil.

Canapés, tapas and/or Cicchetti Bene Ca'

Patatas bravas Bene Ca', Warren Hill rabbit rarebit, North Sea fritto misto, etc . . .

Vegetable and/or vegan options, many and various, e.g.

Benacre asparagus with Benacre rapeseed oil dressing or Hollandaise sauce

Benacre Verdurer's pie – baked veg topped with Benacre rapeseed-oil mashed potatoes

Suffolk French onion soup, with Benacre red onions

Main courses and wild game

*Roast Benacre pheasant with roast Benacre
potatoes, carrots and parsnips*

*Potted Benacre partridge with Benacre pigs-in-
blankets and green beans*

*Benacre gamekeeper's pie, with Benacre rooks,
crows, muntjac and grey squirrels*

*Benacre wildfowlers' pie, with mallard or goose,
and sometimes nothing at all*

*Benacre bacon sandwich, with Benacre free-
range pigs on Benacre wheat or rye bread*

*Benacre bunny, three ways (coney confit, coney
cacciatore, rabbit rarebit), with Benacre carrots
(and so on)*

Pudding

*An assortment of puddings made with
Benacre sugar beet*

Savouries

*Rabbit rarebit, and/or any combination of any
or all of the above Benacre ingredients*

Foraged wild seasonal extras

*Alexanders (angelica), marsh samphire, elderflowers,
greengages, damsons, bullaces, plums, blackberries,
rose hips, chestnuts, nettles, dandelion leaves etc . . .*

Gleaning opportunities after various harvests
Occasionally a few red onions on the footpaths
after the red onion harvest . . .

Occasionally a broken straw bale after the
wheat and barley harvests . . .

Little is missed by modern agricultural machinery, so the ancient rural ritual of gleaning is largely lost.

If all this seems a bit poncey or obscure, McLocal's and pub food is easily done:

Cucina Tipica Bene Ca' fast food and takeaways
Beniburger (venison) and chips, optional onions

Covehithe hot dog (pork) and chips, optional onions

Off-the-beach fish and chips

Baked potato with Bean Acre baked beans

Beer and crisps

Beer and crisps

Beer and crisps

'Every ingredient fresh from the fields of Benacre . . .'

(or the nearest fields to you . . .)

A clod washed away

No man is an island
Entire of itself.
Every man is a piece of the continent,
A part of the main.
If a clod be washed away by the sea,
Europe is the less.
As well as if a promontory were,
As well as if a manor of thy friend's,
Or of thine own were.
Any man's death diminishes me,
Because I am involved in mankind,
And therefore never send to know for whom the bell tolls.
It tolls for thee.

JOHN DONNE (1572–1631). *Meditation 17*

5

MAY

At roughly the same time as absorbing the spirit of the *Spring Gaiety* picture, I learnt as if by osmosis many of the usual doggerels and rhymes of childhood, some of which were in some way usefully informative; for instance a handy guide to the singing and migrating habits of the cuckoo:

> In April, I open my bill.
> In May, I sing night and day.
> In June, I change my tune.
> In July, far far I fly.
> In August, away I must.

Without knowing it, in the 1970s we were connected via the cuckoo to the song *Sumer is icumen in*, dated from around 1300, which features the song of the cuckoo sung as a 'round'. The shared human experience, the relief of spring and the celebration as spring turns to early summer, seems unchanged. Into this quasi-medieval mix of singing and celebration comes May Day, the 'obby 'oss in Padstow, the choir singing from the tower of Magdalen College, Oxford, and bank holidays.

'Virtual May Morning 2020' from Magdalen College, Oxford, was an unexpected little wonder, an ancient rite of spring elevated to something magical by the strange combination of pandemic and panorama, isolation and innovation, Zoom and zooming. Against a backdrop of bells and birdsong, a camera panned across the dreaming spires of Oxford in the manner of *Powers of Ten*. The choir and their conductor popped up, one by one, via Zoom or similar multi-screen tech wizardry. Then at 6am, they began to sing, live, as if from the top of Magdalen Tower as usual. Heartbeats slowed. Blood pressures lowered. People were calmed. Spirits were lifted.

At a moment when global lockdown was on the cusp of veering towards pandemic panic, and with an imminent sense of climate change 'icumen in' never far away, this little vignette appeared as a beacon of civilisation, a reminder of human ingenuity across centuries, and of the speed with which we can adapt, co-operate and innovate, in order to retain that which matters to us, that which makes us human. In the most unlikely way, these improbable pioneers of progress not-singing from Magdalen Tower on that memorable May Day symbolised something greater than mere survival.

The May Day tradition of the choir singing from Magdalen College tower dates from 1505. *Sumer is icumen in* predates this by about two centuries. The temporary loss of the choir singing from Magdalen Tower gave a tiny insight into what it would be like if this arcane little tradition was lost forever, as 'a clod washed away'. *On its own*, the choir may be unknown or insignificant to many people, but as part of civilisation, it starts to matter, as table manners do, as a thank-you letter does, as kindness does. The 'small thing' matters most when it is part of a greater whole. *On its own*, a single thank-you letter might not matter, much, but as part of *courtesy*, this small thing, this 'clod', does start to matter. Ask any aunt what they think of people who don't write thank-you letters, not even emails.

John Donne's *Meditation 17*, the famous 'no man is an island' piece written *c.*1630 or earlier, seems entirely pertinent to the constant loss of land to coastal erosion along the east coast of the UK, as Donne instinctively zooms out in the *Powers of Ten* spirit, as we do, to include Europe and the wider world. At Benacre and Covehithe his seventeenth-century words seem apposite in the twenty-first century. Literally, we witness the clod-by-clod loss of 'a manor of thy friend's', felt almost as poignantly as if it were 'thine own', or mine own. It is almost as if Donne's *Meditation 17* could have been written deliberately and specifically for and about our historic and imminent losses along the whole of the east coast of the UK. If the UK is 'the less', Europe is 'the less'.

The church of St Nicholas at Easton Bavents, formerly the UK's easternmost church, was lost to the sea in a storm shortly after the inauguration of what turned out to be the easternmost parish's last vicar in 1666, forty years or so after John Donne wrote his *Meditation 17*. This was also the year of the Great Fire of Southwold, showing London to be not the only place so afflicted. Our ancestors were evidently also plagued by devastating natural events of many kinds, and with considerably less technology and comfort with which to suffer them.

With his uncannily apt words, John Donne seems,

to those of us who live in places where many a 'clod be washed away by the sea' every year, to speak in a completely contemporary tone. He seems to empathise with modern global feelings of connectedness to our neighbours; East Anglia and mainland Europe being once literally joined by visible and walkable land above sea level – formerly Doggerland, now the Dogger Bank, or the Dogger sea area on the Radio 4 Shipping Forecast. Donne also seems to have an instinctive understanding of the way in which the loss of land belonging to other people, whether family, friends or people we don't know, is often (almost) the same as if it were the loss of land of our own, as if it were the Old Rec and its land being washed away, whether we are talking about acres of Benacre estate farmland and listed buildings being lost to coastal erosion, or a tiny timber retirement house in Hemsby. To the individuals concerned, it is all the same, regrettable, unavoidable, sometimes catastrophic, loss.

The difference between 'ours' and 'theirs' in a rural context is perhaps not as clear as some people may think. Since land is generally held in trust (literally or metaphorically) to be farmed and nurtured and handed on to the next generation, to some extent no land truly feels owned by us, even if legally it is. Therefore, with this attitude of custodianship, and a sense of duty to try and hand everything on in a better condition than we collectively found it, it becomes easy to see how John Donne seems to have intuitively understood, and communicated across the centuries, the nature of the collective loss we feel here along this coast, here and now. John Donne seems to feel the loss of land quite personally and with a degree of patriotic anguish, as the loss of something greater, of country, of continent, that suggests that he may have witnessed similar circumstances of constant and physical loss of land and buildings himself, or if not, would have certainly sympathised with the current lot of those who do.

Moving from Easton Bavents to Covehithe and notionally zooming out to the wider territory of Benacre land, or 'Benacreland', genuinely a little world of its own (in a good way), could be seen as moving out of the frying pan and into the fire, in terms of coastal erosion. Knowing six miles of coastline intimately, from the north boundary of Benacre to the River Blyth, and many more miles of coast convivially but in less detail, has made me peer into the future to try and imagine what will be lost within my natural lifetime, other than 'a clod'. The answer is alarming.

The loss of *architecture* alone will be great, before we even start on the cultural loss of *land*, agriculture, reedbeds, old trees, hedges, farm tracks and so on. There are several historic and/or listed buildings imminently vulnerable to coastal erosion, while others will also be lost eventually, though having slightly longer, perhaps lasting a few decades into the foreseeable future. Many more ordinary buildings, including people's houses, will also be lost to the sea. Almost certainly, judging by current experiences and available realistic technologies, none of these, in the long term, can be saved by sea defences.

In early 2020, a house at Bawdsey was advertised for sale with what was described as an 'armour' of sea defences, officially intended to 'hold the line' (often written as 'HTL' in erosion jargon) for fifty years. At £475,000 the price did not seem to reflect the fact that it is possible, indeed probable, that those sea defences may be washed away, and well before the fifty years is up.

Other houses comparably close to the edge have often

been sold as if on a short lease, with an estimated timescale ultimately dictated by nature. The price of erosion-blighted houses is usually about one tenth of what it might have been without the threat of erosion. Erosion blight is comparable to any other blight, airport noise and so on, coupled with the normal attitudes of a short leasehold. At the right price these doomed houses can still represent good value. They are often romantically placed, and they can offer people a decade or more of an exceptional quality of life. They can actually be a bargain, compared with renting or paying a mortgage on a safe but dull 'normal' house. But *not at the full price*.

At Orford Ness, on 28th June 2013, the lighthouse management people at Trinity House decommissioned Orfordness Lighthouse, ending the working life of another beacon to shipping. This familiar red-and-white-striped landmark has been stuck out there on the shingle outreaches of Suffolk since 1792. This is where the National Trust looks after the former nuclear weapon testing grounds and the concrete 'pagodas'. Orford Ness is a bleak, brutal and Brutalist landscape of rusting barbed wire and gritty coarse-grain concrete, of war and wasteland, water and wader, shingle and shoveller. People who would never consider visiting the farming prairie-lands of Suffolk, or places like The Saints, for some reason are drawn to flock in droves from London and elsewhere to see the landscape of Orford Ness.

In many ways Orford Ness is Suffolk's equivalent of Dungeness. Orfordness Lighthouse conjoins the two words in the same manner as Dungeness, while Orford Ness is the Ness (or 'Nose') itself. But for all its comparable bleakness and shingle, Orford Ness has never been occupied or peppered with non-nuclear civilian human habitation. On the Ness, in the days before the National Trust allowed us to cross the river in a little boat and have a good poke about, there were only ever state secrets and the kinds of people who could keep such secrets for eternity, no artists making rustic rusty gardens, no urban tourists pretending to be pioneering backwoodsmen living in remote black-tarred huts at weekends. Comparisons of Orford Ness with Dungeness are made complete by the looming presence of the dome and hulk of our nuclear power station: Sizewell.

Unpretentious black-tarred huts are plentiful along the Suffolk coast, and so far the architects haven't got to them, mimicked them or replaced them, except on one or two sites a few miles inland. One-off new houses with vertical planks and huge windows tell their own stories, and the story is always the same. Old men with little houses and big log piles die, and their families not unreasonably sell the house so they can share the money. Someone, usually from London, buys the little house for the site, knocks it down and builds an architect-designed house as a second home. Ordinary unpretentious black-tarred huts used for storing fishing gear or selling fish along the shingle beach at Aldeburgh or the harbour-side at Southwold will be among the losses to coastal erosion or inundation. Many may be left unrecorded, except in old photos, which is why I take photographs of 'ordinary beauty'.

Orfordness Lighthouse has been heroically protected by the Orfordness Lighthouse Trust, but it cannot be saved from the waves. There has been much love and expense dedicated to this, including a rescue mission, Geotex sand-sausage sea defences, a plan to move the lighthouse back, books, poems, discussions, funds, fondness, art, articles and outpourings on social media. In the autumn of 2019, the little bungalow cottage beside the lighthouse was almost entirely destroyed by a storm. In February 2020, articles in the local press said the lighthouse itself was damaged around its base and foundations, but because of its remote location, it was not a threat to the public. Although with enough money it might have been be shored up in the short term, in the longer term, realistically its time had come to an end. The owner realised it could not be saved. While artefacts and parts of it were salvaged, this was the beginning of the endgame for the lighthouse.

Our old friends Anglian Demolition were awarded the Orfordness Lighthouse demolition contract. The process of demolition was careful, slow and gentle, involving the architectural salvage of all that could be salvaged. If Anglian Demolition's work demolishing the [then] 'house at the edge of the cliff' near us on the clifftop at Easton Bavents in the summer of 2015 is anything to go by, they will have left no trace. They really will have left nothing but footprints.

There is a stark predictability about coastal erosion, as inevitable as death, and comparable in that the details and timing are left unknowable. 'And never send to know for whom the bell tolls. It tolls for thee.' Along this coast, I have been doing an unofficial architectural survey of buildings of historic or architectural interest that I foresee being lost to erosion in the twenty-first century, and recording what I think is of value about their memory, and when exactly they may be washed away by the sea (or more likely demolished in preparation for same). As previously, when recording this crumbling country, this is largely for the benefit of the people of the future, people we may never meet and who may never show any interest in these lost places or the people who knew them. Once again, it seems sad to think that where all these places and people once were, one day there will be only a particular volume of empty sky over the sea, and the people on the beach will not know.

If we record a little of what we loved about these places though, the people of the future *will* know.

Thorpeness was a once-a-year trip during our summer holidays as children, just one day messing about on boats on the Meare, the shallow lake (mere) on which generations of children have learnt to sail or manhandle a heavy wooden double canoe, in search of the Crocodile. The original wooden Crocodile was a suitably sinister creature, lying low and discreetly difficult to find, in some far-off tree-shaded creek. The Crocodile seemed genuinely miles away from the boathouse, in those hazy days when we took what seemed to be the whole day navigating our way there, guided by little maps of the whole Meare and all its islands and destinations, Wendy's House and so on, the whole place inspired in part by the fact that J. M. Barrie was a family friend of the Ogilvies. Thorpeness includes references to Peter Pan (but not at all in a creepy way as is sometimes the case), hence the Crocodile as an adventurous destination for us all to aim for. The little maps were treasures in themselves, A5 size and printed on glossy magazine paper back in the 1970s. One particular memory of the place is that we were all standing near the little boat-ticket office at Thorpeness when I first heard of Elvis Presley, and the first thing I ever knew about Elvis Presley was that he had just died.

Thorpeness Meare still has the same old wooden rowing boats that my late father remembered from his time at prep school nearby at Orwell House, in the days when all these really quite tiny boys were made to swim in the North Sea every day, presumably for character-building reasons. These same rowing boats are still in use every day on the Meare, from about Easter to the fireworks at the end of Thorpeness Regatta in August. The boats have names like Pip, Squeak and Wilfred, the specific boats we always had to look for, for my father's nostalgic reasons, apparently named after an old cartoon strip featuring a penguin, and now presumably quite arbitrary and meaningless to any modern person who didn't happen to be briefed on the subject in the 1970s.

Architecturally, Thorpeness is a kind of Edwardian half-timbered fantasy holiday village, set around the Meare, the whole place having a consistent if eccentric architectural manner. It is the idealistic realisation of a man who might be called a benevolent dictator, Glencairn Stuart Ogilvie (1858–1932), in the sense that he had the idea and was able to carry it out, on a whim and without opposition, especially as he was paying for it all. The story of the building of Thorpeness is recorded in a book, *One Man's Dream*, by Ailsa Ogilvie de Mille (1996).

The village of Thorpeness itself was opened in 1913. It all began 'on a damp day in November 1910', when Ogilvie decided to turn the desolate, flooded and boggy mere into a proper lake, the Meare. In 2013, we all celebrated the centenary of Thorpeness, but it is difficult to see a similar party happening in 2113. Thorpeness is obviously vulnerable to the sea and to flooding, being both low-lying and historically a wetland, as well as having crumbling cliffs being eaten away by coastal erosion in the few areas of the place which are not dead flat, or wet. Part of the village is on higher ground, or built high, like the various Gothic-style towers, and the House in the Clouds next to the windmill.

The House in the Clouds is a water tower which was originally disguised to look like a cottage in the sky, for fun and to hide the supposed eyesore of it being an honest water tower. It has since been converted into a holiday cottage, so that the top part of it really is now a house in the clouds. The high points and high buildings of Thorpeness may be allowed to survive, subject to dull matters relating to capping off services and the like, which makes imagining the future of the place oddly more interesting than if the village in its entirety were to be decommissioned at the same time, and abandoned to so-called 'managed retreat', to be swiftly overwhelmed by nature and the waves. As a ghost village, sometimes submerged and sometimes revealed, it might become even more of a tourist attraction.

Perhaps a recognisable remnant of Thorpeness, including the towers and the House in the Clouds, may remain for much longer, still to be enjoyed by future London visitors or second-homers over hot, dry summers a century into the future, when whatever remains of every former town or village left on the edge of this coast may by then be reached only by boat. The half-submerged ghosts of Covehithe, Southwold, Walberswick and Aldeburgh may be reminiscent of the romantically ruined and abandoned islands and buildings in the Venetian lagoon, but without the *Serenissima* glamour.

The beach and the Meare at Thorpeness are perhaps more vulnerable to inundation than to coastal erosion, but still, with crumbling cliffs all along this coast, it is all dangerous, all vulnerable, all unpredictable. A few years ago someone was killed by coastal erosion at Thorpeness, buried by chunks of falling sand while walking near the bottom of the cliff, when the beach was narrow at high tide. People desperately tried to dig, but it was futile.

Not far from Thorpeness, a lesser known but more

remarkable building, built by another enterprising Ogilvie, is also likely to be lost. Ness House at Sizewell is a house on the cliff, built of sea pebbles, like flint but not knapped to a flat surface, the stones still rounded as if just picked off the beach. Now in the shadow of the nuclear power station, Ness House was known until the war as the Tea House, for reasons slightly lost in the mists of time, but associated with a folly for having tea at Sizewell Hall or some such tale. Lovely as Ness House may be, and itself vulnerable to the crumbling of the cliff on which it stands, it is not only Ness House which is among the 'heritage' at risk from the sea, but also a building that might be considered its extraordinary offspring.

In the grounds of Ness House there is an architectural gem, a genuinely unique rarity. This architectural gem is a survival of the Edwardian mindset in the built form of a stuffed-bird museum, built to house the taxidermy collection of Dr Fergus Mentieth Ogilvie (1861–1918), one of several brothers of Glencairn Stuart Ogilvie who built Thorpeness. Really this former stuffed-bird museum should be a listed building, but it isn't. In many ways that is a good thing, as it means that it can be freely used and enjoyed by many people, and is not preserved as if in aspic, like some kind of Edwardian confection constructed from the imaginary pages of *Mrs. Beeton's Architectural Management*.

For those interested in taxidermy, the Ogilvie Collection merits a whole separate area of investigation. It was probably the best bird collection in the country, by taxidermist T. E. Gunn, with the birds mounted in flat-fronted cases with duck egg blue backgrounds, all arranged to show the birds at their best and in their natural habitat. The Ogilvie Collection is now in Ipswich Museum, complete with detailed notes and all meticulously catalogued by Fergus Mentieth Ogilvie.

The remarkable former museum building is now headquarters of the Warden's Trust charity, founded by Elspeth (née Ogilvie) and Richard Gimson and now run by other members of the Gimson family. In its fully functioning heyday, full of taxidermy cases, this building must have been spectacular. It is essentially Classical in spirit, with a faint hint of early Brutalism when seen from the outside. The main internal feature is a single large barrel-vaulted area, probably big enough to house an indoor tennis court, and it is this main space which originally would have housed the stuffed birds. To keep the taxidermy in the correct conditions, the building would have had state-of-the-art Edwardian environmental technology including underfloor heating, remote-controlled ventilation, and overhead skylights with blinds to control the sunlight and protect the exhibits from UV light damage. Great banks of top-quality cases housing birds mounted by a leading light in the art of taxidermy would have completed the scene.

This building was and still is a remarkable achievement, in its function, the scope of its intent, and the quality of its technological execution. For these reasons, in its original state it should probably have been listed Grade II*. In fact it is far more in the slightly anarchic Ogilvie spirit, and better for human use, that the building is not listed at all, not even Grade II, so it is free from the constraints of the listed building officer, and freely open for the many disabled people who enjoy holidays there. There also concerts in the main space, to raise the money for the holidays which are the main purpose of the Warden's Trust charity, so the whole building is full of active use. It is also made accessible for use by local people with disabilities who are taken there for weekly baths and showers. In the typical way of Suffolk, when Fergus Ogilvie died in 1918 and the birds were moved, the building was then used variously for the storage of farm machinery and boats, and by the Army.

The Ogilvie Collection of birds was overseen by a warden who lived in a cottage in the grounds, so when the charity was founded, it was called the Warden's Trust and the building generally referred to as Warden's. Personally I prefer to think of it as the stuffed-bird museum, in memory of the considerable combined efforts of both Fergus Ogilvie and T. E. Gunn. Whatever it is called, the Warden's building is not immediately threatened by coastal erosion, but there are places along the coast very near it where chunks of cliff have fallen on to the beach below. It is difficult to see how this magnificent building, and its attractive companion Ness House, plus cottages, can realistically survive to the end of the twenty-first century.

At Covehithe, the situation is arguably even more poignant. The Benacre estate currently loses about thirty to thirty-five acres of good arable and/or nature reserve land a year to coastal erosion, but coming into view is the threat to some important pieces of architecture and rural heritage. Covehithe is tiny, but every single building could be counted as 'good ordinary' or 'good', with most of them listed Grade II, and with a Grade I listed church built within a mightily romantic ruin, the whole composition visible for miles around.

Of the current buildings remaining at Covehithe (others having been lost long ago), in about fifteen years' time, around 2035, a group of attractive listed farm buildings at Church Farm will be the first of the twenty-first century to be lost to the sea. There are also some useful modern farm buildings in the same yard area. In reality, these buildings will probably be carefully dismantled, brick by brick, pantile by pantile, crinkly tin panel by crinkly tin panel, in scenes very similar to those we recently witnessed during the dismantling of the Easternmost House at Easton Bavents for the same reason. The loss of a few old farm buildings might not seem too tragic to some, but they are handsome listed buildings, built of local soft red brick and blue pantiles, which have helped to feed us over the centuries, and which are quintessentially part of Suffolk's agricultural history.

Next, in about twenty years' time, in about 2040, the sea will probably have reached Church Farm itself, meaning the farmhouse. Then comes Anchor House, nearby but a few metres further back down the lane, another good farmhouse type opposite the church. At about the same time, a lovely house of the 'old rectory' type, The Cedars, will also be by then on or near the edge, not merely vulnerable, but inevitably to be demolished and dismantled before its land too is lost to the sea, if no protection or effective sea defences can be summoned. Geotex sand-sausage sea defences work, up to a point, but to protect the whole of Covehithe (population about twenty) would involve vast expense and ongoing maintenance, and even then, there would need to be some kind of causeway along the little road from South Cove to access it. In the end, *the water will come*.

On old maps of Covehithe there is a building marked Coastguard Station and a sizeable-looking house considered important enough by the Victorian cartographer to be marked as Lodge House, which may be the same one an old man told me about, which he described as 'a house with a walled garden'. Both the Coastguard Station and Lodge

House were located far down the track, well beyond the church towards the sea, and both have been long since lost to the sea.

Then comes Covehithe church itself. St Andrew's church, Covehithe, is a little church crouching in the corner at the west end of a magnificent ruin, with vast empty window openings looking out to sea, framed by soaring stone arches, and the whole construction a great credit to the skills of the original builders and stonemasons. The original church was built over many years, with the tower dated as fourteenth-century and the main body fifteenth-century, completed in about 1430. The church, meaning the whole church-and-ruin ensemble, is a Grade I listed building. This alone would make it worth saving from the sea, or at least worth making a strong effort for. But there is a factor other than architecture to take into account when considering its future, and that is what might be called 'human archaeology', and in particular 'modern human archaeology', meaning bones.

There are many graves of our kinsmen, old and new, in the churchyard at Covehithe; these are not appreciably far from the cliff edge even now, and the two are coming ever closer to each other. The first grave, meaning the nearest to the edge, would naturally be reached in about fifteen to twenty years' time, with no intervention. The people in the churchyard are not people who died in 1740. Many of them are people we (collectively, locally) knew. There are a couple of Commonwealth War Graves among them. I recently noticed the grave of a friend's father, whose funeral I attended in 2010 in that church, all of us arriving that eerie day at what seemed like the edge of the known world, into a deep fog, the classic East Anglian coastal haar.

Covehithe church itself currently has a temporary pause in services (separate from the lockdown stoppage of 'social gatherings'), as a huge chunk of plaster ceiling recently fell down, narrowly missing the head of one of our neighbours, an innocent person of the parish who happened to be arranging flowers at the time.

Covehithe church and its graveyard may be deconsecrated, and the people for whom the fever of life is over may be discreetly moved to Wrentham and reburied, but it is an obviously sensitive subject and the whole scenario carries with it thoughts of the future, and of the four-hundred-year long view. At Dunwich, in April 2020, someone tweeted a photograph of a human thigh bone sticking out of the cliff. In the case of the Dunwich cliff, the bone in question belonged to someone buried long ago and exposed by recent erosion, but its presence and visibility prompted thoughts (in me at least) that while there needs to be empathy and sympathy with the kin and friends of the people buried at Covehithe, there will also need to be some fairly decisive action about physically and practically what to do, and when and how to do it. Quite soon, clearly.

Church Farm Cottages will go next, a decent pair of typical Benacre estate cottages built of red brick with blue pantiles, well-maintained with attractive original doors and windows (external doors painted Benacre Green, naturally), and recognisably architectural half-brothers to the Easternmost House at Easton Bavents.

Eventually, in about thirty-five years' time, at some time in about 2055, Corner Cottages will also be lost to the sea. With climate change likely to create more, and more unpredictable, weather events and storms, it is reasonable to suppose that the rate of erosion may continue to accelerate.

But something else will probably have happened to us by 2055, so we will be unlikely to see it, unlikely to have to move out of the way of the waves in short order, ever again.

Inevitably, there is a great deal of bureaucracy and strategic planning relating to What To Do about the impending, now imminent, threat to actual named whole places, small towns and villages, not just the odd clifftop cottage, from coastal erosion, or what officialdom now refers to as 'coastal change', or 'our dynamic coast'.

The Suffolk Shoreline Management Plan (SMP) is intended to be a plan for dealing with the anticipated coastal erosion along the Suffolk coast, specifically from Lowestoft Ness (now the easternmost land point of the UK, although historically the easternmost land point and parish was for centuries Easton Ness at Easton Bavents) to Felixstowe Landguard Point. Attached to this is a Strategic Environmental Assessment (SEA) Report. Acronyms seem inevitable in such contexts, as does nominative determinism, since the document now known as the Shoreline Management Plan and SEA Report was drafted by a Mr Cork, who may well know Phil Dyke, the National Trust's coastal change and water expert.

At this point it is tempting to point out that the fishmonger at the weekly markets in Southwold and Halesworth told me that he goes on his holidays to Sardinia.

The Shoreline Management Plan and SEA Report is a huge and (presumably) carefully researched document, dated January 2010, Reference 9S4 195, replete with spreadsheets, zones in different colours, maps, a particular lexicon of jargon, and so on, outlining proposed policy along 'our dynamic coast' in three 'epochs', up to 2025, 2026–2056 and 2056–2105. The names and dates of these plans and reports may later be changed and updated, but the gist of the thinking is clear.

It is quite enlightening to think ahead into the twenty-second century, to imagine the practical problems that will come with the water invading the land, and it is something that oddly comes quite naturally when you live with such visible erosion. You are forced to look forensically into the future. In tone and density, the Shoreline Management Plan and SEA Report, drawn up in association with the Environment Agency and Natural England, is much like any comparable document, for instance those relating to planning and conservation areas, or agricultural policy bumf. Where the Shoreline Management Plan and SEA Report seems slightly at odds with its own title is in its apparently definitive conclusion.

The conclusion to the Shoreline Management Plan and SEA Report (i.e. the What To Do part) carries echoes of the Lloyd's names small print which warns of 'unlimited liability', in that the official response to devastating impending losses from coastal change can be summarised in two words: 'No intervention.'

The official plan is to Do Nothing. Naturally, some have other ideas.

The water will come

I heard the water lapping on the crag,
And the long ripple washing in the reeds.

ALFRED, LORD TENNYSON (1809–1892),
Morte d'Arthur

6

JUNE

There is no doubt that large parts of East Anglia and especially the easternmost edge of the UK will be underwater within the next century. The precise predictions and extents of the water are shown on what I think of (and refer to) as the 'blue maps'. To gather more detail, searching on the Internet for 'British flooding map 2050', or 'Suffolk flooding map 2050', reveals the landscape of the future. Searching for the 'Shoreline Management Plan' also rewards the effort. A succinct summary of the situation is that where now there are fields of land, soon there will be fields of sea.

These maps and predictions carry with them the fascination of attempting to see what the world will be like, and especially what the parts of the world we know most intimately will be like, after we have died. For similar reasons, I like to imagine with idle curiosity certain predictable dates and celebrations in the future, some of them around or after my presumed date of death: 2039–45, centenary of the Second World War; 2nd April 2077, centenary of Red Rum's third Grand National win; 21st June 2082, Prince (or by then King) William's 100th birthday (or the centenary of his birth), and so on.

It is oddly calming to think ahead, and to realise that the default position of nature and of life is one of constant adaptation and change. What will come is usually comparable to what has already been.

We have some relatively small-scale personal experience of water replacing land, as environmental evacuees and coastal erosion 'experts', in the sense of living with coastal erosion and being affected by it, rather than being actual experts. We had to move sooner than predicted because of a phase of coastal erosion more extreme than previously typical averages. Although our coastal erosion was at least in part historic and foreseeable, my ongoing observations and measurements of the erosion on the cliffs at Easton Bavents over twelve years have led me to believe the rate of erosion is accelerating, and that logically this seems highly likely to be related to rising sea levels and climate change. Therefore it seems likely that in the future there will be others facing similar inconveniences and losses, possibly sooner than they had imagined or planned for. It is not so much that *the water will come*, but that the water is already coming. The real question is, *where* will the water come? Luckily, there are maps which try to preview *where* the water will come. This is where the blue maps become genuinely useful, rather than sensationalist.

At about the same time as our evacuation in early 2020, NASA animations and photographs in the newspapers showed great chunks of polar ice falling into the sea. North Pole and South Pole, Arctic and Antarctic, habitat of polar bears and penguins: ice was filmed melting. Logically, the volume of this melting ice, formerly above the water line in the form of the tips of icebergs, must when it melts join and become part of the main body of water. This will cause sea levels to rise all over the oceans of the globe, as water seeks its own level, including at the bottom of the crumbling cliffs at Covehithe and Benacre. The predicted sea level rises seem insignificant and incremental, measured in millimetres per year or decade, until you multiply them by ten, or a hundred. The spirit of *Powers of Ten* haunts the sea, x10, as the millimetres eventually gather into tens, and eventually become metres. The Suffolk coast has already lost most of Dunwich and Easton Bavents to the sea, and there is much more loss to come.

Add to the ice melting the associated swells in the sea, and the changing nature of more (and more erratic) storms and weather patterns, and it all seems to conspire to create a perfect storm of environmental change, a potentially violent storm to which we must all adapt. And some people are going to have to adapt much more, and more quickly, than others.

Fairbourne in Wales is a village on low-lying land by the sea, popular as a retirement and seaside holiday spot, and charmed with the geographical advantage of facing west, thus giving its residents the daily natural spectacle of the sun setting over the sea. Here on the easternmost edge, we are sunrise people, enjoying the smug rewards of the early riser. But it hardly seems appropriate to watch the sun*rise* with a glass of chilled Chablis, even on Summer Solstice Day, which must surely be chief among the high days and holidays of what might be called the 'sunrise community'. It is not for nothing that a glass of something in the evening, at that witching hour when the working day melts easily into the evening zone of civilisation, is called a 'sundowner'. The west coasts of the world are in many ways a more sensible choice of human habitat than the east coasts.

Fairbourne, like Easton Bavents, is now defined by a natural disadvantage which will finally overwhelm and outlive all its attractive advantages of natural beauty and sunset-watching. The entire village of Fairbourne is due to be decommissioned and abandoned to the sea between about 2052 and 2062, with the more specific date of 2056 being cited in some sources. 'Managed retreat' is the phrase. Like 'no intervention', it really means 'abandonment', when applied to much of the easternmost coast in Suffolk or to our geographically mirroring westernmost coastal allies in Wales.

In early 2020, a BBC Radio 4 series of three features, on *PM* at 5pm, focused its attentions on the problems of Fairbourne specifically, referring to its residents as 'the first climate change evacuees'. While I think that the historically evacuated residents of Easton Bavents may lay claim to at least part of that dubious honour, it was a fair point about Fairbourne. This is to be the first entire village to be deliberately lost, in a planned abandonment, formally attributed to climate change. The village of Derwent was flooded when the Ladybower reservoir was built, and was later exposed as a ghost village when the water level dropped. There is a street of abandoned cottages on the uninhabited island of St Kilda. There are many ruins of crofts abandoned during the clearances in the Highlands. Abandonment of former human settlements is not uncommon, whether great civilisations or tiny cottages. But Fairbourne is unique in its current, very twenty-first-century predicament. There is already huge uncertainty about compensation, the value of houses, and the logistics of relocation.

This is the start of human climate change relocation on a grand scale, likely to happen across Britain and the world, yet the whole phenomenon of climate change relocation seems to have gone largely unnoticed by those not directly affected by it. This 'going largely unnoticed' is one of several reasons why I am drawing attention to climate change relocation on the micro and local scale that will characterise any one individual person's experience of it. At macro and global level, millions of unknown people migrating because of climate change relocation becomes a statistic, just as hundreds of thousands of people dying in a coronavirus pandemic becomes a statistic. At micro and local level, climate change relocation becomes an individual person having to leave this cosy house, their home, tomorrow. At micro and local level, the coronavirus pandemic becomes this particular person's parent having died, isolated and on a ventilator, this morning.

Officialdom had a half-hearted go at the wholesale decommissioning and relocation of Easton Bavents, but it was a fiasco. In 2010, a scheme with the infuriatingly uninformative title *Pathfinder* proposed relocating the entire community of Easton Bavents (including us), and rebuilding all the houses, at the time I think about seven in total, in a field a mile away. There was uproar, opposition and what became known as the Pitchfork Meeting. No one was in favour of it, with the possible exception of two people who used their houses as holiday homes and who were never there.

What the council officials initiating *Pathfinder* didn't really understand was that, although we lived there permanently, all year round, and all knew each other, Easton Bavents wasn't really a community as such, but more of a collection of people who happened to live in the same place. When the time came, we all knew we would have to move, or adjust the farm and the uses of its land and buildings, but it would be our individual problem. We would all want to move to different places or do different things. We were also all opposed to the idiotic idea of rebuilding all the houses on an arable field a mile away, when there were some perfectly good farm buildings a long way back from the cliff which could be converted. Besides, although we enjoyed living at the Easternmost House, if you were designing a house from scratch, you wouldn't rebuild it. All of the houses up on the cliff had ridiculous cupboards in the middle of the kitchen, and all kinds of awkward layouts and inconveniences. When designing (or rebuilding) a normal house, you wouldn't 'start from here'.

Presumably something similar would apply in Fairbourne. Some people might want their house to be compulsorily purchased and rented back to them. Some might want to remain as tenants to the bitter end. Some might see an opportunity for escape and a new start. Some families might have just had a baby. Some people might have just died. When the time comes to prepare for adaptability because of climate change, Fairbourne and Easton Bavents have been envoys, and the first thing that has become obvious is that there is no single pattern that will fit everyone, everywhere.

As much as we can plan ahead in principle, when it comes to the reality on the ground we nearly always have to adjust and work it out on the hoof, and usually, when it happens in real life, dramatic change tends to happen in a manner not conforming to computer models or maths.

Environmental evacuations such as those from Easton Bavents or Fairbourne will logically be likely to become more common. There are thousands of acres of low-lying farmland in Britain, which are increasingly beginning to seem un-farmable in any conventional arable sense. They are under water for too long to make any definite plans about the farming year or find vehicular access for drilling and harvesting and so on. In places like Hebden Bridge, no sooner has the community recovered and refurbished their houses and businesses from the last flood, when another flood inevitably strikes, with six months' worth of rain apparently falling in a day or two, vast volumes of water hurtling down the valleys. Logically, we can't keep on saying 'six months' worth' (or however many months' worth) of rain has fallen in single day, because if this happens often enough, and it does seem to, clearly the new normal is that *what used to be considered to be six months' worth* of rain is now a *new-normal day's worth* of rain.

The current and future impacts of sea level rise on agricultural land in the UK are quantified in the government paper *The Future of Sea Level Rise*. Of the UK's total agricultural land (23.07 million acres) it is calculated that 2 per cent will be lost to the sea. This means that 461,400 acres will be lost (23,070,000 x 2 per cent), if the prediction is correct. But the point about this 461,400 acres is that it will be lost from the east coast not the west, i.e. the 'croppable land' side of the UK. The principle of the matter is the important part of it, the term 'croppable land', rather than the detail. We cannot know exactly what will happen, but we can understand the implications of this loss of productive agricultural land for our food security, and for our attitudes to land use, crops and animals in the twenty-first century.

We can probably help reduce the effects of encroachment by the sea, or coastal erosion, or repeated flooding, but there surely must come a time when such efforts must be accepted as futile in the long term. Groynes, sea defences, river rewiggling, leaky dams, river catchment area tree planting and natural regeneration: all can play their part in mitigating the effects of what is essentially an excess of water in the wrong place. But it seems increasingly likely that some of these places will not be habitable in the long term.

It is clear from the 'blue maps' that much of the landscape of East Anglia and the Fens will be lost, or at least permanently under water. We are living with this first hand, and you would have to 'zoom out' and live quite far inland to be completely unaffected by it in the foreseeable future, meaning the next generation or two. To the familiar experience of coastal erosion, we can add the realistic expectation of imminent inundation of low-lying land, which is obvious when near the sea, but which continues far up the estuaries, marshes and rivers, into areas which look like 'normal farms'.

'Inundation', which seems a more descriptive and expressive word for the anticipated situation than 'flooding', has happened before on this coast, for example in the great floods of 1938 and 1953 which overwhelmed the North Sea coasts, especially East Anglia and Holland. It seems likely that there may come a day in the future when the sea will come in again, on a storm surge or a spring tide, breaching over our beaches onto the reedbeds, marshes and farmland beyond, and overwhelming our fragile estuaries – but this time the water will stay, and the sea will never retreat.

Looking at the 'blue maps', it seems quite easy to predict roughly *where* the water will come, in the UK and across the globe. These maps are based on the best science and modelling available at the time, including topography, and are likely to be reasonably accurate. Realistically, it seems wise to start planning to move away from these places, and for some, sooner rather than later.

Existing places built long ago, which were previously viable but which now find themselves to be in locations with uninhabitable levels of flooding, will need help. One day, in the foreseeable future, within our lifetimes, many places like Fairbourne and Easton Bavents, small convivial places in low-lying countries all over the world, will have been reclaimed by nature and the sea. Where all those generations of people and their (our) ancestors have lived, and where all those built places have been, there will be only houses of air, and empty sky. Specific Pacific islands may vanish. Parts of Venice may be drowned. In the UK, the rich, flat, fertile farmland of the Fens once reclaimed *from* the sea may once again be reclaimed *by* the sea.

The Fens will be allowed to flood, in stages of 'managed retreat' which amount to abandonment. In his book *The Fens* (2019), Francis Pryor comes to the 'when or if' moment. He says that if he had been writing twenty years ago, *c.*2000, he would have said 'if' the Fens are in the future flooded and lost at least to human habitation, but now he reluctantly says 'when'. Francis Pryor is a genuine expert on the Fens, and his anticipation of a managed, staged flooding of vast areas seems realistic. He also remarks on the discreet signs which appeared along a particular road, 'ER', and thought they might be something to do with HM the Queen up the road at Sandringham. In fact it turns out that the ER signs mark the 'Evacuation Route'. Once you know this, the bright red ER signs seem very obvious, and oddly fascinating, if a little sinister.

Having known the Fens myself for many decades, I have seen hundreds of acres underwater from normal seasonal flooding, so it is not difficult to picture the scene in the future. What is remarkable in the Fens is how shrewd our forebears were in building on the 'high ground'.

Guanock House is a well-documented 1699 fenland house with an ever-evolving and now quite famous garden, formerly lived in by garden designer Arne Maynard (an ex-housemate from our architecture student days), and is demonstrably sited at least a metre above the flatlands around it, as are the fenland churches, yet until the place floods, you would never realise their clever sitings. One Easter at Guanock some vet friends living nearby had to rescue horses from treetops in the floods, which covered vast areas of land and gave us a very real insight into the future. The entire landscape had been transformed into fields of sea. Later that evening we created a communal painting of the memorably dramatic flood scenes and events of that weekend, for posterity. The artist Fred Ingrams continually paints the Fens *en plein air*, as an authentically outdoor artist, operating from out of the back of a Land Rover Defender.

Those dark-earthed flatlands of the Fens are a profoundly inspiring creative muse for many, producing from their apparently bleak horizons and geometric vanishing points great surges of art, literature and architecture. (The late Jade Goody who was so unkindly mocked for referring to 'East Angular' on *Big Brother* in the early days of reality TV was not wrong. The fenland landscape is east angular. Jade coined an apt phrase.)

The Fens are topographically to the UK what the Florida peninsula is to the USA, already low-lying land to the extent of barely being above sea level, and it is perhaps worth noting that the author of *The Water Will Come*, Jeff Goodell, uses an animation of the future of Florida, to advertise and illustrate exactly why he wrote the book. In his animation, the land gradually becomes water, the whole map, blue. His point is well made, his warning, graphic.

There is much that can be done in the design of houses and other buildings to make them flood-resilient, as distinct from flood-proof. There are also many ways that new buildings can be designed as 'amphibious'. There are already examples of contemporary architecture embracing the problem of 'flood water ingress'. It is also worth considering the wisdom of traditional and vernacular architecture around the rivers of the world: for instance, the wisdom of building your house on stilts.

Warren House near Covehithe is a house near the reedbeds, overlooking the sea, a seventeenth-century house built of brick and timber, with a thatched roof. It is a listed building, but on the 'Buildings at Risk' list, because of coastal erosion and the inevitability of the sea coming in over the land. It will probably be dismantled, as such lost buildings tend to be, but the case of Warren House is interesting because it is built entirely from materials which come from within a mile of the house. It backs on to woods, overlooks the reedbeds, and is a mile or so from Brick Kiln Farm. If Warren House had been built on stilts from the outset, it could remain a viable house, and would have a strong claim to be one of the most eco-friendly houses in the country, if not the world, if the air miles and carbon footprint of the production and supply of building materials were properly accounted for. Just as 'food miles' are beginning to be taken seriously, so might 'building miles' and particularly 'house miles'.

Warren House is in many ways three centuries ahead of its time. If you were to reimagine its forms and materials in a more contemporary arrangement including, say, rammed earth, and with what might be called the twenty-first-century 'architectural tropes' that many people now demand (kitchen islands, en suite bathrooms, wood-burners hanging from the ceiling, windows the size of a barn door, and so on), it would be the star of many architectural magazines. As it is, Warren House is going to sink gently back into the earthy reedbed bog from where it came.

Sea defences and flood defences are easier talked about than done, and all such constructions are expensive to build and to maintain. There are few, if any, systems of sea defence which work *in the long term*. Among sea defences currently in use to protect very specific coastal structures in Suffolk, the two most effective and currently-approved systems seem to be Geotex sand-sausages, such as those which have protected Orfordness Lighthouse for a few years, and rock 'armour' intended to hold the line, which currently protects Benacre sluice and pumping station at the northern boundary of the Benacre estate. Sometimes there is some combination of these two sea defence systems deployed together, Geotex sand-sausages *and* rock armour, a belt and braces approach.

What demonstrably does not work *in the long term* is any variation on a theme of timber trellis and concrete blocks or triangular 'Toblerones'. I was sent several helpful diagrams of homemade sea defences after *The Easternmost House* was published, but there are many ruins and remains of such 'defences' along the Norfolk and Suffolk coast already, which rather proves that such structures are always either washed away or, in the case of concrete blocks, the cliff behind them is washed away, so that the concrete blocks become merely a marker of where the bottom of the cliff was at the time the person thought to put concrete blocks there.

The most famous example of DIY sea defences was initiated by Peter Boggis at Easton Bavents. As a retired engineer, Peter had the quite rational idea of 'feeding' the cliff with 'clay' (from a mysterious unspecified source), thus keeping his house *in situ* in perpetuity. In theory, and in the neat engineer's drawings showing a section through the cliff and hypothetical defences, this worked. But in real life, the beach became a mass of builders' rubble as an anarchic system evolved over about a decade. Feeding the cliff with clay became chucking any old builders' rubble overboard. Lorry-loads rumbled through the villages. And still the land was lost.

Of all the sea defence systems I have investigated, in an admittedly unprofessional manner, there is one single outstanding system that really seems to work, *in the long term*. It is the 'in the long term' part of the problem that is the real crux of the issue, and the system that seems to work is ... mangroves. The effect of planting mangrove swamps on coastal erosion is impressive. In theory, using drones, we could plant mangrove swamps along the Suffolk coast at a rate of one hectare every eighteen minutes. If the mangrove models worked as well at 1:1, life size, as they do in the scale models to demonstrate the theory, the energy force of the waves would be dissipated through and by the mangrove tree roots, leaving the incoming seawater as still and quiet as a trout pool by the time it lapped at the bottom of the cliffs of Benacre and Covehithe. The Benacre estate office might like to consider the drone-planted mangrove swamp option, perhaps not minding as much as some others about 'sea views', being more concerned about farming and crops and so on. There must surely be some harvestable crop from a mangrove, although sadly actual mangoes seem to be grown in 'mango orchards'.

In Southwold and Aldeburgh, the holidaymakers and beach-hut aficionados would just have to get used to looking out to the Suffolk mangrove swamps instead of the grey North Sea. The resilient mangrove trees with their gnarled roots, somehow able to tolerate rough and salty water, could become the stars of the BBC prime-time Sunday evening television slots, possibly appealing more to the *Springwatch* and *Countryfile* audiences than the *Farming Today* audience, although the retention of farmland through mangrove planting could be a game-changer that would win friends and influence people at the Suffolk Show and the Game Fair. The local wildlife would be bound to adapt in interesting and unforeseen ways. The new eco-tourism opportunities could be lucrative. Visit Suffolk could think up some snappy swampy slogans, reminiscent of those elegant 1930s advertisement posters for train journeys to 'Cornwall: The English Riviera'. Given that there will be Venetian levels of water, 'Suffolk: The English *Serenissima*' might be a romantic start. 'Visit Suffolk: stomp around our swamp.' 'Visit Suffolk: pomp and swamp.'

The future of Southwold and Aldeburgh on the blue maps looks literally insular. These two seaside towns are genuinely going to become islands. As the erosion of the farm at Easton Bavents continues, and it will, Southwold will be bordered and raided by the sea from the north, as well as from the east. Southwold Harbour will be inundated and will eventually be completely underwater. The Harbour Inn at Southwold Harbour may perish, although as it floods regularly and dramatically already, it may yet find a way to adapt. Raising the plug sockets and light fittings by a couple more metres would at least buy some time.

The *Isola d'Ischia* and the *Presqu'île de Crozon* might provide chic inspiration for the newly-formed Isola da Southwold and the Presqu'île d'Aldeburgh. Something like this really will happen. The water really will come. The most successful creatures in nature are not necessarily the biggest, strongest or fastest, but those most adaptable to change, and so it must be with human animals.

Looking at the blue maps, there will be remnants of the landscape as we know it, but we might need a boat system to navigate the more fragmented easternmost edges. The northern part of the Suffolk coast and islands, from Lowestoft to Southwold, including the isles of Benacre and Covehithe, could perhaps be known as the Northern Lagoon, just as Murano, Burano and Torcello are to the main 'fish' of central Venice. The southern part of the Suffolk coast and islands, from Walberswick to Orford, including the isles of Thorpeness and Aldeburgh, could be known as the Southern Lagoon, as the Lido and Choggia are to Venice. For local transport between the islands, there could be water-buses like *vaporetti*, or a fleet of fast RIBs (rigid inflatable boats) like Coastal Voyager, which currently operates out of Southwold Harbour. Private boats might be allowed for residents, just as Francesco da Mosto always seems to drive his own little red and blue boat around Venice whenever he appears on the telly to tell us interesting things about its (and his) noble history. The Venetian farming island of Sant'Erasmo is already so like Suffolk in spirit that our island future seems already laid out there for our inspiration, for a glimpse of the watery landscape to come.

The food of the Suffolk *Serenissima* would be naturally

local and seasonal, just as it is now, but perhaps with Adnams brewery and distillery diversifying into uplifting aperitifs like Aperol, so that the Suffolk Venetians (especially the holidaymakers and second-homers from London) could make a locally produced approximation of an Aperol spritz. *Cicchetti* would be no problem at all, since we already have local pigs, cattle, sheep, muntjac, roe and red deer, fish, vegetables, cheese and wine, all of which could be tweaked into all manner of tidy little *tapas*. *Fritto misto* would simply be a slightly more delicate version of our existing fish 'n' chips, using a lighter tempura batter, and perhaps some spidery squid and shellfish instead of a gigantic slab of slithery fish, but still locally caught, and still dunked in the sizzling oil of Mark's Fish and Chip Shop or the Harbour Inn deep-fat fryers. Sadly the Harbour Inn deep-fat fryers might by then be either in the attic bedroom, or even, notionally, underwater. Nowhere. Gone.

Thorpeness and Aldeburgh could see similar scenes, and in either case the inspiration of France or Italy, or anywhere else in the world, would be entirely welcome and without fear of accusations of cultural appropriation. Besides, when it comes to navigating around a series of islands, the children and grandchildren of Thorpeness would have the Venetian children's advantage, the advantage of having already been for several generations steering their way around the wet islands of the Meare, small children in small boats, in search of the Crocodile.

In terms of the future of wildlife, the East Anglian wetlands, lagoons and even mangrove swamps could actually benefit certain birds and animals. Our existing deer, herons and bitterns are apparently well-adapted to the mangrove swamp habitats elsewhere in the world, as are egrets and spoonbills. The storks which used to nest on a particular chimney at Easton Bavents might also find such a habitat to their liking. Storks are already nesting at Knepp Castle in Sussex, albeit as a reintroduction project rather than because the storks have chosen the place themselves. Animals have an uncanny knack of finding what they need, moving around, drifting inland if they find that the fresh-water boards at Benacre and Covehithe are breached and have become permanently brackish saltwater lakes.

At Heveningham Hall near Halesworth in Suffolk, a few miles inland from this easternmost coastal edge of the UK, there are several thousand acres of newly formed habitat awaiting the environmental evacuees from the animal kingdom, in anticipation of this coast being underwater in the future. On a scale comparable to the ambitious land-scapes laid out in the eighteenth century, Jon Hunt has had the foresight, and the money, to rewiggle a river and form part of it into a lake, to a design found on an original drawing by Capability Brown (Lancelot Brown, 1716–1783). Reedbeds have been encouraged to spread so that the bitterns will have somewhere to retreat to when the inundation crashes over the gentle widescreen panoramas of the Benacre reedbeds, and then the Easton reedbeds, and then the Hen reedbeds. At Heveningham, millions of trees have been planted, to become acres of woodland over the next hundred years or so. Permanent pasture (aka 'wildflower meadow' in the modern eco-lexicon) and historic oak-planted parkland has been nurtured. Bog habitat ('wetland') has been created and restored. Nature will be given more space in our farmed landscape in the next century than it was in the post-war half of the last.

There is often a small fly in the ointment of any overt

expression of optimism in the face of obvious crisis. In the context of coastal change (and several other kinds of major change) along the Suffolk coast, that 'fly' might be Sizewell Nuclear Power Station. There it sits, and we have all grown used to it. The dome is one of my architectural guilty pleasures. Undoubtedly the nuclear energy it produces keeps the lights on, and the reliable electricity it produces is from a natural, renewable source. But there is quite a big *but* coming, and it comes under the understated heading, 'Catastrophic Accident Risk'. Someone who really knows about nuclear power stations has been looking at our 'blue maps'.

'Sizewell will become an island, defences eroded before the end of its natural life,' a structural engineer called Nick Scarr of Nuclear Consulting Group told the *Climate News Network*, in the spring of 2020 (for the record). Dunwich, which disappeared in about 1338, is less than ten miles from the Sizewell Nuclear Power Station site. 'We' collectively are not NIMBYs about the nuclear power station. The Ogilvie family, who built Thorpeness and the stuffed-bird museum at Ness House, in the shadow of the nuclear power station, actually gave the land for Sizewell. We slightly admire the army of pylons which march to and from it, carrying the cosy electricity of the Internet and television to the houses of many streets we cannot see. In the era of coronavirus lockdown and Zoom meetings, 'our' nuclear power station is nurturing human contact.

People often say that tidal power 'will never be economically viable'. Twenty years ago people said much the same about wind and solar power. Wind and solar power now provide roughly a quarter of our electricity, at a cost that is below nuclear power or that from most fossil fuels. Tidal power could eventually be the same. A watery land of wave power and wetland wildlife awaits us.

With a little imagination and a willingness to adapt, Suffolk may find that when the water comes, parts of this landscape are presented with an opportunity, not a disaster. But the final words of Nick Scarr, the structural engineer, will echo the deeply understood certainties of anyone with even the lightest understanding of this coast, anyone who has been to sea in a boat of any kind out of Southwold Harbour, anyone who has studied the blue maps: *Any sailor, or lifeboat crew, knows that east coast banks need respect – they have dynamic patterns, and even the latest charts cannot be accurate for long . . .*

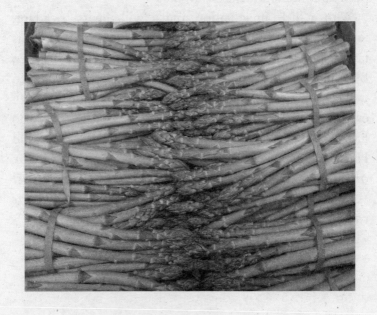

Strawberry fields

Curly-locks, Curly-locks, wilt thou be mine?
Thou shalt not wash dishes, nor yet feed the swine,
But sit on a cushion and sew a fine seam,
And dine upon strawberries, sugar and cream.

Traditional English Nursery Rhyme
(probably seventeenth or eighteenth century)

7

JULY

Curly-locks, the girl in the old nursery rhyme, evidently has a natural physical attribute considered beautiful at the time of the rhyme's origin. In return for giving her beauty to her suitor, Curly-locks is going to be let off ever having to do any kind of hard manual chore, apparently for the rest of her life.

This is an enticing offer, and one which has been exploited by young women with any kind of asset (beauty, aristocratic lineage, a title, land, money, etc.) for hundreds if not thousands of years, probably since we gathered round the fires in our animal-painted caves. The 'Curly-locks Scenario' over many centuries essentially led to my mother and her ilk being debutantes in the 1950s, and provides the engine for some of the most predictable stories in the whole of literature, most notably *Cinderella* and *Pride and Prejudice*.

The cultural expectations this has subtly spawned down the generations may also reflect the unwillingness of many people to work outdoors, in the asparagus fields and strawberry fields, or the leafy vegetable fields, or the orchards and vineyards, or indeed any fields at all. There seem to be perpetual reports of a shortage of manual labour to pick crops. Outdoor work is deemed unappealing at any price, and has low status. Apparently the Duke of Devonshire is often seen litter-picking around Chatsworth, which anecdotally at least gives credence to the third clause of an aphorism of a previous era, referring to litter: *The lower classes drop their litter, the middle classes take their litter home and the upper classes pick up other people's.*

Having spent many days picking various crops at different ages and stages of my life, and for different reasons, as a teenager in the summer holidays or as an adult resolving to earn a living without having to set foot in an office ever again, I can easily see why jobs involving manual labour might seem unappealing. They are exhausting, and often cold and wet. I would personally be delighted never to have to work again at all, but if work must be done, I would rather be in a cold, wet field, chatting to a fellow picker across the rows of a crop, than have a 'water-cooler conversation' in an office of any kind. Having done both kinds of work, and several others, I truly understand the allure of the warm, dry office, with computers and meetings and proper coffee, and the *not-having-to-do* the cold, wet routines of animal husbandry. Horses, hay nets, mucking out, feeding sheep, or hours of crop picking, especially when they are all on the same day, day after day, can begin to pall.

Yet many of us would still choose the purple-sprayed hands and snatched mug of instant coffee after a morning dealing with animals in the rain, over a 'flat white' in the flat white world of the office. In the contemporary culture of working from home, being able to continue to work in the usual way has become more appealing. However, days in fields of any kind, picking crops of any kind, seem long and hard, and they also require a degree of skill and knowledge, as well as physical fitness and a certain kind of mental resilience. Crop-picking resilience is the resilience of Boxer, the carthorse in *Animal Farm* by George Orwell, the ability to trudge on for the last hour.

I have derived enormous satisfaction from working in various jobs or careers (never sure which is which or what the difference is), mainly as a rural architect, but also as a writer, cartoonist, illustrator, crop picker, gardener, sheep wrangler, horse exerciser, skipper's mate on a boat, and so on, but the downside of all jobs is that they go on too long. If I didn't have to stay on for that last hour or two, I would probably have gone home. Given absolute freedom and choice, I might have done some (certainly not all!) of these jobs, but only for perhaps four or five hours at a time, and then I'd have gone off to ride my dun pony (if I had one), purely for the pleasure of it. It is the *having to stay at work for days on end* that I think we all find a bit laborious, not the concept of work, or the nature of the work itself. It is the metaphorical *ploughing on for two hours longer than we would choose to* that requires the mental resilience of the carthorse.

Most of us can be easily trained to do most jobs, and can pass on our skills to others, but it is understandable that not everyone wants to be so trained, to be able to recognise the pollinators of a different breed of apple, planted among the main crop in a diamond pattern, while picking the main 'heritage' crop of Egremont Russet. Not everyone wants to know their Bacchus grapes from their *Pinot Meunier* in a chilly Suffolk vineyard in October. It turns out that most people don't even want to pick attractive, glamorous crops, like strawberries or asparagus.

When I was a child, a friend's father grew commercial strawberries on his Suffolk farm. In those days, there was a 'Pick Your Own' (PYO) market in strawberries, where the public at large would come and pick a few punnets of strawberries for personal use, and pay by weight, thus cutting out several middlemen (pickers, packers, transport, refrigeration, supermarket shelf-stackers, the 'man from Del Monte' in charge of quality control, the man who creams off the profit, and so on). As teenagers, and possibly as children, in the summer holidays the friend and I would sometimes pick properly for the farm, or be put in charge of handing out empty punnets (little rectangular baskets, made of woven ribbon-like slivers of pale wood, with flat silvery metal handles, and no plastic about them at all), weighing the full punnets and taking the money. We were also notionally in charge of telling the public at large not to eat too many strawberries in the fields, thus literally eating into (actually, stealing) the profit income of the farm.

Over the years, the public at large must have eaten too many strawberries without paying, because the sight of a 'PYO Strawbs' sign on the side of a road is now a rare sight indeed. These normal country scenes of the 1970s and 1980s seem as quaint and outdated as the harvest scenes in books now considered twentieth-century rural classics, *Corduroy* by Adrian Bell, or *Akenfield* by Ronald Blythe.

The Suffolk element of the national UK strawberry crop is now picked by efficient itinerant teams of professional pickers, often from EU countries, and sold in little strawberry-shaped red huts beside rural main roads, reminiscent of those hot-dog-shaped hot dog stalls found along the emptier highway routes of America. The loss of the PYO farms is a tiny erosion of both freedom (based on trust) and British culture, but the public may have eaten just too many strawberries in the strawberry fields. What might be called *The Parable of the Strawberry Fields* probably carries a warning and a lesson within it, or several, but it is also just an opportunity to idly reflect on the Culture of the British Strawberry, and the Place of the Strawberry in British Culture.

It must surely be the commercial strawberry that makes the real money. Strawberries are *everywhere* in a typical British summer, as reliably present as the rain lashing down against the roof of the marquee or the racecourse grand-stand. It will always be 'raining cats and dogs' in the dog days of a British summer, even though such an expression seems to have escaped from a French child's English lessons. French people love telling us how recently they and their children were taught to say 'raining cats and dogs'. *Ha ha ha! C'est formidable, non? Chats et chiens!*

Strawberries seem to be everywhere in a British winter now too, an offshoot of the hyper-globalisation which ironi-cally led us all into a pandemic semi-lockdown summer.

Just as the PYO strawberry culture seemed to have vanished forever, the Internet craze concept of 'cottagecore' came to the fore, and people suddenly started seeing cottages and a cosy countryside image as an identifiable TikTok and Instagram trend. Teenagers became entranced with 'pastoral fantasy landscapes'. Urban men started wearing tweed and old jerseys, in London. The *Guardian* described a stick as a 'scythe', but no one cared, just as no one cares when straw bales are captioned as 'hay bales'. In the grand scheme of things, and in such an urban age, anything that indicates the wider public valuing country things, even if only for a moment, must be seen as good and wholesome.

Essentially the British strawberry season is the bedrock of what is still called 'The Season'. Some may think it anachronistic, but in real life The Season exists and happens. For those unfamiliar with the concept, The Season goes roughly as follows, like clockwork every year, only being paused for war or pandemic:

March

Cheltenham Festival; National Hunt racing, Cheltenham; The Boat Race, Rowing, Oxford v. Cambridge, London

April

The Grand National Meeting, National Hunt racing, Aintree

May

Badminton Horse Trials, Eventing, Badminton, Gloucestershire; Royal Windsor Horse Show, Windsor Great Park; RHS Chelsea Flower Show, London

June

The Fourth of June, Eton College (usually not on 4th June); The Derby, flat racing, Epsom; Trooping the Colour, The Queen's Birthday Parade, London; Royal Ascot, flat racing, Ascot; Wimbledon Tennis, All England Club, Wimbledon; RA Summer Exhibition, Royal Academy, Piccadilly; Glastonbury, Latitude etc., assorted festivals on dairy farms and estates etc. (not strictly 'Season' but now comparably established)

July

Henley Royal Regatta, Henley; The Proms, Royal Albert Hall

August

Glorious Goodwood, Flat racing, Goodwood; The Game Fair, various, Blenheim Palace etc.; The Glorious 12th, grouse shooting season starts (traditionally the end of 'The Season')

September

Burghley Horse Trials, Eventing, Burghley House, Lincolnshire; Last Night of the Proms, Royal Albert Hall

Although Cheltenham Festival and the Last Night of the Proms are clearly outside the core dates of the British strawberry-crop season, all these events are without exception highly likely to serve strawberries among their offerings. Whether in a pre-frozen *jus* alongside a teeny triangle of lemon cheesecake for pudding, or in a cocktail at Aintree, or as unadulterated fresh berries and cream, strawberries will be there. There are various other events throughout the summer, which may not count as part of The Season, for instance polo, Glyndebourne opera and the Old Rec (and other village) cricket matches, but strawberries will be there too.

Strawberries are a symbol of summer and of enjoyment and of sociability. Strawberry fields forever, as the Beatles might say. The song was apparently inspired by the garden of a Salvation Army children's home called Strawberry Field, a reminder that life is a lottery, and children cannot choose whether their alma mater turns out to be set among the playing fields of Eton or the garden of Strawberry Field.

While no one wants to ban strawberries, there are people who want to ban all or most of the events of The Season as listed above, for reasons usually related to animals or politics, and often both simultaneously.

As we are anyway living through a phase of great change, this seems a good moment to consider the long-term future, to think about which changes we might make for the better in the long term. All the events of The Season could continue, not least for reasons of diversity (which must include diversity of experience and opinion) and enjoyment, adding to the gaiety of the nation and so on. There is potentially huge capacity for change, which could be managed as a kind of phased 'cultural erosion', so that any change evolves naturally and does not result in the loss of cultural 'land' in the form of the loss of these events altogether. This may be a literally crumbling country but it is not a culturally crumbling country. Like the landscape, we are constantly adapting, evolving and changing.

Ethical changes could in many cases make life better. We could change the rules of racing, redesign the inflatable whip, or run certain races with no whips at all (subject to safety factors), rather than banning the entire sport and culture of racing, leaving only its memories in the museum at Palace House in Newmarket, its history on the Heath, the stables empty, the gallops silent, Tattersall's buried under an anonymous new townscape. Some people would not be happy until every horse was 'free' (meaning, never born at all), but they are few.

The same goes for animal agriculture. We could radically reduce intensive indoor animal farming while retaining the benefits of grazing herbivores for conservation, permanent pasture, wildflower-rich hay meadows, and so on. Some people might prefer it if we all went completely vegan, but many, if not most, would not. Gradual change and cultural balance could be achievable. We should not just presume to follow the creed of 'we've always done it this way', if there is a better, kinder way.

The most successful animals are the ones most adaptable to change.

Unprecedented levels of cultural and behavioural change happened in a matter of days when the coronavirus outbreak turned into a pandemic and global lockdown. We used to smoke on aeroplanes and on the Tube in London. We used not to wear seat belts. Why not capitalise on our recently learned lockdown capacity for radical change? Why not reduce our flying habit for good? Why not ration air miles? Why not remove the presumed right to own a second home and keep it empty for fifty weeks a year? Pollution levels were measurably lower in lockdown, and it wasn't because we switched off all the cows. Perhaps it never really was cattle that were the major cause of pollution, CO_2 and climate change in the first place. Instead of living with ongoing cultural tensions, we could make radical changes now, and then live peaceably with the consequences for the next half-century, saving time not arguing.

Libertarians are *in theory* philosophically against draconian measures which curtail people's freedom to live as they wish (subject to not harming others in the process), but *in practice* we don't seem to mind. No one rioted against draconian coronavirus lockdown measures. Perhaps we are now in a state of preparedness, in a good frame of mind for more permanent positive change.

No one has the right 'not to be offended', but when we stroll past the outdoor free-range pigs, and when I look them in the eye as I used to look our Jacob sheep in the eye, I consider every pig to be as much of a sentient being as I am. I would not consider the pig exactly my 'equal', in the sense that faced with killing a pig or a human, I would consider taking the pig's life to somehow be morally (as distinct from legally) the lesser crime. But I could also think killing a pig, the pig, for any reason, at some fundamental level, 'wrong'. As someone with farming experience, who has grown up in the country, surrounded by the life and death of wild and domestic animals all my life, this sense of killing any animal as 'wrong', sits uneasily with everything I know and live among. Perhaps among the radical changes we have made, increased empathy could be uppermost.

In many ways, those who shoot and kill their own food have much in common with vegans, in the sense of having a connection with nature, a conscience, and a sense of personal responsibility.

It so happens that I committed a pig-related crime recently, albeit without knowing that it was a crime. I was also once threatened by the RSPCA with being accused of 'stealing a pig' if I organised for a particular neglected pig to be rehomed, but that is a past near-crime, whereas my more recent encounter with a piglet was a real crime, a crime which went unreported.

While we were still living on the crumbling cliff at Easton Bavents, after the publication of *The Easternmost House*, there was a rap on the kitchen window. A couple of walkers told me there was a piglet on the farm track, so I came out to have a look and help catch it. From their slightly alarmed manner, and my general knowledge of the local lie of the land and the word 'piglet', I had rather imagined a smallish actual pig, just as the word 'lamb' is often used to describe quite a big animal. I was already working out how to herd a large-ish piglet into an enclosed part of the garden, perhaps using my white chopping board as a pig guider, in the manner of the pig handlers at the Suffolk Show (or any other agricultural show), where it seems to be 'correct form' for handlers to wear a white coat and guide their pigs round the show ring using what looks like a white chopping board.

When I finally found the piglet, I was mildly surprised to see that it was tiny. It was about the size of a Jack Russell terrier or thereabouts, pink, portable and utterly piglet-like. Naturally, I picked it up. This seemed the obvious thing to do bearing in mind, a) it wasn't my piglet, and therefore, b) I would need to return it to its rightful owner, who I presumed to be our neighbouring farm, albeit that was quite a long way for such a tiny piglet to run away from, or back to. Besides, how would it know the way?

To my surprise, the walkers who had alerted me to its presence seemed appalled when I picked up the piglet and proffered it to them with a view to thinking they might like to say hello to it, perhaps stroking it and thinking 'how sweet', and so on. They backed off, as if I were holding a half-grown baby crocodile, not a tiny little piglet. There was a small speck of blood from a minuscule puncture-type injury on the piglet's back. It didn't seem to bother the piglet at all, but perhaps it was this tiny red dot, hinting at injury and blood, which bothered the walkers.

I thanked the nervous walkers very much for alerting me to the piglet, and said I would put the mini-pig in the

Mighty Jimny and take it home, obviously meaning the piglet's home, not mine. The walkers looked horrified. But I don't know what they thought I should do instead of taking it home, to its mother, its only source of food and warmth. I was tempted to ask the walkers what they would have done, or thought I should do, but I let it go. Did they think I should 'save' the pig? Take it to a 'sanctuary'? The vet? Keep it? I regret not asking what they thought I should have done.

The tiny piglet, by now in the car boot (the dog-friendly kind of boot with windows, like a mini Land Rover, not the enclosed kind of boot), suddenly burst into impressively strong and vigorous life. Squealing like a child being murdered, it hurtled down the side of the front passenger seat, into the footwell, across the gear stick and back into the boot, so I found a cardboard box and a dog blanket, and made the piglet a little nest, to contain it and calm it down.

Then I drove down the track, turned left onto the 'public highway', drove along the road for a few hundred yards, turned left into the neighbouring farm, and returned 'my' piglet to its rightful owner. By this time I was quite fond of the piglet, and on the way home I slightly regretted having given away such an opportunity for a pet pig, the founding pig of my herd, so lightly. Then I thought of Defra movement bureaucracy, ear tags and all that, and felt relieved again. But in the driving of a live pig in a domestic vehicle, I had committed a crime, although I only discovered this later, by accident. You'd think it would be the driving of someone else's pig along the 'public highway' that might be the cause of consternation in law, but apparently it is the style of vehicle rather than the route or the ownership of the pig. Even if I had taken the pig down the farm track and entered the neighbouring farm through a gap in the boundary hedge, it would have been a crime.

By law, pigs require a licence if being moved to another premises. It is illegal to transport pigs in any vehicle that has not been properly constructed to carry them. Pigs must be transported in accordance with the Welfare of Animals (Transport) Order 2006 . . .

The Animal Welfare Act 2006 does its best to formally protect and promote the welfare of animals, but it seems quite obvious that the law on its own is not enough. There are gaps, not so much regarding transport arrangements but for instance in the matter of *housing* for farm animals.

I have a long-standing interest in architecture for animals, to the extent that it has been a significant part of my job as an architect. One of my specific areas of interest is stables, and if anyone is interested in the history of stables, the definitive book on the subject is *The British Stable*, by the late Giles Worsley. It is a scholarly tome, with notable photographs by William Curtis Rolf. Another book with satisfying photographs is *Beastly Buildings* (updated as *Palaces for Pigs*) by Lucinda Lambton, which celebrates the heyday of grand architecture for animals, mostly in the eighteenth century, when there was a fashion among the aristocracy to build deliberately beautiful buildings for creatures of all kinds, menageries, hunt kennels, dovecotes, cowsheds, and so on. My own personal architectural hero is Thomas Wright (1711–1786), who built castles for cows at Badminton, among many other endearing things he did in his life. He was known as The Wizard of Durham, an eighteenth-century architect, astronomer and mathematician, author of *Universal Architecture* and many beautifully illustrated astronomical tomes. I was struck by a kind of *coup de foudre* in my early twenties, but this was no foolish love affair, and I still love Thomas Wright so much that I have written a so-far unpublished book about him, *The Wizard of Durham*.

From time to time I post examples on Twitter, using the hashtag #ArchitectureForAnimals. Sometimes my #ArchitectureForAnimals shows attractive old cowsheds, pigsties and so on, but there is a more serious underlying point. I believe that the lives of millions of animals could be greatly improved by alteration of the Building Regulations. Currently there are hundreds of recommendations about light, space, ventilation and so on, particularly with regard to the housing of farm animals, but probably also for zoos and other places where animals are kept, for whatever reason. Architecture for animals is a subject which I believe could and should be taken more seriously, as it has been in the past.

Commercial chicken sheds could be required to have more natural light and *enrichment* for the chickens in the form of old chairs for them to climb on, and dust baths in tyres. Small changes and the idea of *enrichment* could improve animals' lives so much. You only have to see the pleasure given to cows using the Happy Cow scratchy brushes now commonplace on farms to see the benefits of enrichment. Swift boxes, sparrow boxes and hedgehog holes in fences should be required in all new-build housing. Bat boxes and barn owl boxes seem to genuinely help these animals find homes.

I believe the design of buildings for animals could be greatly improved, not least by looking at the requirements of the animals *from the animals' point of view*, not from the point of view of human perceptions of architectural beauty. William Kent's stables for the Household Cavalry, still in daily use at Horse Guards, are undoubtedly beautiful and can be seen by the public through a window in the Household Cavalry Museum, but from the cavalry blacks' point of view (i.e. the horses' point of view), they would probably prefer loose boxes to stalls. Even in a stable, horses ideally need to be able to turn round, lie down, move around freely, and roll.

But back to the piglet...

It occurred to me later that my piglet might have been picked up in the talons of a bird of prey, and dropped. We had a number of large birds of prey at Easton Bavents, buzzards, marsh harriers, hen harriers and the like, and the same here at Benacre, and it seemed unlikely that such a tiny piglet would run so far from the warmth of its mother and piglet-siblings, all cosily in a row beside her.

A few years ago there was a plan to introduce sea eagles along this coast, and every single landowner and farmer had big signs up in fields along the roads, saying something along the lines of NO SEA EAGLES HERE in big letters. I think someone gave us a sign to put up too. The local reasoning was that the sea eagles would take valuable lambs and piglets. Bearing in mind the number of pubs called The Eagle and Child, I think they might have had a point. With hindsight, and thinking about the neat little puncture wound on its back, I feel sure that 'my' tiny piglet was taken by a bird of prey, and literally dropped into my life. The tiny red dot was literally the mark of nature red in tooth and *claw*.

I sometimes think I should have broken all the rules and kept my little pig, in the grass yard and pigsty at the Old Rec. A lucky pig. A pig from heaven. The pig of Fate.

Honesty boxes

Whatsoever things are true, whatsoever things are honest,
whatsoever things are just, whatsoever things are pure,
whatsoever things are lovely, whatsoever things are of
　　good report;
if there be any virtue, and if there be any praise, think on
　　these things.

Philippians 4:8

8

AUGUST

A few years ago, Suffolk won an award for its regional food, being the best county for butchers, bakers, game dealers, and all that sort of thing. Among the plaudits was a flattering article in a broadsheet newspaper, pointing out that this win was no accident, that it was not because of luck that the county had won.

It was because Suffolk still has good fish huts, and livestock and dairy farmers, because the local people still value these things, and they (that is, we) vote with their feet and put their money where their mouth is, and so on. We continue to buy locally caught fish from black-tarred fish huts, and Blythburgh free-range pork from independent butchers, and milk cheese from named and known dairy farmers like Baron Bigod, whose cows could be seen grazing on the marshes, and who sells milk directly on the farm from a hut painted like a cow. All of which is true, which is why it all survives. Tiny bit by tiny bit, little amounts, bought often, by many people.

One of the more satisfying nuggets of this memorable

article was that it pointed out that Suffolk people are active and enthusiastic users of roadside honesty boxes, meaning those homemade stalls selling home-grown veg, eggs and slightly random seasonal items like redcurrant jelly. It was pointed out that this active use is precisely why there are still so many honesty boxes on the sides of the rural roads of Suffolk, honesty boxes which have disappeared from many other seemingly more sophisticated counties.

In the language of *Powers of Ten*, honesty boxes represent zooming *in*, to examine at molecular level the home-grown nourishment that they offer, of body (in veg) and soul (in honesty-testing).

The people of Suffolk who read this article must surely have felt a fleeting momentary puff of personal pride in this tiny fact, in print, thinking of all the times when we personally have put the money in the cash box, or the slot, or the old ice-cream tub provided at the business end of these enterprises, sometimes rounding *up* (as distinct from rounding down or leaving an IOU) if we don't have the right money. The honesty-box detail felt like a little feather in our collective cap, for being on the whole, or at least when faced with the identifiable efforts of real people rather than faceless institutions, honest. 'Whatsoever is honest, whatsoever is lovely ... think on these things,' says the Bible. We did. And still do.

The sad thing is, recently and since that award and that article, standards have somehow lapsed. Until recently there used to be a keen sense of anticipation for the Sea Breeze Asparagus sign which would go up near the south lodge of Benacre Hall around St George's Day, and until approximately the summer solstice on 21st June. SEA BREEZE ASPARAGUS in big black block letters with a neat arrow was a marker buoy in the year. We put our money in the slot and took however many bunches of asparagus, always tied up with red elastic bands, which we were encouraged to save and bring back. For an extra £1 or however much, you could also buy a Sea Breeze Asparagus branded cardboard box, so that you could give people a box of asparagus bunches instead of a box of Bendick's if you were asked to dinner. Then someone stole the money, and now it is all over.

You can still buy Benacre asparagus in the local shops, but it is not called Sea Breeze Asparagus any more, and you can't give people a box of asparagus when you go to their house for dinner. In a year when it seemed as if we might never go to dinner with anyone again, this appeared a minor matter. But it is the collapse of our collective honesty which stings. 'Whatsoever *was* lovely ... whatsoever *was* honest ... look on these things', as the twenty-first-century Amended Version of the Bible might say. Insult was added to injury when some friends with a proper commercial egg farm had to change their farm gate system to a vending machine, as people had begun not to pay. We still have plenty of honesty boxes in Suffolk, but it is easy to imagine a future when they might no longer exist, and it would be no small loss.

At about the same time as the honesty-box article, we happened to go to a wedding in the Cotswolds, and as lovely as that honey-stoned part of the world undoubtedly is, it was noticeable for an absence of something we take for granted in Suffolk: scruffiness. Everything from the tiniest terraced cottages to the most done-up barns seemed smart, tidy and Farrow-and-Balled to within an inch of its lock-up-and-leave life. Suddenly I appreciated the literally lived-in scruffiness of Suffolk as never before. The scruffiness of Suffolk is a sign that most of the cottages and houses, at least away from the coastal towns and villages, are still lived in full time, all year round and in all weathers. It is obvious really. It is also obvious that not too long ago, the scruffiness of Suffolk would have still been evident in every rural county, which leads to thoughts about change, and whether improvement is inevitably better.

If you live somewhere all the time, but are not a proper farmer, you can still have chickens and geese and guinea fowl, grow vegetables, keep sheep, set up a homemade honesty-box stall, and at least partly, live off the land. This is true whether the land of the not-proper farmer is measured in hundreds or tens of acres, or small fractions of acres, or window boxes. It is largely a matter of attitude. When I lived in London I routinely grew 'crops', guerrilla gardening on an improvised rough roof garden in Stockwell and in neglected concrete planters in Pimlico. My bicycles were often stolen, but oddly never my crops, which amounted to quite significant allotment quantities of spinach, lettuce, rocket, courgettes, mint and so on. Perhaps the local Londoners didn't recognise them as crops. Perhaps they were super honest, or rich enough to buy their own greens, or committed non-vegans. Even the tomatoes were never stolen, although they were more publicly arrayed, in a tumbling tangle of reds and yellows of different shapes and sizes, by the door. Perhaps you'd have to be a pretty brazen thief to dare to nick such obviously loved tomatoes.

This ad hoc cropping system produced useful amounts of food, so at some level it was genuine urban farming. If many people grew similar amounts of food in planters and pots here and there in cities, and if ad hoc cropping became a 'thing' (e.g. on social media), it could add up to a significant percentage of every grower's individual total food. It could also improve emotional wellbeing, as well as fostering community spirit in the form of ad hoc crop-swapping. It is another good reason (or food reason) to make it part of the Building Regulations that all new housing of any type must have access to some kind of outdoor space. The global lockdown experience has made the benefits of access to outdoor space abundantly clear. Even a tiny balcony opens up a world of new perspectives, *at best* access to fresh air, sky, ad hoc cropping, daylight, sunlight and Vitamin D, and *at worst* to a reconnection with bad weather and unsolicited neighbourly musical enterprises.

Village gardens used to be productive allotments, almost mini farms, long before and after the wartime Dig For Victory campaigns, and some of them still are. If you are only there (rather than 'here') for occasional weekends, and you have a lock-up-and-leave arrangement, it becomes impossible to keep chickens and geese and grow vegetables, so the honesty boxes naturally disappear from the sides of the roads. I hadn't noticed the peculiar lack of honesty-box stalls in that part of the Cotswolds, until I suddenly did notice. And once I had noticed this idiosyncratic absence, I couldn't stop noticing it everywhere, or, more accurately, nowhere.

The neat village houses with their doors painted in subtle stone-coloured hues, or that greyish-green Londoners seem to favour, were almost all second homes. The total lack of chickens, and of scruffiness, and of people, told the tale. I know for certain that in other parts of the Cotswolds, and the home counties, there are still plenty of permanent people, and proper farmers, but they may be becoming a rare breed, and we must be careful not to lose them through neglect. The easiest way to not-neglect farmers of any kind is to buy their produce, buy British, 'shop local'. Buying British doesn't preclude buying food from the rest of the world. It just means thinking a bit harder about provenance. It is a luxury to have the choice, just as it is a luxury to have the choice to be vegan.

There are people in the world who live entirely on reindeer, converting inedible lichens and moss into meat, milk, clothes, reindeer-horn jewellery etc., and apparently thriving, but they have no choice in the matter, in that place. Those of us who can shop locally and buy food from honesty boxes, farm shops and game dealers are at some level the equivalent of the reindeer people, in that eating local and wild food, for instance muntjac venison and pheasants, is an entirely logical way for us to obtain food, but it makes us marginal statistically. This is a sustainable way to feed local people, but it won't feed the world. Zooming away from the picnic scene in *Powers of Ten*, the enormity of the population and the necessity for a diversity of ways of feeding us all becomes immediately apparent, and with this kind of diversity comes some food that some people will disapprove of: the hunted, the stalked, the culled, the shot, the foraged.

It used to drive me slightly mad as a tidy-minded teenager, with an eye for a good building even then, how scruffy Suffolk was, compared with, say, Norfolk. Suffolk was scattered with what I thought of as 'shack land', with small-scale patches of land harbouring chickens and geese, and barns and sheds full of goodness knows what; whereas Norfolk, or at least the Norfolk I knew, was efficient and farmer-ish and grand and feudal. (Here it might be relevant to mention that as small children we used to spend Christmas with cousins who then lived at Anmer Hall, now home to Prince William and the Cambridge family, in the shadow of

Sandringham, and with the large estates of Houghton and Holkham down the road, the tentacles of their collective formality felt in subtle ways for miles around.) Despite its relatively grand architecture, and the fact that the address says it is in Norfolk even though it is in Suffolk, the Old Rec and its farmyard area has always operated more in the chaotic 'Suffolk shack land' way than in the efficient Norfolk manner. And it still does.

Now, I see the error of my teenage ways in not appreciating the wonders of the smallholdings, and the quite-large-holdings, of Suffolk. With the benefit of hindsight, I think the scruffiness might have been a relic left over from the war, of necessity being the mother of invention. The later scruffiness that I remember, the scruffiness of the 1970s and 1980s and beyond, has accidentally been a vital and beneficial counterpoint to the industrial-scale arable farming going on around us.

What might be called the scruffiness of the immediate Old Rec territory itself, for instance the wilder parts of the garden, the un-done-up barns and outbuildings, the quiet moat and its wooded 'island' (really just a large horseshoe-shaped pond, and such moats are ten a penny in this part of Suffolk if you look at the map), the high hedges round the orchards, the four old dew ponds, the nettle patches and scraps of scrubby undergrowth in odd corners, have all been a haven for wildlife all these years. The Old Rec is an oasis amid a desert of efficient barley, a tropical island paradise set in a sea of wheat. The farming around the Old Rec is notable even among what might be called the arable community as an unusually prairie-like monoculture of what the professionals refer to as 'combinable crops', quite unlike our surroundings only a few miles away on the coast at Benacre.

The scruffier kinds of smallholdings and quite-large-holdings of Suffolk have kept rare breeds of farm animal alive, fed us from honesty boxes, nurtured a love of animals in the children who grew up on them, ethically reduced food miles, provided habitat for wildlife and generally been an ongoing productive national treasure, a hive of living rural history. Here is the kind of diversity that neither seeks nor receives the attention of the mainstream media. It just trundles on. The Prince of Wales has been right about many things, particularly relating to farming and ecology (and the criminal undervaluing of wool), so it would be precisely the *scruffiness* of Suffolk's smaller family farms and larger smallholdings that ought to delight him, agriculturally and ecologically. Feudal Norfolk has its place, particularly in the arena of grand eighteenth-century Palladian country house architecture and large estates, but the 1970s and 1980s 'shack land' of smallholder Suffolk hid a richness of life that I didn't fully appreciate as a child and teenager.

Now that so many of the old barns and sheds have been done up and are no longer 'unspoilt', and the land around them made tidy as second homes, I realise how wrong I was in the olden days to be annoyed by the scruffiness that was actually just the outward signs of our active country life, places and things in daily use. At the Old Rec, there was and still is stuff everywhere, and some of it is scruffy, but it is the paraphernalia of a real rural life that itself feels almost endangered now: animal-feed sacks and sheep-worming, purple vet spray and binder-twine, buckets and bales, horses and hay-nets, apple boxes and barrows, and the endless timber and lumber that haunts every un-mucked-about-with barn in the country, stacks and lengths of old timber from other projects, waiting about, waiting for the day it might all be useful again. There is a deep peace in the generosity of space and time in a barn still used as a barn. Things quietly wait for decades, half-centuries. A good barn is as beautiful and important as a cathedral. And arguably more useful.

Perhaps the greatest compliment you could now pay to places like the Old Rec is that it is a bit scruffy. Its land, left a bit rough round the edges, is now wildlife friendly. Its outbuildings, un-mucked-about-with, are now *unspoilt*. Although it is currently going through a natural phase of relative quietness compared with the industrious days of the past, with the rumble of tractors and apple harvests and lambing and horses clattering about, the Old Rec is still known and used by hundreds of people in any given year, through garden open day, cricket matches, people who come ferreting, people who rent grazing, and so on. There are still coots and moorhens on the moat, still rooks nesting high on the island, still ducklings being frogmarched from pond to pond, still dragonflies over the dark water at dusk, still snails in the soft grass and bats in the belfry. We never appreciated that by doing nothing, we were actually doing everything for nature.

I still have the instinct that errs towards what horsey people call 'yard discipline', in that I like a tidy tack room or a shipshape tool shed, with not a blade of straw in the water buckets. I am congenitally allergic to bad fencing, while still appreciating the ingenuity of a good binder-twine fix-up. There is a difference between benevolent, beautiful, nature-friendly scruffiness and the malign scruffiness of old traffic cones and dead caravans lying about, or old machinery and scrap metal, neither used nor removed nor recycled.

I have personally been ordering the outbuildings of the

Old Rec since I was a small child, so that the paraphernalia of, say, cider making, looks professional and efficient, the old apple boxes stacked properly, cobwebby apple-picking 'hods' hung up, weighing scales neatly stacked, all the spanners in one box, all the hammers in another, screws and nails sorted, and so on. But now, against a backdrop of seemingly desperate loss of nature and wildlife within my lifetime, I appreciate more than ever the people of my childhood, like the Bradstreet brothers who farmed the land adjacent to the Old Rec on one side, in a slightly scruffy manner. Or people like Harold Page who kept those 1970s smallholdings.

Harold Page was a relation of 'Shrimp', Sir Alfred Munnings's early pony-painting model whose real name was Fountain Page, and who is immortalised in early paintings like *Shrimp on a White Welsh Pony*, the pony being a similarly recognisable and often-used model, a much admired grey pony called Augerau. Munnings loved greys, and thought them 'very paintable'. He was born at Mendham Mill, only about three miles from the Old Rec, and lived his early life there. Anecdotes about him were still quite common in the 1970s, when he was still someone in 'local living memory'. We rode around his territory as children, on ponies like Augerau. That picture in the nursery, *After The Race*, was signed by the artist in pencil. As a child I used to endlessly attempt to draw horses, inspired by Munnings, who was a formative presence in my life. A BBC art presenter and *Guardian* journalist has scoffed 'Liking Munnings doesn't count' (as proper art appreciation), apparently associating him only with horses, and not acknowledging the river paintings, trees, cows, landscapes, skies, portraits of people, dogs and country houses, nor the bounteous humour and genius gift for life of 'AJM'. It seems borderline philistine to write any acknowledged artist off so completely, and not even *half*-jokingly, but Munnings has the last laugh in the salerooms. He was known by the gypsies as 'Mr Money' even in his own lifetime, as he paid them so well to be models for him.

I miss Harold Page enormously. He was a great one for 'mardling', chatting for what seemed like hours, putting the world to rights, and even until quite recently telling me strange and clever things 'the old boys' used to do with a Suffolk horse or a partridge or a willow tree. I thought of Harold as an 'old boy', and felt a bit guilty about it on the grounds of both ageism and stereotyping, so I was relieved when he used the phrase himself, about an even older 'Suffolk boi' of the same ilk.

I think it was Harold who told me that the way the 'rum 'uns' used to steal guinea fowl was to soak a handful of raisins in a drop of whisky and scatter them under the trees where the guinea fowl roosted, until the guinea fowl were drunk. Then you could just pick the guinea fowl up and take them home. Harold recounted this poultry-thieving ploy to me in 2012, but it reminded me of a forgotten incident in the late 1970s, when all our Old Rec guinea fowl suddenly vanished overnight. I didn't like to mention this, just in case it was Harold who stole them. 'Rum 'uns' is Suffolk for 'loveable rogues', and it so happens that Harold's nearest village was Rumburgh. Perhaps Rumburgh was the borough in which the rum 'uns congregated in the days of yore, possibly in the Rumburgh Buck. Alfred Munnings used to go out with Lord Stradbroke's Harriers, and mentions a meet at the Rumburgh Buck in his three-volume autobiography. Someone should have recorded Harold Page for posterity, but somehow it would have seemed patronising to have suggested it. Instead, he is remembered here.

The Bradstreets seemed, even in the 1970s, from another age, from the past, almost from another century, from what I thought of as 'the olden days'. I now see the 1970s as a kind of personal 'golden olden days', my age of innocence, but obviously at the time it all seemed quite modern, at least in comparison with the Bradstreets. The two Bradstreet brothers communicated in an apparent sign language imperceptible to others, or perhaps by some kind of osmosis. The larger Bradstreet seemed big and strong and brown and healthy, like a story-book farmer, but I can't remember his name. The smaller Bradstreet was called Kenny, and seemed almost completely silent.

Together, at hay-time, the Bradstreets used to cut various people's hay, including their own and ours, using what seemed to be farming 'bygones' as their normal everyday machinery. One of my favourite book titles (as distinct from the actual book) is *Ask The Fellows Who Cut The Hay* (along with *Ring of Bright Water* and *Light on a Dark Horse*), and the Bradstreets were quintessentially such 'fellows'. I wish I had been older, so my life could have overlapped a bit more with such people, so I could have asked them so much more. As it is, I remember just enough of that era and its people to realise how much has since changed. Looking at the blue maps of where the water will come, and thinking about the coastal, climate and cultural changes that are already lapping at the edges of this crumbling country, the changes coming in the next fifty to a hundred years may well be even greater than the changes of a comparable timescale in the century that has just passed.

The Bradstreets had been in the Suffolk Regiment in the

war, and at some time during the 1970s Old Rec haymaking, one of them happened to mention to my (ex-Army) father how they had recently met up with some men from 'The Suffolks' at a regimental reunion somewhere in France. As the conversation progressed, everyone listened with a kind of enchantment, not so much at the story of the Suffolk Regiment's contribution to the war effort, nor the reunion itself, but in fascination that these men, who had lived barely five miles apart from each other all their lives and for over forty years in peacetime, had not once seen each other in all the intervening years since the war, not at the livestock markets, not at the Suffolk Show, not even in church at harvest festival, until that regimental reunion of The Suffolks, in France. I remember being pedantically indignant that they claimed that the reunion was the first time they had been abroad. I wanted to say that it can't have been. It must have been the second time. The war must have been the first time. But evidently the war somehow didn't count, and luckily I had the common sense to let it go. Perhaps the agrarian ancestry of their brains had somehow automatically filed such non-agricultural experiences of land, of the wartime *paysage* of France, in a separate place altogether. Perhaps it was why Kenny Bradstreet was so silent.

The Old Rec was a land girls' hostel during the war, described as the 'most remote land girls' hostel in East Anglia', which perhaps gives some idea of cultural context. But still, even as a child, I somehow picked up with my sixth sense (then quite noticeable) the fact that the Bradstreets were unusual, even for Suffolk, even for that remote and by reputation backward backwoods area knowns as The Saints. As I was the youngest person in the village (St Margaret South Elmham, for the geographically interested) at the time of the Queen's Silver Jubilee celebrations in 1977, and the Bradstreets didn't seem to have any wives or children, one day I may be the last person alive ever to remember them, and I *will remember them*. I learnt a great deal from people like the Bradstreets, without either them or me ever realising it.

As a child I was a bit of a spook, somehow seeming to know things before they happened, or being able to pick up on the atmosphere of buildings and places, especially the ancient commons around us and a particular door and outbuilding at the end of the kitchen garden. I think the sixth sense, extrasensory perception, and the appearance of seeming to have it, is simply an offshoot of being observant. For instance, as a child I used to be able to tell when a car was turning off the road and into the Old Rec drive, and would casually mention it. Five minutes later, the guests would duly arrive, and the grown-ups would look oddly, sideways, at me as if I were some kind of soothsayer or perhaps a 1970s modern child-witch. But all it was (and still is) is that I could feel subtle changes in vibrations underfoot, and I just 'knew', just as eighteenth-century astronomers 'knew' how to appear to extinguish the sun, when a solar eclipse was about to happen.

This happens in other ways. Some people seem more able than others to 'see' things before they should logically be able to. This is quite separate from the architect's ability to visualise a building before it is built. It is more akin to that fascinating television programme, *Tomorrow's World*, where scientists would foresee various contraptions that they thought would become our everyday future. Looking back, it seems comical, as the inventions were often clunky and impractical, as if constructed from Heath Robinson

186

drawings, but now that we are living in 'the future', it may be that buried somewhere in the archives of *Tomorrow's World* is something like the iPhone, Twitter or Zoom. Certainly the concept of the Video Telephone kept popping up, alongside the Paperless Office.

One of the more memorable of the many changes brought about by the coronavirus pandemic is that people of all ages started drawing and writing by hand again, drawing thank-you rainbows and writing messages on paper, just as we used to write messages on paper in 'the past', meaning as long ago as the 1970s, the 1980s, and even the *1990s*. The pre-iPhone millennium year 2000 now genuinely seems like 'the olden days'.

I think the ability to 'see' the future, the genuinely useful inventions, the likely social changes and so on, is a combination of being observant, having a visual imagination and perhaps a little knowledge and open-mindedness. For instance, it is quite easy to see in advance the watery future of Suffolk, with much of the land underwater and Southwold and Aldeburgh as islands. It is also quite easy to see how the currently predominantly urban desire for the romance of rewilding and veganism might develop and gain traction. Acknowledgement of urban attitudes has the effect of foreseeing and presaging how existing rural businesses and country people might adjust and adapt to accommodate these attitudes, or how new country people may be attracted to live in rural areas, and therefore how all this seems likely to change the *landscape* of the British countryside (e.g. farming) and the *culture* of country life (e.g. shooting) over the next fifty to a hundred years. Generally, adding the word 'wilder' seems to hint at the future of the rural scene.

You don't need to be a spook to see that these changes are likely, even probable. The real question is what, if anything, we should do about it now. Perhaps it will all just evolve naturally, as it has before, over centuries and generations. Sometimes, what seems like a new cultural fixture quite soon fizzles out, just as clean eating seems to have come and gone on the wind. And spiralising. And smoothies. Rewilding may turn out to be a passing phase rather than a permanent way of life, like the memory of animals running amok 'in the wrong place' during lockdown.

Because of the coronavirus lockdown and the wide-reaching global adjustments, large numbers of oil tankers gradually began to gather in and haunt the North Sea, many of them visible to us off the coast of Suffolk. In the evenings, seen from the high ground and farm tracks around the Rubbing-Down House, these oil tankers begin to turn on their lights. From a distance, and with a bit of imagination, the scene on the sea takes on the twinkling appearance of a marooned but easily reachable watery civilisation, of Venice at dusk as seen across the lagoon, or of Southwold as an island in the imaginable and not-too-distant future.

When you walk back towards Covehithe, two great white wind turbines rise up over Kessingland in the distance, but the view is foreshortened and distorted by the combined visual forces of perspective, open landscape and unlikely juxtapositions of scale, so that from certain angles and in the particular East Anglian light, these lofty bright white turbines seem to spring from among the medieval ruins of Covehithe church. The foreground detail seems greatly enlarged by the optical illusion of proximity, so that the whole ensemble gives a strange vision of 'the future' as seen from the past.

At Pakefield church, just up the coast to the north, a master thatcher has recently been rethatching the church roof, in an almost defiant act of optimism given the proximity of this church to the crumbling coast, and the proximity of the thatcher's ancient craft to the slick technology of the vast white wind turbines. Yet as the master thatcher tweets his progress on his iPhone, accompanied by his faithful dog, we can see both past and future simultaneously, just as to see Venice today is to see both its past and its future simultaneously. This vertigo of time makes it easy to see that there is nothing to fear from the future, or from the state of *not being*. At *Powers of Ten* molecular level there is some solace in returning to become once again truly *a part of* nature, rather than *apart from* nature, a peaceful place where the fever of life is over, and there is no more weather for us.

The fat of the land

Ye shall live off the fat of the land.

Genesis 45:18

9

SEPTEMBER

On 5th January 2020, the environmental campaigner and journalist George Monbiot made public his vision of the future of food, which included the prediction that 'farming will more or less end':

> On Wednesday, at 10pm, our film #ApocalypseCow premieres on Channel 4. It argues that farming will more or less come to an end within a few decades. All our food except fruit and veg will be produced by completely different means. Yes, I mean farming – not just livestock farming.

Having grown up in an extended family and a local community involved in farming for generations, I found this 'farming will end' announcement more thought-provoking than alarming. Here on the edge of Suffolk, we live surrounded by food, in its farmed, pre-harvested and pre-supermarket state, in the fields all around us. Off the top of my head (and without thinking too hard about it so as not to labour the point), within a mile of this kitchen table, and depending on the seasons, there are reliable supplies of wheat (bread), barley (beer), sugar beet (sugar), oilseed rape (rapeseed oil), onions, parsnips, carrots, potatoes, peas, beans, asparagus, pork, bacon, sausages, lamb, pheasant, partridge, venison (roe and muntjac), wild goose, wild duck, sea bass, cod, plaice, haddock, sole, skate, crabs, lobsters and a few domestic or forageable extras such as herbs, marsh samphire, apples and blackberries.

I have deliberately taken some trouble to find out how coastal change will affect the UK over the next fifty to one hundred years or so. I have also taken a keen interest in what might be called social change, including a rise in veganism, concern for animal welfare, increasing environmental awareness, and a predominantly urban population increasingly now seeing nature and the countryside as something to visit rather than to be deeply embedded in and part of – hence the rise in the popularity of rewilding and related romanticised ideals. But among all my digging, reading, research and thoughts about 'adapting to change', I had never come across a serious prediction of 'the end of farming as we know it' before.

The very name of the estate on which we live, Benacre, is roughly derived from 'cultivated land where beans are grown', or 'bean acres'. Acre may in turn be derived from acorn, with acre-men (and surnames approximating to acre-man) granted rights to feed acorns to pigs. This is a farmed landscape that our eighteenth-century ancestors would have no trouble recognising. The immediate landscape today still bears a strong resemblance from particular viewpoints to a painting by Thomas Gainsborough (1727–1788), *Mr and Mrs Andrews* (*c.*1750) or similar, with ancient oak trees framing wheat and barley crops, and the whole scene arranged on a gently sloping topography.

Zooming in the *Powers of Ten* manner back in time, rather than through space and scale, this landscape would also be quite familiar to people from 1600, 1500 and 1400, who would largely have navigated the land by the same byways, farmsteads and church towers as we do today. The people of even the more distant past, say 1300 and 1200, would recognise the natural routes born out of the original human desire lines and sheep-trod paths between farm and church, pub and village. The crops and essential rhythms which still apply to much of our local farming today would be familiar to people living at roughly the time of the Bible, because the rhythms of the seasons, animals, food crops and vineyards can only be tinkered with so much. In the end, the keeping of 'swine' has barely changed, at least in the outdoor and nature-friendly manner favoured in this area. There is a long-established block of woodland nearby called Hog Pen Belt. At times you can practically feel the work of our ancestors in the living soil.

Around and between the farming of crops and livestock, and notionally zooming *in* to examine the detail here and now around the farmland at Benacre, as distinct from in the world at large, there is a textbook mosaic of various habitats, holding healthy populations of wildlife, alongside the crops. We regularly hear bitterns booming in the reedbeds, and see roe deer leaping about in the barley like gazelles, albeit slightly in the wrong place (the barley). Sand martins return every summer to live and breed in deep holes all along the crumbling cliffs. Nightingales nest in the low-level scrub habitat which would be seen by many less enlightened landowners to be a waste of land. Parts of the estate could be a model for illustrations of the prevailing taste for rewilding, although it would not be called rewilding here.

The management that has produced this effect, creating deliberate areas of dense woodland or low-level scrub, pre-dates the words 'wilding' or 'rewilding' by at least a century, more of which later. Admittedly a large estate is not necessarily typical of all farming, because there is a long enough history of private ownership, and a large enough tract of land, to be able to 'waste' some and give it over to nature. Seen through the businesslike lens of return on investment and the production of commercial crops, nature has not traditionally been a product that pays. Increasingly, the intrinsic value of nature is being valued once again, after the post-war concentration on high yields and intensive food production. Most farmers have a vested interest in nature and wildlife, and take a personal pride in the state of nature on their own farms, whether as owner or tenant. If the public is prepared to pay for 'nature' alongside food, e.g. via subsidies or higher food prices, then rural landscapes may change, and lost species may return from the bottom up, starting with 'mini-fauna' rather than megafauna, an increased diversity of insects, butterflies and worms, feeding songbirds, voles and hedgehogs, feeding owls, raptors, foxes and badgers, and millions of cats.

Evidently George Monbiot's vision of 'the end of farming' will, or *would*, have a considerable impact on the *Powers of Ten* zoomed-*out* function and appearance of the farmed landscapes of Suffolk ... the UK ... Europe ... and the world. And that is before you take into account the enormous *cultural changes* implied in his proposal, considering how farming has moulded the countryside, and its culture, history and people, for centuries. An underlying preoccupation of mine is to scrutinise the idea of change and adapting to change, with a particular interest in change brought about by or relating to nature, and likely to occur in the foreseeable future. The idea of the end of farming is clearly within this remit, and merits some zoomed-*in* investigation.

But first, to be rigorous and fair, we need to define our terms.

The Pocket Oxford Dictionary defines the concepts of farming as follows:

Farm 1 n. area of land and its buildings used under one management for growing crops, rearing animals, etc.; any place for breeding animals; farmhouse.
2 v. use (land) for growing crops, rearing animals, etc.
[F *ferme* f. L *firma* fixed payment].

Farmer n. owner or manager of farm.

'Farm*ing*', therefore, and fairly obviously, is the action of using land for growing crops and rearing animals etc., to which I would add the phrase, *'for food or other human uses'*. For instance, alpacas or cashmere goats are farmed primarily for their unusually soft wool, rather than for their meat, therefore any alpaca or goat meat produced from these animals is the by-product of the more valuable wool, rather than the wool or leather being the by-product of the meat and milk, as would normally be the case with sheep, cattle, goats and most other animals ever farmed in human history. The ethics of all this comes a bit later. The first phase is to examine exactly what George Monbiot, and the philosophy he represents, thinks is going to 'end'. What is farming? What exactly will end? And what will replace it?

It turns out that, in summary, the Monbiot model for the

end of farming, as outlined in his film *Apocalypse Cow*, involves certain key principles, the main one being defining different land uses as separate activities from each other, each allocated an estimated percentage of the whole, for instance woodland *or* livestock farming. At one key point in *Apocalypse Cow* there is a representation of a simplified map-model of the UK and all its land uses, each with its percentage of the total: farming at x per cent, livestock farming x per cent, woodland x per cent, moorland x per cent and so on. Each landscape is seen as a single, separate use, and each is given a percentage of the total land area. This leads to an 'end of farming' film sequence in *Apocalypse Cow* in which the 'undesirable' land uses are systematically removed, and the resulting now-empty x per cent land is notionally given back to nature.

For instance, all of the livestock farming x per cent element is removed, because it is considered undesirable, which leaves the vast x per cent area of land where animals used to graze now free for nature and rewilding. The proposal then counter-intuitively suggests that whatever farming is left should be intensified, to allow even more room for nature. The basic idea, in the style of a snappy slogan, could be summarised as: *Go vegan. Stop breeding livestock. Rewild the farmland.*

To anyone who follows the ongoing environmental discourses about the British landscape, particularly those involving the countryside, country life and farming, George Monbiot is well known for his particular disapproval of sheep. George has often expressed his desire for the removal of *all* sheep from the British uplands, because the sheep have 'sheep-wrecked' the landscape of, say, Wales, Cumbria and Swaledale. The uplands to the west of the UK should by rights be British rainforest, part of which is still visible in the remnants of the original Atlantic rainforest, if allowed to naturally regenerate. Remove the sheep and the rainforest will return.

Understandably, the hill farmers of Wales, Cumbria and Swaledale object to an outsider wanting to entirely remove their livelihood and their whole way of life from the notional *Global Map of Indigenous Peoples and their Cultures*. If these British hill farmers were farming llamas in the hills of Bolivia instead of sheep in the hills and moors of Snowdonia and Swaledale, their culture would probably be internationally protected as UNESCO intangible heritage. The farmhouses, drystone walls, barns, owl holes and smoat holes would feature on Survival International merchandise, alongside details of other photogenic indigenous dwellings. But the end of the uplands livestock marts (markets) and the Muker Tup Show is the price we will have to pay (or *they*, since it is the hill farmers who will pay, by being culturally cleansed from the landscape) in order to reap the unquantified hypothetical benefits of the return of the British rainforest. At least, according to the thesis set out in *Apocalypse Cow*. But there are many small flies in this ointment.

The film then comes to the crux of the matter, which involves the replacement of livestock farming with lab-grown 'meat'. This does not involve replacing identifiable cuts of real meat from an identifiable carcass, as in a traditional Sunday roast, since that would be impossible. What is proposed is a new way of making the processed 'shaped' kinds of meat, and meat-like foods, such as burgers, sausages, nuggets, mince and so on, the resultant 'meat stuff' aimed at the mass market. These burgers (for the sake of argument) may be made from animal cells, or they may be plant-based. It doesn't really matter, because it is the *lab-grown, non-farmed* principle that seems to matter, not the small detail of what it actually is. Exactly what the lab-grown 'meat stuff' in the film was made of is slightly unclear, but there was a tiny sample of the resultant 'stuff' ready for Monbiot to taste on film. So he did. And for that I think he deserves some credit. At least he was prepared to put his money where his mouth is, or more accurately *his mouth where the money is*. Realistically, the primary motive for manufacturing any of this stuff will surely be raw capitalist profit, cooked.

It would be very easy to mock this scenario with sharp comic satire, and it turns out that someone already did, in the 1970s. The scene where George Monbiot tastes the unidentified stuff-burger was reminiscent of a 1970s sci-fi film called *Soylent Green*, which is before my time but is apparently about a population going mad for some worthy food product made from soya and lentils, hence 'Soylent', and especially the 'Green' variety, which turns out to be somehow made out of processed people, in a plot reminiscent of *A Modest Proposal* by Jonathan Swift. The plot sounds as dire as the fictional foodstuff, but the satirical point, the unidentifiability and the sinister name of the 'stuff', is accurately ridiculous.

Similarly sinister is the foodstuff Quorn, which has nothing to do with 'corn', since it is made from some kind of fungi, again suffering from the unidentifiability of ingredients which haunts so many similar highly processed products. Oddly, for what seems to present itself as a vegan brand, Quorn shares the name with one of the smartest packs of fox hounds in Leicestershire. I'm sure many people

other than me have been puzzled or amused by the word
Quorn being associated with a vegan foodstuff. For those
interested in the identifiability of ingredients, Quorn is
made of: 'mycoprotein derived from fermented fungi, bound
with egg albumen or potato protein'. So perhaps it is not
actually vegan, but vegetarian. What happens to the male
chicks that result from the production of the 'egg albumen'
that binds the 'mycoprotein' together? I am not being glib.
It genuinely matters to know and to take responsibility for
these living creatures, if you, we, I, purport to care about
animal welfare, and about the circle of life.

The 'Apocalypse Cow thesis' espoused and promoted
by George Monbiot in summary advocates that we should
stop livestock farming altogether, and increase farming
intensity of those crops which we will continue to farm,
such as vegetables, thus releasing the previously farmed
land for more 'nature'. There are some fundamental flaws
in this argument, at least in the manner it was presented
in *Apocalypse Cow*, the main one being that 'farmed land'
and especially 'grazed land' is *not separate from* 'nature'.
Witness the hundreds of ancient oak trees along the hedge
lines around the barley and other 'farmed land' of Benacre.
Witness our scrub and woodland alongside the pigs.

The separation of the x per cent livestock farming and
x per cent nature makes *Apocalypse Cow* fundamentally
flawed from the outset, since our farmed and landscape uses
are layered over and alongside each other, nature *and* livestock *and* crops, not one *or* the other, as if entirely separable
and apart. For all its intellectual and factual flaws, to be fair,
Apocalypse Cow makes an important and valid point. We
could accommodate vastly more nature in our landscape.

Yes, there may be mountain and moorland areas which

are overgrazed, and some places could benefit from the complete removal of sheep. But there are countless studies, not to mention the evidence of our own eyes, which show the benefits and carbon sequestration capacity of farmed and grazed landscapes: the measurable biodiversity of plants, birds, small mammals and insects on permanent pasture, and those wildflower-rich hay meadows, which are directly connected with livestock farming. Pasture-grazed animals tread in and spread seeds; they provide habitat for dung beetles. Why does a dung beetle colony in a *cow pat* not count as nature in the *Apocalypse Cow* scenario? Who decides what is the right kind of nature and what is the wrong kind?

Of course pasture-grazed farm animals (and therefore grass-fed meat) should continue to exist. The Twitter hashtag #FarmingWithNature illustrates many such farmed landscapes teeming with nature. Nature is not a *separate place* to be visited. We are embedded in it, and part of it.

It would be easy to disagree with George Monbiot and to disapprove of his lab-grown 'meat stuff' and 'stuff-burgers', but I am an unlikely advocate for it. I genuinely think lab-grown 'meat stuff' is a brilliant and necessary idea, subject to the crucial condition (mine), that it is not *instead of* traditional grass-fed farming, but *as well as*. The kind of farming that the lab-grown *meat stuff* should be *instead of* is the intensive indoor kind of farming, the kind that might be called factory farming, if only we knew what we really mean by that hackneyed and depressing phrase. Farmers with intensive chicken sheds and so on (and I know some of them personally), object to the term factory farming. Factory farming, like civilisation, is difficult to define, but we know it when we see it. Or, more accurately, don't see it.

It is the invisible animals we should worry about, not the ones we see grazing in the fields. All animals benefit from 'Dr Green and the sun on their backs'. It is the invisible animals whose welfare is severely compromised, to the point of only ticking certain theoretical boxes relating to their most basic physical needs, for water and so on. The 'cage age' will surely end in the twenty-first century. We have taken our dominion over the animals too far, by far. This is the kind of farming that George Monbiot's *meat stuff* could end. This is why I support the concept of what I call Monbiot Meat or Monbiot Mince. It is practically a brand already: Mon Bio mEAT™.

George Monbiot thinks that the trouble with farming starts with the storybook version of the farm presented to children. There are actually still plenty of British farms which look like the farms in children's picture books, but George has a point in that no child is ever presented with a story set on a factory farm, against an architectural background of vast grey sheds and crinkly-tin feed-store towers.

George may be pleased to know that as a child I had (and still have) a book called *The Effluent Society* (1971) by Norman Thelwell, which depicted, in Thelwell's inimitably well-drawn cartoon style, factory farms in all their horror and glory, alongside cartoons about pollution and environmental carnage, and an amusing line in the hypocrisies of hordes of people visiting the countryside while simultaneously ruining it, causing traffic jams, picking bluebells, leaving litter, and so on. Thelwell is best known for drawing cartoons about country life, and in particular the exploits of children on fat ponies, but actually Norman Thelwell was also a serious painter and environmental campaigner, quietly drawing (literally) our attention to the environmental disasters which concern us today, an unlikely precursor to George Monbiot, decades ahead of his time.

To conclude his '*Apocalypse Cow* thesis', George Monbiot pointed out that the deer population of the UK is too high because of the absence of wolves and other 'apex predators'. He then shot a deer and ate part of it in a bun, as a kind of venison burger but without the deer having been 'burgered'. Naturally this incited the wrath of his followers (which at times can seem a bit like a discipleship) and set alight almost every corner of Twitter against George, on the one side for his genuinely held desire to 'end farming', and on the other, for not being a proper vegan, and for shooting and eating a deer. Probably among the general public, if you could ask them in a representative way, there would be vastly greater understanding, at least of the eating of the deer. But part of the problem of discussing these things in the era of social media is that every debate immediately becomes so polarised that the silent majority no longer dares or bothers to speak.

We have become accustomed to being told that 'veganism is sky-rocketing', e.g. 'from half a million to more than 3.5 million – 5 per cent of our population – today' (according to Isabella Tree in The *Guardian*, 25th August 2018). The 5 per cent vegan statistic was debunked, because it turned out that it included people who said that they *have been vegan* or *were vegan* when asked if they had *ever been vegan*. The statistics are variable, depending on the survey and the source, but it seems that about 1 per cent of the UK population is truly, consistently, long-term vegan (540,000 vegans out of a 66 million population, according to The Vegan Society). The vast majority of the public either seasonally dabble with the idea, perhaps trying to do Veganuary, or they don't think about it at all. This matters, because it means that even if we generously say that 5 per cent are vegan rather than 1 per cent, it still means that the vast majority, 95 to 99 per cent, are not vegan. Realistically, the 99 per cent need to be fed. This is why I am perhaps an unexpected supporter of the part of the 'Apocalypse Cow thesis' which includes George Monbiot's vision of lab-grown 'meat stuff' and 'stuff-burgers'.

When I take the train from Suffolk to London, as I approach Liverpool Street I am always struck by the sheer volume of people, evident in the vast architecture of their housing. I know about it and expect it, but it is still startling, every time. The density of population in places like Hackney, Tower Hamlets, Stratford and Poplar makes feeding people locally and seasonally completely unfeasible. If a large percentage of the population enjoys eating burgers, chicken nuggets, kebabs, lasagne and various other food involving meat or 'meat stuff' in shaped and minced form, then George Monbiot's meat-stuff and stuff-burgers may well provide an answer, at least for one aspect of the total food supply, and a vast one at that: the fast food and convenience food markets. This is why so many vegan products come in recognisable forms: sausages and burgers. They are at least partly aimed at meat-eaters. Witness the success of the Gregg's vegan sausage roll.

It makes absolute sense to try and make cruelty-free *meat stuff*. The small family farm or the traditional Sunday roast is not truly threatened by the 'Apocalypse Cow thesis'. It is not the grass-fed cow you see in a field that is the problem, nor the chicken scratching around in the farmyard. The problem, causing untold damage to both the environment and animal welfare, is the feed-lot beef cattle in the former rainforest, the billions of factory-farmed shed-chickens, the invisible animals across the world.

To put my own food-and-farming cards on the metaphorical table for scrutiny, I have taken an interest in food and farming for most of my life. As children we had no choice in what we ate, at home or at (boarding) school, so food was neither a particular interest nor a notable pleasure. Since then, a whole world of food has gradually opened up to me, including ethics, animal husbandry, animal welfare, architecture for animals, land use, and the feeding of crops to animals or directly to humans, as well as the more colourful aspects of food, the lemon and garlic, the heat and dust, the smells, the souk, the sweat, the spice, the travelling and cooking and eating of unfamiliar ingredients, the morals, the taboos, the 'uneatable', the culture, the death.

Two of the most startling books about food and farming that I have read are *Food for a Future* (1975) by Jon Wynne-Tyson and *Diet for a Small Planet* (1971) by Frances Moore Lappé, old copies of which are by my side as I write. Until I had read these books, years ago as a student, I had not really considered the land-use aspect of livestock farming, the production of crops as animal food rather than people food. The sheep at home ate grass, hay and sugar-beet pulp, so the issue didn't really arise. The ponies and even the horses ate much the same, perhaps with a sack of Spiller's Pony Cubes or a few oats if they (or we) were feeling adventurous. Coming from a rainy country, I had never really considered the water consumption involved in food. So these two books opened my eyes.

I was accidentally vegan for five years as a student, partly because I liked the Indian vegan food that was readily available in those parts, but mainly because I had a vegetarian flatmate who would not allow any 'unapproved' food into the house or his orbit in the first place. In fact, my memories from that era do not include any memories of eating anything at all, but I suppose we must have eaten something, sometimes. Mainly, we smoked and drank black coffee. My flatmate lent me his well-thumbed copy of *Diet for a Small Planet*, and insisted that everyone in the world, or at least 'everyone in this house' should henceforth be vegetarian.

Seeing an opportunity to bring a bit of rural realism into the 'debate', and to highlight an almost unseen food dilemma with which I am perpetually preoccupied, I glibly called his bluff by mentioning that surely we should go *vegan* rather than merely vegetarian, because what are you going to do with the male calves, the billy kids and cockerels, if not eat them, or let me eat them for you? So that is what we did. We went completely vegan.

I freely admit that I didn't really mean to go vegan for five years, but the fact is I did, and I didn't mind at all. It was an education and a pleasure. There were rare exceptions, when I went home for the holidays or attended occasional formal social gatherings, weddings, dinners and so on, when differentiating my own entirely voluntary and non-medical 'dietary requirements' would have seemed (to me) intolerably rude to my host, but these were anomalies, quirks. At least half of the food I typically make now is still genuinely animal-free, without even thinking about it or making an effort to be so, and I could happily cook for a houseful of vegans for a weekend or party. The point is that it is easy to accommodate significant change, without going the whole hog, as it were. But this vegan-friendly cook also wears a wool jersey and a leather polo belt every day, and leather shoes. To me it would be immoral *not* to wear these natural materials.

I believe that wearing wool and leather while cooking animal-free food is precisely the kind of absence of fundamentalism, whether about food and farming or about anything else, that can bring about the greatest overall change, and which could cause the least conflict and fewest unintended consequences, in the coming decades. If added together, my non-animal food days would be roughly equivalent to 'the whole life so far' of a Gen Z climate-strike protester, for example. Incremental change makes a difference. A small change that is sustainable over a long time, might be better than a more absolute and perfect change, that is unsustainable. Human nature and behavioural science have to be taken into account.

Removing all the sheep from, say, one-fifth of the uplands might be more beneficial than removing one-fifth of the sheep from all of the hill farms, and certainly more beneficial than removing all of the sheep from all of the hill farms, as in *Apocalypse Cow*. To be fair, the proposal is not to remove and kill any sheep or other livestock, but simply to stop everyone ever breeding any Herdwick or Swaledale lambs, or any Hereford or Longhorn calves, or any Tamworth or Gloucester Old Spot or Oxford Sandy and Black piglets, ever again. That's all. The animals and farmers will naturally 'die out'. It will be completely humane, at least to the non-human animals involved in this 'vision'.

Perhaps the Rare Breed Survival Trust may be allowed to keep some sample farm animals of all these long-established native breeds, in a kind of museum-farm. *Apocalypse Cow* didn't mention the native horse and pony breeds, but perhaps we might be allowed to keep a breeding pair or two, of the Eriskay and others, in our museum-farm, a twenty-first-century Noah's Ark. The proposed extinction of native breeds seems to be the wrong kind of extinction to rebel against, Extinction Rebellion-style.

If millions of people who might normally eat actual beefburgers, or chicken-shop buckets of finger-lickin' actual chicken bits, or home-cooked lasagne made from supermarket mince, were to convert to George Monbiot's lab-grown stuff-burgers, meat stuff or stuff-mince, for, say, three to five days a week, this incremental change could over the course of all our lifetimes make vastly more of a difference than for a tiny percentage of people to go completely vegan for what after all can only ever be one lifetime each. Subject to 'identifiability' and understanding what the actual ingredients are or were, in theory I would happily cook (and eat) a lasagne made with Monbiot Mince.

The shunning of animal-derived products like wool, leather or fertiliser, may be more practically fraught. For instance, a mushroom farm near here uses the muck heaps from a hunting yard as the growing medium for the mushrooms. This arrangement is on at least its second generations, and the tractor and trailer collecting and delivering the horse muck from the hunters (mostly ex-racehorses) is familiar sight. A photograph of Mr Constance standing at the top of the muck heap appeared on the back of the service sheet at his funeral, so entrenched was the 'mushroom muck round' as part of his identity. It is one of the main things we all remember him for. Given that vegans (among others) are against both racing and hunting, can these particular mushrooms ever be considered vegan by purists? Does it matter whether the end-user mushroom-eaters know the horsey provenance of their mushroom muck?

Similarly, the muck from the high-welfare, free-range, outdoor pigs all around us is spread on the surrounding fields as fertiliser. Given that the pig muck is essential to the health of the soil, are the resulting arable and supermarket-vegetable crops, onions, parsnips, carrots and the like, grown on the same land, truly vegan?

For most people, this is easy. The mushrooms, arable and vegetable crops are vegan, and the pigs are not, regardless of which animal muck-heaps have been involved in their production. Yet these vignettes offer a glimpse of the complexity of the problems we may face if we were to truly aim for a largely animal-free future, especially a meat-free future. What would happen to the health of the soil without animals? The book *The Living Soil* (1943) by Lady Eve Balfour, the Suffolk organic farmer who founded the Soil Association in 1946, demonstrates the degree to which healthy fertile soil is alive with living organisms. And soil can die.

It is also quite easy to make the case that wearing wool and leather is a choice that can be made for 'ethical reasons', being natural materials, biodegradable, by-products, and so on. The Prince of Wales's Campaign for Wool actively promotes wool as an ethically and ecologically sound product. The non-use of animals doesn't have a monopoly on morality. The point is, long-term ethical vegans have a serious point, a good point well made, and deserve great respect for their consistency and ethical stance. But there is obviously a 'but' coming, and it is quite a big 'but' ...

The logistical factors resulting from just-enough, just-in-time supermarket deliveries are also fraught with fragility, as was shown in the early days of the coronavirus lock-down, when supermarket shelves were bare. Whether it was because of stockpiling tinned tomatoes and dry pasta, or because of a lack of lorry drivers, is not really the issue. We may have come close to the 'nine missed meals to anarchy' scenario in some places. The vast majority of people do not live near where their food is produced, and obviously cannot just pootle down the road to the farm shop or to an honesty box.

The practical flaws and moral hypocrisies (including my own) embedded within our global food economies and personal choices can be highlighted by *The Parable of the Vegetarian Guest*, a Suffolk food parable in three parts. Once upon a time, I was house-sitting at the Old Rec, as has happened regularly over the years, and I had a succession of guests to stay over three consecutive weekends, for whom the provision of food could be seen as a food morality play in three acts.

Act 1. The first weekend was a full house, convivially disposed, and fed predominantly on one of our own home-bred, home-reared Jacob-cross lambs, slow cooked into various dishes of loosely traditional Moroccan or British character, using lemons and garlic and olives and rosemary and the like. The same animal, a full-grown sheep, made an appearance in various guises for several different dinners and lunches, feeding about twelve people several times. The food-miles distance of the main ingredient was under a mile, a few hundred yards in fact, with the added advantage that we knew (or at least I did) exactly how the Jacob-cross lamb had lived and died.

Friends have occasionally asked how we can eat our own lambs when we have seen them frolicking about outside. But it is precisely because we have seen them frolicking, and sometimes gambolling, that we are more at ease with eating them. Generally I am more comfortable eating meat I have 'known alive' than the unknown unknowns that are more usual to most people. There also are several food items I avoid altogether, for ethical reasons.

Act 2. The second weekend in the Suffolk trilogy was a less full house, involving a 'Vegetarian Guest' who had specifically requested shellfish, particularly prawns, to be on the menu. This is not my idea of being vegetarian, but I liked the person, and the customer is always right. There was a freezer full of home-produced lamb and wild game, which at that particular time of year happened to be muntjac venison, but in order to be a good host, I set off (on an unnecessary petrol-burning journey) in search of my friends at World of Fish and Morrisons on the industrial estate in Lowestoft. In the event I bought an assortment of beautiful crustaceans from around the globe, at what seemed to be vast expense, and a couple of packets of industrially frozen prawns as backup. The resulting 'seafood platter' was like a painting inspired by the Rialto Fish Market in Venice, the whole composition artfully adorned using lemons and garlic (again), and parsley and crusty bread and so on. The 'Vegetarian Guest' was delighted.

Whether the non-meat option was truly more ethical than the home-bred one-food-mile lamb, or the wild muntjac in the freezer, is debatable. Actually it is not really 'debatable'. The muntjac venison would have had a vastly lower carbon footprint than the globally transported shellfish, and would have incidentally benefited the nightingale. The industrially frozen prawns could be seen as a lower life form, but there were many more of them, more 'animal souls', and therefore many more deaths, than would be the case with the single muntjac or the single lamb, feeding many people.

Act 3. The third weekend of the trilogy was easier, and the guests were easier too. They were fed on the frozen leftovers from the previous two weekends, variously disguised as tagines, paella, *chiccetti*, and whatever else you could make with the remnants of a lamb and some seafood from around the world. In all three 'acts', the vegetable family provided an element of local colour.

The Parable of the Vegetarian Guest illustrates the vast variations in distance travelled by our food, from the just-in-time industrially frozen packets of prawns from the other side of the world, to the home-bred lamb who lived his whole life in the field outside. Distance alone does not negate the case for eating both or neither. But anyone who eats prawns of any kind is not a vegetarian.

Mr McGregor in *The Tale of Peter Rabbit* (1902), by Beatrix Potter, is as good a vegetable-growing role model as any, demonstrating the efficient management of an old-fashioned kitchen garden and its associated sheds, paraphernalia and tools. Mr McGregor is in some ways a role model who could inspire any allotment, veg patch or plant pot. From the evidence in the book, he grew lettuces and French beans, radishes, parsley, cucumber (in a 'cucumber frame') and cabbages, since he was 'planting out young cabbages' when he espied Peter Rabbit. Mr McGregor also grew potatoes, gooseberries and blackcurrants (or 'black-currants'), and red geraniums in beautifully weathered old flower pots.

While Mr McGregor is a fine role model for those with ambitions to be at least partly self-sufficient and/or vegan, he did reveal the inevitable flaws inherent in human nature when he put Peter's father ('Your Father had an accident') in a pie.

Not long ago I was behind someone in a shopping queue, and noticed that her pineapple was £1. If someone had offered 'a penny for your (that is, my) thoughts', they might reasonably have been slightly startled by the resulting *Potted History of the Pineapple* and associated imagery that came cascading into my mind at the sight of such a cheap pineapple: the eighteenth-century Pineapple Folly at Dunmore now a Landmark Trust holiday let; the £10,000 it cost to grow a single pineapple in the country-house glasshouses of England; the grand hostesses renting a pineapple for one evening as dining-room table centrepiece; the architectural symbolism of the pineapple on a gatepost; modern 'pleather' (fake leather) made of pineapple skins. The history of the pineapple really is remarkable. I loathe pineapples, but when I later saw an advertisement for a supermarket, which included a picture of punkish pineapple alongside the caption *selected fruit 60p*, I felt oddly sad for the pineapple, for it and its kind having travelled so far, both literally and metaphorically. I hope we do not replicate the lost cultural capital of the pineapple in other visions relating to food and farming, for the loss of our treasured farm animals would be a vastly greater cultural loss than the fall from grace of the wretched pineapple.

There are many ethical food dilemmas arising in the hyper-globalised world, and eating only plants does not let anyone off the hook, at least not in the developed Western world. 'Plant-based' food (often just a plant, or its fruit) comes with its own moral maelstrom of undesirable side effects, for instance avocados are associated with deforestation, ecosystem destruction, water shortages and human rights issues. Soaring demand for quinoa in the urban 'quinoa belt' has allegedly caused shortages among the Peruvians who produce it. A region of southern Spain seems to be entirely covered with glasshouses and solar panels, if the images from Google Earth are to be believed. An article in The *Guardian* 'debunked' these uncomfortable facts as so-called myths, but then the article itself was 'debunked', so there are awkward truths embedded in all these 'myths'.

Palm oil is ubiquitous these days. The palm plantations are destroying the rainforest habitat of the orang-utan, and all this devastation allegedly arose from a scare surrounding saturated fat, mostly meaning butter, originating in the 1970s or 1980s, when everyone was instructed to convert to plant-based oily spreads. Perhaps we should have stuck to eating butter from Baron Bigod's cows on the marshes after all. In fact, many of us did.

Despite, or perhaps because of, converting to low-fat, unsaturated-fat spreads, approximately 30 per cent of adults in the UK are now deemed officially obese, and a further 35 per cent overweight, leaving only about 35 to 40 per cent deemed neither obese nor overweight. As always, the methodology and timing of the statistics is slightly variable, and underlying mental health issues may account for some people's epicurean habits, but the basic message is clear.

We were supposed to live off the fat of the land. We weren't supposed to *be* the fat of the land.

Pigs in the park

Oh for a lodge in some vast wilderness,
Some boundless contiguity of shade,
Where rumour of oppression and deceit,
Of unsuccessful or successful war,
Might never reach me more!

WILLIAM COWPER (1731–1800)

10

OCTOBER

In the unlikely event that I were suddenly to change tack and do something truly worthwhile in my life, to the extent that I might be honoured with an invitation to appear on *Desert Island Discs*, I would seriously consider taking as my chosen book *The Penguin Complete Saki*, a fat tome which includes the collection of short stories *Beasts and Super Beasts* (1914), by 'Saki'.

Every single story of *Beasts and Super Beasts* is a comic masterpiece, usually involving the pricking of pomposity, and large animals in the wrong place, often quite a grand wrong place, such as a drawing room. Hidden among the wonders of *Beasts and Super Beasts* is a story with the uncharacteristically beast-free title *The Story-Teller*, but it is worth digging out because, among its many unexpected virtues, it paints a remarkable picture of pigs in a park.

The scenario of *The Story-Teller* is that some bored but inquisitive children are on a train journey with an unimaginative and irritable aunt (Saki hates aunts, having been partly brought up by a particularly vicious one). The aunt has just told the children a 'deplorably uninteresting' story, in the company of a bachelor who was 'a stranger to their party', but who happened to be in the same carriage. The bachelor breaks his long-suffering silence by pointing out that the aunt doesn't seem to be much of a success as a story-teller, prompting the aunt to challenge the bachelor to tell a better story. So he does. It is worth quoting a sentence or two *verbatim*, to capture the quality of what literary agents and publishers might call the 'narrative arc':

'Was the Prince killed by a sheep or a clock?' asked Cyril.

'He is still alive, so we can't tell whether the dream will come true,' said the bachelor unconcernedly; 'anyway, there were no sheep in the park, but there were lots of little pigs running all over the place.'

'What colour were they?'

'Black with white faces, white with black spots, black all over, grey with white patches, and some were white all over.'

The story-teller paused to let the full idea of the park's treasure sink into the children's imaginations; then he resumed . . .

The story continues, to describe how there were no flowers in the park because the pigs had eaten them all, the Prince having been told that he couldn't have pigs and flowers, so he decided to have pigs and no flowers.

There was a murmur of approval at the excellence of the Prince's decision; so many people would have decided the other way.

The story ends with the 'horribly good' little girl who is the main protagonist (antagonist) being killed by a wolf, alerted to her presence by her three clanking 'medals for goodness'. The children conclude that it is the most beautiful story they have ever heard. The aunt predictably declares it 'a most improper story'.

With its depiction of a wolf and some pigs in a park, this dormant Edwardian story seems suddenly to have acquired a fresh relevance to the British countryside, particularly to the modern twenty-first-century British countryside, and specifically to the current fashion for rewilding. Rewilding (or 'wilding'), in its current variably defined form, does seem to have much in common with a fashion, or a popular movement, and even among some followers of its creed something bordering on a religion or a cult. But rewilding may turn out to be a fashion (or a fad or a movement) that stands the test of time.

For anyone interested in adapting to change, particularly change relating to nature and the foreseeable future, rewilding cannot be ignored. This is a movement that could change the function, character and appearance of the British landscape more than any other in several hundred years. In that sense, rewilding has much in common with the fashion for naturalistic landscapes of the eighteenth century, most notably those laid out by Capability Brown, but also part of a whole movement with many proponents at the time, which mimicked a romanticised version of nature and eschewed the formal gardens and landscapes which had gone before. Rewilding also has some echoes of the post-war 1950s and 1960s era when the more enterprising owners of those country houses suddenly started introducing safari parks and modern activities like water-skiing to their estates, in their efforts to make such inheritances financially viable in the face of vast debts and expenses. There is something of the 'lions of Longleat' about rewilding at its most extreme. Rewilding has also been criticised for being anything from 'a petting zoo' to 'eco-gentrification', and both seem fair comments. Sometimes, rewilding is really just a photogenic kind of farm diversification, exploiting shrewd knowledge of grants and conservation subsidies.

Rewilding has many merits and is gaining traction as a popular ideal, while not yet having many established practical examples at landscape scale to learn from. Some of the most notable examples of rewilding in practice (so far) are at Knepp in Sussex, Hovingham in Yorkshire, Holkham and Raveningham in Norfolk, and Somerleyton in Suffolk. All these are large, inherited, privately owned estates able to devote at least a proportion (typically about 20 per cent) of their several thousand acres to rewilding. For the purposes of clarity and brevity, here we will refer to them as rewilding estates, although, in fact, most of them contain a complex patchwork of land uses. The Hepple estate of 3,500 acres in Northumberland is also an advanced example of rewilding, having removed fences and reduced the number of sheep from 2,000 to about 150. Among other benefits, this allows a profusion of juniper to flourish and find its way into the rewilded gin industry. Of all these rewilding estates, probably the one that has most completely captured the public popular imagination is Knepp, which I will come back to.

The Benacre estate demonstrates many of the same characteristics, practices and resultant benefits to wildlife as these 'official' rewilding estates. At Benacre the effect of rewilding is actually the result of centuries of active land management in this manner rather than a recently contrived project. It cannot really be counted a 'rewilding estate' in the same sense as the ones above, although the measurable benefits to flora and fauna are the same.

There are also vast areas of the Scottish Highlands which have been bought for the purposes of rewilding as what might accurately be called a hobby, albeit a hobby on a seriously grand scale and one which will leave a lasting legacy for generations. Among the most notable of these modern landowners are Danish billionaire Anders Povlsen, who has bought over 200,000 acres of the Scottish Highlands, and members of the Rausing family who have bought the Corrour estate. Both estates have a strong emphasis on wilderness. It is interesting to note that both of the websites promoting these newly bought estates as wilderness holiday destinations depict in their opening sequences a man with a gun, perhaps a ghillie, perhaps a stalker, but either way, an indication that the new owners are not shying away from such an image.

For many years, the Duke of Westminster and the Duke of Buccleuch were always the standard answer to the question, who owns the most land in Britain? Now, some of the modern landowners buying rewilding estates are out-landowning even the oldest established ducal domains. If anyone thinks that change never seems to happen in the British countryside, perhaps they haven't been paying attention to *The Times Rich List*. There has already been enormous change in British rural culture, landscape and ownership over the past twenty years or so, roughly since the year 2000, but much greater change is yet to come, and soon.

Rewilding seems at first glance to be a win-win situation which can only benefit depleted nature and wildlife habitats, and certainly it has some fanatical advocates and supporters. But rewilding also has many knowledgeable and articulate doubters and detractors. Not everything is entirely rosy in the modern Garden of Eden that is the British countryside. Rewilding is not a magic solution that rights all wrongs. 'Nature' may not always balance itself or behave in the way people wish it to, and there are already subtle but observable differences among and between the various tribes, e.g. wilding, Wilding, rewilding, Rewilding, and an articulate contingent, anti-rewilding.

To understand the pros and cons of rewilding, first we must define our terms. 'Rewilding' entered the dictionary in 2011 (*Chambers*, 12th edition), but what does it actually mean?

There are two books which might be considered the original and best 'sacred texts' of rewilding, the first, *Feral* (2013) by George Monbiot, and the second, *Wilding* (2018) by Isabella Tree, so it is to these texts and their definitions of rewilding that it makes most sense to turn.

In *Feral*, George Monbiot starts by saying, by way of explanation for his entire rewilding philosophy and enterprise, 'I believe I was ecologically bored'. He favours two definitions of rewilding, the first being *to permit ecological processes to resume* and the second being *the rewilding of human life*. Leaving aside the pedantic logical wrongness of using the word *rewilding* in a definition of rewilding, we can immediately grasp the gist of this outlook.

In *Wilding*, Isabella Tree quotes a letter of intent to Natural England from her husband Charlie Burrell who is what might be called 'the enabler' (i.e. the landowner), setting out their plans for wilding the Knepp estate where they live. This letter of intent serves as a definition of what they mean by rewilding, or wilding. Their stated intention is 'to establish a biodiverse wilderness area in the Low Weald of Sussex'. The letter goes on to include phrases like 'land management experiment' and 'mix of free-roaming grazing animals'. Isabella also adds near the start of the book, 'We were seeking funding to ring-fence the entire 3,500 acres of the estate, take up all 200 miles of fencing, leaving only fences around houses and buildings ... so that animals could traverse the whole area'.

Charlie Burrell and Isabella Tree sportingly admit that there might be 'minor problems' involving weeds and the public distaste for rotting carcasses, but they hope that these are not insurmountable. The whole Knepp enterprise is deeply endearing, but it must also be mentioned that it is at large scale, privately owned, in the home counties (meaning easy to reach and therefore feasible for eco-tourism), and is supported financially by various grants and countryside stewardship schemes funded by large sums of public money. Essentially, the public pays out some money, and the Knepp estate delivers back some nature.

Whatever success Knepp Safaris and the wild meat business now enjoys, it was a brave move to turn such an estate to 'wildland'. The wilding of Knepp replaced a debt-ridden, loss-making farm, dairy and ice-cream enterprise, but it would be unfair to suggest that there was nothing more to lose. There was plenty to lose, including the goodwill of their farming and landowning neighbours (some of them family members), who saw their vision and the resulting scruffy land as an affront to the efforts of every self-respecting farmer, an immoral waste of land, an assault on Britishness itself.

For all its romance and good intentions, this little vignette about the reaction of Knepp's neighbours illustrates how the word rewilding is considered a toxic brand in some quarters of rural Britain, and why it is no accident that the book *Wilding* is called *Wilding* and not *Rewilding*. Having drawn attention to the nature of the resistance to both the word and the attitude, for simplicity, in this chapter, from now on, rewilding will be the word used, without further qualification. But the antagonism associated with the word rewilding among many country people, and the deliberate rejection of it as the title of the *Wilding* book, should not be underestimated.

These definitions-cum-descriptions of rewilding together give a clear enough picture of the intentions for these two books, or their authors and enablers, to serve as what might be called the founder members of the Modern Rewilding Movement, just as the book *Vers Une Architecture* served to install its author Le Corbusier as the unofficial founder member of the Modern Movement and Modernism in architecture. And just as with modernism in the European urban landscape, so it is with rewilding in the British rural landscape, in that some of the lesser impersonators are poor relations of the original concept. Some of the so-called rewilded land is just neglected. Some of the so-called modernist blocks of flats are just vertical slums.

To return to the pigs in the park and the wolf in the Saki story, one of the central desires of the rewilding purist is to 'reintroduce apex predators', meaning to release lynxes and wolves, and for purists ideally also bears, into the British landscape. Typical headlines include: *Let lynx roam free to keep deer in check, says wildlife chief*. The release of apex predators is intended to spark a trophic cascade, meaning one animal eating another, thus setting off the ecological processes that will naturally occur as a result, such as decay and the provision of carcasses as carrion.

The most widely cited example of trophic cascade in practice is the film of what happened when wolves were released in Yellowstone National Park. While the details of this film have been widely discredited, it does still serve to illustrate some useful principles bound up in the phrase *trophic cascade*.

There is an obvious problem with some of the language used around the subject of rewilding, and the problem is one of what I would call *eco-parlance*. Normal people, and especially normal country people, on the whole do not speak in this way. Such language tends to be a marker of people who have studied ecology mainly from books and screens. We need qualified ecologists, to do thorough surveys of insects and bats and plant species in a meadow and so on, but we also need people with hands-on practical knowledge of rural life on the ground, like 'the fellows who cut the hay', or gamekeepers. Paradoxically, if you want to know exactly where the nightingale nests, or where the hare will return to her leveret, any gamekeeper will almost certainly be able to tell you, in detail, about the observable habits of the wildlife on their patch. But they might choose not to.

People normally use words like 'maggots' or 'rotting' or 'dead' to describe something natural but slightly gross to behold, not *trophic ecosystems*, or *meso predators*, or *ecosystem engineering*, or *niche construction*. The use of jargon and eco-parlance is comparable to management-speak gobbledegook in office life, or psychobabble in mindfulness circles. It is like the jargon which describes coastal erosion as coastal change. All of this jargon is useful and accurate in the right place, but it can also alienate people.

Eco-parlance may be one of the more subtle and seemingly insignificant antagonisms of rewilding among country people (here meaning anyone who is either part of, or supportive of, traditional country life as it currently exists), but eco-parlance rubs people up the wrong way from the start. For this reason alone, the lexicon and over-use of eco-parlance can be unhelpful.

Here is a working everyday example of an exchange about eco-parlance on Twitter, to illustrate the point:

SC, Rewilder: Fully occupied, fully functioning trophic ecosystems . . . Surely that should be the goal, wouldn't you agree?

PG, Country Person: I think, in the nicest possible way, you are balls deep in an ecofantasy.

Person 3: As are most rewilders! In the country perhaps; of the country, almost never.

At the heart of eco-parlance antagonism is the strong sense that the person using the ecology textbook jargon has learnt everything from books and not 'in the field', and in addition, has no 'skin in the game': no land to rewild, no problems to solve, no real-life decisions to make about anything connected with land at all. It feels like keyboard-warrior-ism, and criticism from afar. The voices demanding more rewilding (voices which incidentally tend to be louder on social media than in real life) could surely crowdfund among their collective followers to put their money where their mouth is and *buy some land* to rewild. The Langholm Moor community buyout is a rare real-life example of this in practice, but it was hardly overrun with would-be rewilders actually donating to the fund. The collective social media followers of the more vocal rewilding advocates could have bought the whole moor for about £10 each in the week it was on offer, but they didn't.

The author of *Inglorious* (2015), Mark Avery, formerly of the RSPB, is one such voice on, in his case, the rewilding of grouse moors. He wobbles at the outset, marvelling at the bird life on a grouse moor. Mark is straightforwardly honest and reasonable in his acknowledgement that on the particular day that he visited a grouse moor in Weardale, it was a 'hot-spot for ground-nesting birds', adding that this situation is 'hardly matched in Britain'. He generously adds that this is 'one of the inconvenient truths'. He could have chosen not to mention any of this, to suit his argument, so it is to his credit that he sets such an attractive existing moorland bird scene. Because hen harriers have historically been killed on grouse moors to protect grouse (a separate subject to which I will only suggest the words 'vicarious liability', meaning holding the landowners responsible), Dr Avery decides only a page later to come down on the side of raptors (hen harriers) rather than waders (lapwings, curlews, plovers etc.), and starts an e-petition demanding a complete ban on driven grouse shooting ('#bandgs'), and a call to rewild the grouse moors. But even for him, it was a genuine moral dilemma.

The resulting debate in parliament produced no real-life votes for a ban on driven grouse shooting, but it suggested that the level of argument could be raised and would be more impressive if Dr Avery and those who signed his petition had crowdfunded to buy some land. He or they could then write a follow-up book, *How to Rewild a Grouse*

Moor, with 'not like that, like this' practical lessons learnt from their crowdfunded demonstration moor, highlighting problems and best rewilding practice. If a wildfire starts naturally, do you put it out? Are you allowed to feed hen harriers? Do eco-tourists need accommodation, car parks, loos, a cafe, hen harrier T-shirts? What if the resulting bracken and succession scrub turns out to be measurably worse for local wildlife than managed heather moorland? Complexity and contradiction abounds. Besides, the silent majority may secretly love the heather moorland as it is.

It is the theoretical and distant nature of criticism from afar which grates. Rewilding enthusiasts sometimes seem keen to tell other people what to do, and how and when to do it, without themselves having any practical experience of doing what they suggest. The rewilding answer to everything seems to be 'natural succession' or 'leave it to nature'. When asked what wildlife management methods would be acceptable to control, say, foxes, to protect, say, curlews, the answer is always 'nature will balance populations'. But the British landscape has not been 'natural' for centuries.

Native water voles (Ratty in *The Wind in the Willows*) are still being eaten by American mink, descended from those released from fur farms by animal rights activists in the 1990s. The fur farms were vile, but the devastation caused by releasing mink into the New Forest, from where they spread out along all our river systems, still continues. Predation of native species by mink has become a permanent part of modern riparian life in many parts of the British countryside.

When we were children, there were strange animals called South American coypu out on the marshes all over East Anglia. Fleets of Coypu Patrol vans were out in force, and the aim was not to balance UK coypu populations but to eradicate them. Eradication of any species as the stated aim is extremely rare in conservation, but the same could and should happen with UK mink. The entire situation is sad, as mink are attractive beady-eyed little beasts, and it is not the mink's fault they were farmed and released in the first place. But there are times when nature doesn't actually balance populations.

American grey squirrels ousting native red squirrels is a similar vexation. A grey squirrel in St James's Park is a delight, but in a red squirrel woodland, it is a menace. We have to harden our hearts, rewild ourselves, reconnect with *our role as an apex predator*, and *eat* grey squirrels for the sake of the reds, just as we have a duty to *eat* muntjac to save the nightingale habitat.

Somerleyton is one of the large estates currently being officially rewilded, and is a neighbour of Benacre here in Suffolk (albeit that Somerleyton is half the size, about 3,500 acres against Benacre's nearly 7,000 acres). Zooming out in the manner of *Powers of Ten*, these estates add up to large areas of land, nationally and globally significant acreages of both productive farmland and particular kinds of wildlife habitat. But for rewilding to work at landscape scale it needs large areas of land in the same ownership. Professor Alastair Driver, who advises some of these estates about rewilding, only takes on people who have 1,000 acres or more. This doesn't mean that all of the acres are to be rewilded, but it does indicate that you need a certain amount of land realistically to be able to afford to 'waste' any of it (as those Knepp farming and landowning neighbours worded it), and for the roaming animals to have enough space to roam.

Considering that rewilding demands such large amounts

of usually private land, it could accurately be described as a rich man's game. Most estates (not all) are owned by men, because of primogeniture and inheritance conventions, so this is also a gender-accurate observation. It is therefore quite surprising that rewilding has gained most of its popular support from an urban section of the public, generally with strongly left-leaning tendencies politically, including many people who consider that all private land was stolen from 'the people' in the first place. Urban socialist activists at first seem unlikely allies of the aristocratic owners of rewilding estates, especially as rewilding estates and their owners are not exclusively devoted to rewilding, but tend also to be deeply involved in all the other traditional rural activities that take place on land. Many of the people who clamour for rewilding also actively campaign *against* the other activities which take place on these rewilding estates. It is often precisely these 'other activities' that make the rewilding element financially viable, most notably field sports – meaning shooting, stalking, fishing and so on.

It may turn out to be useful that rewilding is one area where the Venn diagram of divisions and opposing tribes relating to country life may just about manage to find a few tiny 'fingernails' of overlap, as the circles of their various, usually conflicting, interests now find themselves in the rare position of being overlaid on the same piece of land. For example, Chris Packham, the BBC presenter and naturalist, has made many public speeches and videos against hunting, and has publicly denounced the people who do this as 'the nasty brigade' and 'psychopaths'. He has also declared himself vegan. Yet paradoxically, Chris Packham has also written a glowing 'puff' on the back cover of the *Wilding* book about Knepp, saying 'this should be conservation's salvation; this should be its future; this is a new hope'.

On the face of it, Chris Packham would in theory seem to be 'anti-Knepp', since the Knepp estate is inherently *not* vegan, as the free-roaming animals are sold as wild meat, and Charlie and Isabella host the Crawley and Horsham hunt for their Opening Meet and Boxing Day Meet among other such days. Chris Packham must know that Knepp produces meat and hosts the Crawley and Horsham hunt, as meat and trail hunting are clearly present and searchable on the Knepp estate website, yet he has chosen to praise the book and the rewilding it describes anyway.

Instead of being in entirely separate bubbles, pro- or anti-animals as meat, pro- or anti-hounds, and so on, it may turn out that rewilding in general, and Knepp in particular, could be one area where for once these notionally conflicting bubbles can actually overlap in relative peace. This is a rare enough occurrence to be worthy of comment.

There is almost no common ground between the urban and rural outlook on certain issues, particularly with regard to hunting and shooting. If rewilding can provide even one tiny area of common ground, perhaps a place to meet halfway, this could be hugely helpful to those of us who are keen to start building lasting bridges between these disparate tribes. We have to get along. Of course there are some traditional country people who are anti-Chris Packham *and* anti-rewilding, just as there are some urban socialists who think rewilding estates are just a way for rich people to banish people from their land and get richer without doing very much. But both these groups would now represent a minority of their own minority. Most people, whether from town or country in more general outlook, seem to be now at least *slightly* interested in rewilding *some of the land*, and prepared to give it a chance. Almost everyone seems to support wilder farming and farming with and for nature. Most people are also softer in many ways than their ancestors of even a hundred years ago were, and we tend to be collectively less tolerant of cruelty, to animals or people. This is not a fault but an evolution, progress.

If most people have at least some sympathy for rewilding, there are still a few details to clear up with regard to the degree of wildness we would tolerate or enjoy. George Monbiot is in favour of releasing wolves in remoter parts of the British landscape (as distinct from the more managed and populated lowland countryside), so that the wolves eat some of the deer, so that more trees can grow. He might surprise that section of his followers who have not actually read his books, as he actively *advocates the shooting of wolves* if ever they are released (*Feral*, 2013). Some rewilding purists would also like to see bears in Britain. Humouring Monbiot's eco-fantasy, and hypothetically zooming out into a feral future without sheep and with the new British rainforest, in a few hundred years this imagined wild scene may seem less mad than it does now. Many people would draw the line at releasing wolves, but might have some sympathy with releasing lynxes, and certainly with preserving the existing indigenous Scottish wildcat.

In early 2020, a spoof Hampshire Hyena Project, #Hyenas4Hampshire, was launched by Matt Cross, a rural investigative journalist. The Hampshire Hyena Project poked fun at the more extreme end of the wolf-and-bear-releasing rewilding aficionados, and it garnered huge support in the tweedier corners of Twitter in only a few days. In reality, while more than happy to mob it up as a joke, most people even in rural areas seem now to see the serious points and the advantages of sensible versions of rewilding in appropriate places, ideally connected together by wildlife corridors. When asked whether they are 'in' or 'out', most are essentially 'in'.

Hugh Somerleyton, the current Lord Somerleyton, who is rewilding part of his patch of Suffolk, literally has pigs in the park, in the manner of the Prince in the Saki story. Apart from being amusing to see pigs truffling around in conventional parkland around the house, there is a sound rewilding reason for this unconventional arrangement. The idea is that pigs truffle around and disturb some of the earth in the grass. If there is only a light population of pigs, the parkland will not be 'damaged' (although there is no such word as 'damage' in rewilding circles, if the damage is done naturally and by an animal). The disturbance of the earth by the pigs resembles the work of porcine messy-minded moles, but spaced far apart leaving plenty of 'proper parkland' in between. The disturbed earth will be receptive to seeds and acorns dropped by passing birds, resulting in a naturally regenerated scrub and eventually broadleaf woodland. Brambles and thorns are nature's barbed wire, and will act as biodegradable tree guards, protecting the wild saplings from being nibbled by rabbits and deer. At least that is the theory.

Obviously it is not hard to find people who have difficulty adapting to change in this particular context, since the pigs in the park have quite a dramatic effect on what the park actually looks like. If you have known the place all your life, this visual adjustment can at first be slightly startling. And this is only the beginning... Over the next fifty years, there will be much greater changes to come, especially since the Somerleyton estate includes large areas of marshland and is near the coast, on the 'blue maps', where the water will come. The name Somerleyton itself suggests only summer grazing, Summer Ley, the low land perhaps historically flooding in winter. Hugh and his wife Lara's long-term vision for Somerleyton, and for a more nature-rich world their children's generation might inherit, is genuinely admirable, the benefits likely to be felt far into the future.

At Knepp, Tamworth pigs replicate the ancient woodland pigs or wild boar that would have roamed Britain in earlier times, just as Longhorn cattle replicate the aurochs. At Somerleyton, there is a plan to introduce either European bison or water buffalo for the same reason: large herbivores, or in fact, VERY LARGE HERBIVORES. Most of the rewilding estates also accommodate free-roaming herds of Exmoor ponies, and for this reason alone they would deserve our support. There is an awkward moral and cultural dilemma coming, about what to do with 'the 10 per cent' of the Exmoor ponies. It is beneficial to rewilding for various reasons to have an Exmoor stallion running with the mares, as it affects the way the ponies move around the land, how they approach water, how they leave tracks for other animals, how the stallions paw the ground, and so on. But if you have stallions you will have foals. Which means you will have 10 per cent of ponies who are, in the ecological rewilding sense, 'surplus'.

What shall we say to these things? We are culturally averse to ponies of any kind going 'into the food chain', especially Exmoor ponies whose relations and ancestors we have known personally, as childhood friends and allies of the highest order. It seems unthinkable to eat pony meat. Yet a friend sells Dartmoor taffety (pony meat) for the counter-intuitive benefit of the Dartmoor hill ponies, so perhaps if we are serious about the other benefits to nature at large, we should open our minds and eat 'the 10 per cent'. We long ago made a pact with the horse. We promised not to eat him in return for a few favours. Then we elevated him to a god. We have an unusual predator-prey relationship with the horse, and occasionally we return to our basic roots. But in general we stick to our ancient promise. I certainly don't want to eat Exmoor ponies 'surplus' to rewilding enterprises, but in theory I would. We might have to start a discreet box scheme, and give it an abstract name (like keen rewilder Derek Gow, who offers 'cheval'), to play our part in the circle of life.

There are rewilding detractors, and there are good reasons to resist rewilding in certain places, or if overused as a cudgel with which to impose an essentially urban agenda on a rural community from outside. At Knepp, Charlie and Isabella seem to have won their detractors over, with charm, over time. They are no longer seen by their rural neighbours as thistle-farming pariahs, 'wasting the land'. But the mental adjustments that will be needed when faced with real changes in the countryside may be considerable, and we can't start rewilding *too* much of the best lowland farmland of the UK, much of it in Norfolk and Suffolk: we need conventional farming because we *still need to eat*. If nothing else, the coronavirus pandemic has shown us the vulnerability of hyper-globalised logistics, and just-enough, just-in-time supermarket supply chains, whether for food or for anything else.

A proposed rewilding project in Wales, called *Summit to Sea*, was roundly rejected by the sheep farmers whose lives and livelihoods would have been affected, if not removed, by it. At its worst, rewilding can seem like the historic clearances of indigenous people, by haughty outsiders who know nothing about local cultures or land, turning people off the farms that their families have been farming for hundreds of years, and imposing urban values about nature as a place to be visited rather than something to be part of, in a manner that could be called eco-colonialism. Farming is in the blood. It is integral to identity. Bloodlines of sheep flocks may have been nurtured for generations. Tread softly for you tread on my dreams, or the dreams of our great-great grandfathers. Or yours.

Rewilding attracts a few fanatics, and it doesn't take much for the pronouncements of someone from outside to cause outrage by referring to what *to the outsider* might seem to be empty and bleak places as a 'blank canvas' that would be ripe *from the outsider's point of view* for rewilding. Nowhere is a blank canvas to the people who live and work there.

The fetishisation of the Scottish Highlands as a romantic wilderness has much to answer for, given that plenty of people live and work there, whether as professional stalkers or publishers. Not every gamekeeper on a grouse moor wants to retrain as an eco-tourism guide or a wildlife ranger, and it is also quite possible that a former gamekeeper might be treated with contempt by eco-tourists, given some of the views expressed in certain vociferous quarters now. Some cultural sensitivity and a real acknowledgement of the deep pool of knowledge and experience held by the people of the countryside would not go amiss. Spectacular reintroductions are inherently alien to the working British countryside. Big wild animals have been absent for hundreds of years, and perhaps there was a good reason why our ancestors were apparently happy to let them go.

As most rewilding estates tend to introduce an element of eco-tourism – safaris, camping and that sort of thing – it will be interesting to see how tourists will fare if they come across the large herbivores when they are introduced. There they will be, idly sipping a chilled glass of wine on the deck or balcony of their wilderness lodge or 'retreat', as the sun goes down, when CRASH!, out of the undergrowth will come a gigantic water buffalo heading for the watering hole in the evening light. In the morning, as the tourists plunge the plunger of their highly civilised and urbane camping coffee (not Camp Coffee), CRASH! a European bison will suddenly appear and bid them good morning.

At Somerleyton Hall in Suffolk, there are two stuffed polar bears standing upright in the hall by the front door, a slightly alarming greeting if you are not used to them. These polar bears were shot in a different era by Sir Savile Crossley, the great-grandfather of the present incumbent, Hugh Somerleyton. As a child I used to imagine what it would be like to be so close to these polar bears if they were alive, and whether they would eat me, and then I would imagine what that might be like. If nothing else, these polar bears serve as a reminder of how greatly our attitudes have changed in only three generations, standing as they do at the front door of what is now Wild East UK HQ. The Wild East rewilding project initiated by Hugh Somerleyton is hugely ambitious. It aims to link up landowners of various kinds across East Anglia and persuade them to devote about 20 per cent of their land to 'nature', creating a connected area 'the size of Dorset' for wildlife. This is rewilding on a grand scale, but more importantly these landowners haven't lost sight of the fact that they are also farmers. We still need to eat. East Anglia's arable land is among the most productive, but also historically the most nature-depleted since the war. Over the next fifty years or so the changes across Norfolk and Suffolk as a result of this collective ambition should be tangible, visible and enjoyable. This is *regenerative farming,* not an agricultural monastery. It is allowed to be fun.

The Prince in the Saki story was right to choose pigs in the park over flowers, but if regenerative farming and rewilding can work together, in the future we may be able to enjoy pigs *and* flowers.

Venison and venery

Now therefore, please take your weapons, your quiver
      and your bow,
and go out into the fields and take some venison for me.

Genesis 27:3

11

NOVEMBER

You can't set out to write a book about rural life and adapting to change with any authenticity or country credibility, without considering the ancient subject of hunting, and its more *arriviste* son, shooting. Without hunting and shooting, it could be a book about nature, or the countryside, but it could not be truly *of* the country. Fishing is slightly separate, not least because many more people have first-hand experience and therefore some understanding of fishing, whereas hunting and shooting are participated in by far fewer.

If you were a culturally neutral and curious visiting alien anthropologist from another planet, it would immediately be obvious that this thing these Earth people call 'hunting' is an important rite of social bonding, and of great significance to the people participating. You would observe that hunting shares many of the traits and 'otherness' associated with religions: formality, ritual courtesy, smart turnout, peculiar clothing, arcane language, and a kind of complicated choreography. These are the same details of rite and ritual that you would notice if you (still in your role as the alien anthropologist) attended Trooping of the Colour or went racing at Ascot. You could be forgiven for concluding in your alien anthropologist's notebook that the Queen was a minor deity and that we actually worshipped The Horse as our principal god.

Hunting has for centuries been symbolically associated with landownership and power, alongside theoretically existing for the sole purpose of catching our food. With the Norman conquest came a particular kind of venery. The word *venison* comes from the Latin *venari*, to chase or pursue, and *venatio*, hunting. From this comes the old French *venerie*, aka *venery*, hunting, and *veneur*, hunter. Old French *venesoun* becomes the English *venison*. There is subtlety even in the translation of these words. The word *venery* in English includes a suggestion of 'the art of hunting', not merely 'the act or action of hunting'. *Venison* means something close to 'meat from large game', meaning a large hunted animal but not necessarily a deer.

The richest man in Britain was for many years (if not still) the Duke of Westminster, whose family name is Grosvenor. *Gros veneur*, great hunter. Many British surnames and place names include suggestions of Fox or Tod. Hunting is deeply embedded.

Understanding some of the nuance of the language of hunting gives insight into the culture of hunting itself. This is easier if you are separated from your own culture, and so can cast the forensic eye of the alien *anthropologist*, rather than the over-familiar eye that some might call the personally involved *apologist*. As a teenager I spent several months in the Ardennes, ostensibly as an au pair, a phrase which roughly translates as 'on a par' with or 'as an equal' to the family the au pair is living with. To picture the scene, 'my family' could fairly be imagined as The Belgian Mitfords. For reasons too dull to relate, I had left school at sixteen (having taken A-levels, including French, early), and had no clue what to do next. So, naturally, I went to Belgium, as you do.

Finding myself surrounded by *la chasse* and *sangliers* (wild boar) in the depths of the forest of the Ardennes in winter, I briefly became preoccupied with trying to read about the history of *la chasse* in French. This was noticed by the patriarch of the Belgian Mitfords, who gave me chapter and verse on his specialist subject, as well as access to his hunting library. I think he was glad to have someone other than Aicha, his dog, who was prepared to listen to his extensive opinions and erudition on the subject. All the other 'Mitfords' in the house had long since tired of the history and theory of hunting, if not the practice.

There were stags' heads on the walls in the largest of the stone-walled rooms, frequent thunderstorms and a general atmosphere of 'chic gaiety'. They had frites even at formal dinners. Letters arrived romantically addressed to *Le Chevalier* . . . It was as if we were all suspended in a perpetual state of animated rehearsal for a BBC Sunday evening version of *Pride and Prejudice*, filmed on an old set built for *War and Peace*, and inexplicably rendered in comedy French accents.

La chasse in France and Belgium takes many forms, but one thing I noticed was that many of the men at dinner had scars of one sort or another. They casually related stories of how they had been 'glanced' or 'peppered' with shot, or accidentally let their loaded gun off while cleaning it. They asked about gun safety *en Angleterre*, and I ridiculously attempted to translate the poem that begins, Never, never let your gun, pointed be at anyone . . . *Jamais, jamais laissez votre fusil* . . . etc. A man with a patch over his eye warned me that French horses would fall over if you asked them to canter round corners. Apparently they can only trot. On high days and holidays, the Belgian Mitfords' patriarch would perform his party trick and play the *trompe de chasse*, the theatrical kind of horn that coils round in a great circle, rather than the little English hunting horn kind.

I spent a large amount of my time as an au pair trying not to get the giggles, amid what seemed to be a constant supply of comedic prompts. But I did learn a great deal about hunting, and the red blood in the veins: if not in me, then in many of the people and animals around me, and across the wider world. Even the word *sanglier* seems related to *sang*, blood.

Whatever your opinion of it, hunting cannot easily be dismissed, banned or ignored. To consider the place of hunting in the modern world, in an era yearning to heal the natural world, first we have to define our terms.

The word hunting has different meanings across the world, but in Britain it normally means either *historic hunting, usually of deer* or *hunting with hounds, within the law* (as distinct from 'fox hunting', which is very specific and, at least theoretically, historic, redundant). Shooting normally means *shooting animals or birds with a shotgun or rifle, as game, for food, within the law*. Hunting is not normally used to mean shooting in Britain. Context usually makes it plain whether the word 'hunting' actually refers to shooting. The language alone causes misunderstandings.

In the twenty-first century, a rougher, wilder form of shooting, that is genuinely much closer to the original concept of hunting – having to find, track and work for your dinner – is likely to become the norm. The public at large, and the shooting community in particular, is increasingly uncomfortable with (or appalled by) big bag driven days, as distinct from rough, walked-up, wilder shooting. Whether on the grouse moors of the uplands or the pheasant shoots of the lowlands, the mood is to go wilder and rougher, shooting fewer birds or other game, crucially shooting only a sustainable 'shootable surplus' and only in numbers proven to be compatible with demand from diners. Those who continue to expect unnaturally large numbers of birds to fly over their peg are likely to find themselves increasingly ostracised, and eventually, banned.

Obviously, the very word hunting is itself divisive. People tend not to change sides on the subject once they have made up their minds, though many sit on the fence. Whether you like it or not, hunting and shooting in their modern lawful forms are still as much a part of British rural life as farming or walking the dog. If we were starting from scratch we would not invent hunting with hounds, or even guns. But we didn't invent it, we inherited it, so we have to start from here, in the real world.

The sounds of the hunting horn and the gun are as much a part of the rural soundscape as church bells or the cock crowing in the morning. These sounds may be man-made, but they are now part of the collective human (not just rural) psyche. Leicester City Football Club uses the *Post Horn Gallop* as a kind of theme tune at matches, a musical choice which is completely connected to the fact that the county road signs of Leicestershire carry a picture of a perky fox. Leicestershire was the cream of fox hunting country, a fact of its history now, whatever changes may come.

The architecture of hunting and shooting is as clearly present in the landscape as barns, church towers or village signs, if you know what to look for. Many buildings relating to hunting and shooting are listed buildings, for example Georgian stables and kennels. The Belvoir hunt kennels at Belvoir Castle are an exemplar of the type, but these buildings are 'hidden in plain sight' all over the country. The language of hunting, including falconry, is specific and arcane, but it is also part of everyday life: hoodwinked, under your thumb, Chief Whip, Soho, and so on.

November is the month culturally most associated with hunting. The patron saint of hunting is St Hubert or Hubertus (656–727). St Hubert's Day is November 3rd. In the UK, opening meets happen in November and the shooting season is in full swing.

St Hubert's story is an interesting one in that it resonates with contemporary attitudes and disquiet. The nub of the story is that after his wife died giving birth to their son, Hubert retreated to the forest and gave himself up entirely to hunting. One day, he allegedly saw a vision of a crucifix entwined in a stag's antlers, and had a kind of Damascene conversion. His encounter with 'Christ' results not in Hubert suddenly giving up hunting, as might be expected in a modern morality-tale version of the story, but the rather more nuanced and interesting outcome of Hubert coming up with a kind of *Code of Good Practice for Hunting*. St Hubert lived and died about 1300 years ago, but his *Code* includes recognisably contemporary ethics, e.g.: *Only kill when a clean and quick kill is assured; only kill stags who are old, sick or injured; do not kill females with young at foot.*

Obviously, some people cannot condone St Hubert (or

anyone else) killing any animal at all, ever, for any reason. But given that statistically more people eat meat than don't, many more may have some sympathy with St Hubert's *Code*, especially as it was conceived so long ago. The modern *Code of Good Practice for Hunting* (and another *for Shooting*) owes much to this ancient legacy. What the mythical and apocryphal story of St Hubert really hints at is that humans have probably had a sense of fair play and correct conduct in relation to hunting from the outset. Hunting was never without some restraint, forethought and discipline. It was never 'killing for fun'. There was always a ritual courtesy and an arcane morality to uphold. And there still is.

In his TV documentary series *Stiff Upper Lip: An Emotional History of Britain* (2012), Ian Hislop examined the habitual British inability to express emotions, starting with tiny children being sent away to boarding school at prep-school age, and continuing through an alarmingly familiar panoply of public school mannerisms, trunks, prayer books, compulsory chapel, peculiar disciplines, and what might be Empire Training, including footage of the Household Cavalry at Horse Guards. The very word 'trunk' holds a particular sense of dread for anyone who went to boarding school at a young age, and who still remembers the countdown to the end of the summer holidays, cruelly timed by history to coincide with the end of the harvest, just as the countryside of 'home' was at its most glorious, all stubble fields and sunshine.

In *Stiff Upper Lip*, A. N. Wilson makes the shrewd observation, 'only the British could use the word *pathetic* as an insult'. The word *pathetic* is related to *pathos*. *Pathos* is related to *empathy*, which means putting ourselves in someone else's place, imagining how it feels to be them.

Calling someone *pathetic* as an insult is almost the same as calling them *empathetic* as an insult. Pathos and empathy are essentially why we have collectively, gradually, moved away from feeling at ease or at home with the idea of hunting in any form. This discomfort is especially true in a modern urban age, when most people never see what happens to animals who live out their natural life to die a 'natural death'. Natural deaths can be brutal, but most of us rarely see much evidence of nature killing animals in everyday life, although the owners of the more 'hunting' kinds of cats see more of it than most.

Wild animals in the countryside are usually eaten or cleared away by scavengers before we see evidence of their fates. Wild animals are also noticeably either healthy or dead. Philosophically, nature cannot be cruel, because nature itself is amoral. It is the human perspective which allocates the concept of cruelty, for instance to death by predation and starvation. We feel an innate empathy with another creature's suffering. As mammals, humans retain a deep fear of death by predation or starvation, perhaps as a kind of genetic memory of what killed us before cancer and viruses. In nature, predation or starvation are the main killers of mammals, yet these routine natural processes are now startling to us when applied to human mammals. Someone I knew as a teenager became prey to a predator when he was killed by a crocodile. The 1972 Andes plane crash was a profoundly affecting story because of the threat of human starvation at its heart, and the obvious but unusual way the survivors overcame it.

We have become separated from the alternatives that await animals if we do not kill them, so that the stalker killing an aged stag with a rifle is seen by some as reprehensible, when an alternative death from natural starvation might be far worse, from the stag's point of view. Professional stalkers find satisfaction in finding a stag's teeth are down to the gums as it indicates that the stag had lived his longest possible natural life, and died instantly, just before the inevitable processes of starvation had begun to kill him slowly. The stag's death by predation, for instance by the reintroduction of wolves by rewilding purists, would also seem more cruel than by rifle shot.

It is a curious anomaly that many people talk about stalking, shooting etc. as replacing natural predation, or being an alternative to nature where we have no apex predators. If you see humans as being an animal, a mammal playing its part in the hierarchy of nature, then human beings *are* the contemporary apex predator, a predator incidentally a great deal more humane than some of our predecessors with big teeth. Several non-human animals and birds use tools to kill their prey or crack open shells, so it is intellectually inconsistent for human animals to be seen as 'apart from' nature rather than 'a part of' nature when they too choose to use tools to kill their prey, whether with spear, bow and arrow, bird of prey, dog or gun. Antipathy towards hunting, or specifically towards *hunters*, comes from the question of *why* the human predator kills other animals: for food, for sport or for some other reason. It's their enjoyment in doing so that repels those opposed to it.

One of the most poignant scenes of a wild animal's death, that still haunts me, is that of a swan killed on a busy road leading out of London near Canary Wharf. The disorientated swan must have mistaken the metallic road for a body of water on which to land. That particular death of that individual swan still seems an utter tragedy, so directly caused by cars, and so near the wild wetlands of Essex.

Pathos has played a part in some famous cases of a more conventional kind of conversion: the straightforward conversion of a person away from hunting or shooting and towards empathy, without the complexities of St Hubert and his rule book. This suits the simplistic story setup more conveniently, but is usually more nuanced than it first appears. One of the better known of the conversion stories is that of Sir Peter Scott (1909–1989), best known as a wild-fowler, conservationist and artist. He was a famously keen wildfowler in his youth, shooting wild geese over marshes and wetlands 'for the pot', as people still do today. In later life Sir Peter founded the Wildfowl and Wetlands Trust at Slimbridge, and was a co-founder of the World Wildlife Fund (as the WWF was originally called). Many people (including my father) who are considered to be a good shot in their prime, give up as they reach middle to old age, often because they feel they are becoming less accurate, and thus less humane. The idea that shooters are thoughtlessly killing for fun is misleading and inaccurate.

Sir Peter Scott also designed the WWF panda logo. It is no coincidence that pandas, badgers and lapwings are used as 'logo animals'. The WWF freely admits that a black and white 'logo animal' saves money on printing, and shows up well on photocopies. Imagine the 'logo animal' meetings and dilemmas, having to choose between a zebra and a dairy cow. Most modern wildfowlers (and old-school hunting and shooting people) would find no contradiction between wildfowling and active conservation. In fact, for many, conservation is a significant part of the point of it all. This is a separate and expansive subject, but a list of relevant books and organisations are included as an appendix, as a setting-out point leading to more detailed knowledge and information, if anyone feels inclined to explore it.

A word translated as 'venison' appears in the book of Genesis, right at the beginning of the Bible. It may be referring to Arabian oryx, or a similar animal of the Middle East two-thousand-odd years ago, but whichever the animal, the context suggests that it would (and should) be hunted for food. It is when the hunting *for food* becomes conflated with some form of celebration of the finding and catching of it, that the trouble begins. For within the word 'venison' lies the concept of 'venery', the art of hunting, and within the 'art of hunting' lies the origin of hunting *for sport*.

Picture the scene. There we all were, a few thousand years ago, or perhaps not long after 1066, gathering and meeting somewhere like the New Forest or the Knepp estate, or Cnappe as it then was. We set off in search of a deer or some other quarry we could eat, perhaps a pony or a wild boar. We found a deer, we followed it, we were interested in where it led us, we managed eventually to catch and kill it. By the end of this tiring but interesting day, we were able to gather round the fire and feed ourselves, and our assembled tribe of friends, neighbours and extended family, or whoever was passing by and accepted or honoured as a guest. One day, someone might have suggested that perhaps we could turn the occasion into a bit more of a feast, a celebration of both the food and the beast which had provided it. So we did.

Has anyone who ever enjoyed any part of this sequence, whether the tracking, the view, the chase, the kill, the cooking over the fire, or the feasting itself, crossed a moral line? Your pleasure in the day was not *purely for the food* that it has procured. If the exertion or the experience of being a participant in nature, rather than an observer, has enhanced your enjoyment of life in any way, you have crossed that invisible line. Like Sir Peter Scott, you have shot a creature, at least in part, *for sport* as well as *for food*. This complex nuance is one of the principal sources of conflict *in* or at least *about* the modern countryside, including *about* rewilding and the estates on which such wilding currently takes place.

The echoes of the fine line between hunting for food and hunting for sport still resonate today in attitudes to shooting. In the twenty-first century, many people can live with the idea of shooting *for food*, but not *for sport*. Right there is the root of much of the conflict about the whole subject, for it is almost always impossible to separate the two completely. There is not a single day of formal or walked-up shooting of any kind in Britain without pickers-up and gundogs – Labradors, spaniels and so on – always present with the intention to retrieve all the shot game *for food*. The Labrador *retriever* is the full name of the breed. Every gun, beater, picker-up and bystander on a day's shooting is drilled to watch carefully, to mark where every single bird falls, so that every bird can be retrieved and hung on the game cart, as food. The guns themselves, meaning the people who actually shoot the birds, are (or should be) personally responsible for marking and finding their own shot birds, and for ensuring their destiny as food.

Without the caveat that it is at least the *intention* that every single bird must become food, there is no justification for shooting a living creature at all. And even with the caveat that every creature shot becomes food, as in game, for human consumption, some people will still think it wrong to shoot it at all. Certainly there are discussions to be had about numbers, ecology, ethics and sustainability.

The formal protection of mountain hares in Scotland demonstrates the already established direction of flow. Our relationship with other animals as quarry is evolving towards greater *empathy*.

Small pellets of lead shot (as in the metal, *Pb*) occasionally being left in birds has allowed opponents of shooting to mischievously label all feathered game as 'poisonous'. This will soon end, as the shooting community is adapting to change by changing from lead shot to steel. One cartridge manufacturer advertises copper shot for use on the grouse moors with the caption, '*Cu* on the moor'. This seemingly tiny detail is actually a significant change, with enormously positive implications for the marketing of game as food. Yet hardly anyone seems to have noticed it. Barely a word on the move away from lead shot has appeared in the mainstream media. It's almost as if no one cares that much about the *for food* aspect of shooting after all. If they did care, and for those who do care, the move away from lead shot represents serious progress.

Pb or *Cu* matters, because if lead is perceived to be (or actually is) 'poisonous', even in the tiniest trace quantities, it affects the marketability of high-quality game meat. The perceived presence of lead effectively keeps the consumption of game quite *niche*, mostly sold and eaten among the existing traditional game aficionados, typically those who live in the country and who are close to shooting (literally or socially). In fact 'wild game' is compatible with a general modern desire for more traceable and high-welfare food, and it could be enjoyed by more people and bought from mainstream shops, including supermarkets. Some people may flinch at the idea of any animal being shot at all, but many may appreciate that the game meat lives the most natural of lives, compared with other animals from which we more usually source our meat: for instance, chickens.

It would be a reasonable question to ask why we do not farm pheasants for meat, like free-range chickens, leaving out the shooting altogether, but that is a question no one seems to ask. In the real world as it currently is, it makes sense to market game meat in convenient and conventional forms: pheasant breast, legs, thighs, wings, sausages and pheasi-burgers. Muntjac-in-a-Box™ ready meals, veni-burgers, lasagne, stalker's pie, and so on, could be a wilder alternative to beef. It makes total sense to be more connected with the source of meat, and for that meat to live a good life, if we are to continue eating meat at all. It also makes sense to eat invasive species.

The destiny to become food is true of every deer shot, whether by a stalker or by a professional marksman on an RSPB reserve for conservation. Some people object to a stalker paying to shoot a red stag, but not to a professional marksman being paid to shoot a muntjac for conservation reasons, yet these are the same person. I know someone who is a recreational stalker in the *Monarch of the Glen* tradition, and a marksman for the RSPB, sometimes on the same day. The distinction between shooting *for sport* or *for conservation* is unclear, especially since every deer shot for either reason goes into the game larder as food.

There are habitat and biodiversity net gains associated with hunting and shooting, so with our caring-about-climate-change hats on we need to keep a cool head. There are about 600,000 shotgun licences in the UK, with many more people involved as beaters, keepers etc., and millions more involved in the eating of the resulting game. In a 2020 survey, of the 5,000 or so RSPB members who responded, only 14 per cent of this actively interested group supported some form of ban on shooting. This seems a surprisingly low number, but it represents life in the real world as distinct from the Internet. This suggests that some of the conflict surrounding shooting exists in online echo chambers, the voices of a few people magnified and distorted by social media. It may also be that some RSPB members want to ban grouse shooting, but might also enjoy a venison pie, giving them a dilemma as they hover over the 'ban' button.

The *for food* or *for sport* aspect is usually at the heart of any discomfort around shooting, but it needn't be. Most of the estates involved in rewilding typically include shooting on their land, while still retaining their biodiversity net gains. This suggests to an open-minded person that it is possible to be involved in both rewilding *and* shooting. Rewilding is usually connected with shooting, even though many visitors to such estates may not realise it, or might disapprove. This is another good reason to roll with the nuances and grey areas of life, especially when it comes to nature and the environment.

It is entirely reasonable to be vegan and supportive of rewilding, while not approving of shooting. But it would be a shame if the distant activities of people they will never meet caused some people to boycott this or that estate, or this or that organisation. It is the bigger picture that matters, the overall net benefit to nature and wildlife. For example, in the grand scheme of things the National Trust generally does terrific work that we should all feel inclined to support at least in principle, even though we may personally disapprove of some decisions, or some of the activities they allow (or don't allow) on National Trust land. We have to zoom out to see the bigger picture.

Glastonbury Festival is held on a dairy farm, therefore is also inherently not vegan, yet it supports many brilliant vegan food stalls. Knepp Safaris are held on a rewilding estate which also hosts shooting, polo and trail hunting. Knepp hedges historically left in for the hunt to jump, at a time when hedges were typically being grubbed-up to make bigger fields, are beneficial to birds and small animals. The Holkham and Somerleyton estates are hailed as epicentres of rewilding, eco-tourism and regenerative or restorative farming, but they are also famous for their shoots and traditional hospitality. These moral conflicts are normal. Just as *context and intent* must be scrutinised in cases of allegedly inappropriate words or opinions, almost nothing is without nuance. Almost nothing is absolute. There is *almost always* some subtlety, some reasonable middle ground, something we can find in common.

The debate about hunting with hounds was essentially or at least legally settled with the Hunting With Dogs Act (2004), so is not a debate to continue here. Hunting still causes a great deal of confusion and conflict, despite having been banned in its traditional form nearly twenty years ago.

The word 'hunting' alone is often used as a kind of shorthand to convey stereotypes, without even adding any props. For instance, in a BBC Radio 4 comedy sketch, the writer included the phrase *grouse hunting* (i.e. shooting) to indicate that the character had been method acting a Tory. While in a wilder future rough 'grouse hunting' may become commonplace, in real life in the UK, *grouse hunting* is a noticeably abnormal term. This trivial detail is typical of the casual ignorance and/or prejudice about country things which often crops up in the mainstream media and online. Individually these don't matter at all, but as a pattern, they start to add up.

Examples of this pattern are everywhere, but go largely unnoticed in an urban age. Fox cubs being fed by a vixen are captioned on Twitter as 'orphan bears'. Kids, as in baby goats, are captioned 'baby donkeys'. Straw bales are captioned 'hay bales'. A shotgun is a 'rifle'. A swan is kicked because someone mistakes its attempt at mating for an attack on its mate. People refer to released, farmed or imported grouse, when grouse are always native wild birds. The hunting ban is routinely referred to as the fox hunting ban, when other forms of hunting are included in the Hunting Act. When Jack Charlton died, a national treasure of 1966 World Cup fame, he was described online as an animal abuser, because he had enjoyed shooting and fishing as well as football, a legacy of a country childhood and wartime rationing, when wild game was not rationed.

At a National Trust house, a deer died after people fed it, despite signs saying 'Please do not feed the deer'. The people apparently thought the sign meant not to feed the deer 'inappropriate food like chocolate and doughnuts', rather than what it actually said. The sign could not have been clearer. Horses have died from being fed by visiting picnickers. People release great bunches of balloons into the sky 'as a tribute' to someone or something, not thinking of balloons and their strings as litter which can kill livestock and wildlife. Ditto sky lanterns. Wild camping has suddenly become fly camping, with whole campsites of kit just left abandoned in beautiful places. Littering is rife. Even the word yokels is misspelt as 'yocals', oddly diminishing the insult. On it goes. The old Country Code needs to make a comeback. 'Leave no trace' should be the absolute norm. Perhaps the fashion for cottagecore could include helpful hints on rural behaviour as well as how to get the *look*. This pattern of ignorance and prejudice is indicative of disconnect, not malice.

The Hunting Act (2004) came into force on 18th February 2005, and it still causes conflict in the shires and confusion among the online anti-hunting community.

The Hunting Act makes a hunting activity *illegal* if:

a) a *person* engages in pursuit of a *wild* animal, and

b) one or more *dogs* are employed in that pursuit.

The crime is *pursuit*. There is no crime of *not laying a trail*. Whether a trail is laid or not does not matter in the eyes of the law. The onus of proof of intentional pursuit of a wild animal is on the accuser to prove guilt, not the accused to prove innocence.

It is not illegal to hold a meet in front of a pub or a big house, nor to wear odd clothes, nor to gallop around the countryside on horses, nor even to kill a fox in certain circumstances. One of the more eccentric exemptions is that it is legal to flush a fox or hare to be killed by a bird of prey. No one ever seems to object to hunting with birds of prey, which seems odd, from the point of view of the quarry.

In order to commit a crime under the Hunting Act, there must be evidence of a dog chasing a wild animal. There must also be unedited evidence of the time, date and location. The ambiguity of the law causes people to report, for example, '... illegal fox hunt meeting outside the Fox & Goose pub in Tottering-by-Gently'... when the existence of hunts, with names and staff and hounds and kennels, is not illegal. The meet is by definition not illegal, since there is no pursuit when everyone is literally at a standstill. These misunderstandings exacerbate (and even cause) an unhelpful rural-urban divide at a time when people crave nature and open space. The Hunting Act is badly worded, almost as if it was deliberately designed to be unenforceable and awry.

To clarify terms, and to explain what might be happening if you see what appears to be an 'illegal fox hunt', there are three main types of *legal* hunting with hounds:

Trail hunting. An animal-based trail is laid by a person on a horse or a quad bike or on foot, for hounds and mounted field to follow. The trail is usually made of something which smells of an animal, often mixed with vegetable oil to make it 'sticky'. The scent may be obtained from a dead fox shot legally, for instance by a gamekeeper. The scent could be anything, if hounds had been rewarded for following that smell. Hounds, like most dogs, respond to praise, not necessarily 'treats'. Hunt saboteurs aim to disrupt trail hunting, seeing it as a post-ban cover for illegal hunting (of a wild animal). While often malicious or mischievous for reasons related to *gros veneur* issues, power, class, landownership and so on, to be scrupulously fair, the accusers sometimes have a point. There are still too many trail hunting 'accidents', and foxes, hares and deer are still killed.

Drag hunting. A non-animal scent, often aniseed-based, is laid across the country for hounds and the mounted field to follow, as above. Drag hunts have historically always hunted an artificial scent, not foxes etc. Drag hunting is often confused or conflated with hunting with blood-hounds on social media, but drag hunting and hunting with bloodhounds are distinctly different, with separate histories.

Bloodhounds, bloodhounding or '*hunting the clean boot*'. A human runner (or several) runs across the country to be hunted, and leaves a scent, for instance of a sweaty old T-shirt and the runner's natural body scents. The human scent is then followed by the bloodhounds and the usual formal hierarchy of hunt staff and field, the whole scene *resembling* a traditional hunting scene, but with black-and-tan bloodhounds, rather than the more typical tri-coloured fox hounds, harriers or beagles.

The Mitford children were famously hunted by their father with his bloodhounds, leading the late, great Debo, Duchess of Devonshire, to comment on a review in *The Times* of the TV adaptation of *Love in a Cold Climate*: 'He [the reviewer] disapproves in a governessy way of the idea of my father hunting my sisters with his bloodhounds for fun. What else would he have done it for? I know that some misguided people are against hunting foxes, but surely children are fair game?'

Dr Brian May, the Queen guitarist (and astrophysicist, and anti-hunting and anti-badger cull campaigner) is a new convert to bloodhounds, having sportingly accepted an invitation to visit a pack and see what they did. After his day out with the Three Counties Bloodhounds on Boxing Day 2019, Brian May referred to hunting with bloodhounds as 'the humane face of hunting' with 'all the fun and pageantry of hunting but without the cruelty'.

There is much to say about the culture of hounds, 'hound work', bloodlines, pedigrees, puppy shows, the architecture of hunt kennels, history and so on, but that would be a whole library of separate books, which already exist. The main point is that hunting has been adapting to change more in the past two hundred years, with the loss of land and the arrival of motorways, barbed wire and railways. One day, all that remains of the heyday of fox hunting may be the famous woodland coverts and the surviving architecture of hunt kennels. But not just yet.

I grew up with hunting. My mother's father was mad keen on hunting and everything relating to hounds. Until he was killed in the war, hunting was all he lived for, or was at least the main part of his enjoyment of life. He dragged Granny off (fairly willingly it seems) from their comfortable abode at Adbury Park in Berkshire, to Monmouthshire several hours away in Wales, to hunt with Lady Curre's hounds, come rain or shine. There are paintings of them 'living their best life', painted by Michael Lyne, just before the war. Granny is easily recognisable in these scenes, with her bowler hat, on her flashy-faced horse. This was in the 1930s, so these must have been long and tiring days.

During these long hunting days, the children (my mother and her brother and sister) were left at home at Adbury, based in the upstairs nursery with Nanny and Mr Keefy, an Irish wolfhound, going on long walks and later having boiled eggs and soldiers by the fire, being read to and doing the other cosy Nanny things of the time. The 'nursery fender' was an anchoring place of safety, an inanimate object which still has a comforting significance for my mother, now in her late eighties. When Granny died, her children had no hesitation in choosing as their special treasures their own 1930s nursery egg cups, each an animal with a strangely peculiar 1930s pearlescent glaze, which I think might correctly be called 'Lustreware'. Valuable antiques and paintings seemed to resonate far less personally than their old nursery egg cups and photos of Nanny. It was a telling detail.

My mother's father's name was William Herbert Fox, and when he was killed in the war on 1st June 1940, he was buried where he fell in France instead of joining the stack of his ancestors, also called William Fox, who are buried and remembered in and around Burghlere church near Adbury, at home. Adbury was and is not far from Highclere Castle, where the TV series *Downton Abbey* was filmed. Culturally, my mother's childhood and later family life at Adbury seems to have been much closer to that of the upstairs contingent of *Downton Abbey* than to our lives today. The Fox family had a visiting seamstress, a supremely skilled Cockney tailor who had been a suffragette, called Elsie Goss. 'Gossie' stayed with them for half the year after the war, just to make dresses for debutante dances and events like Royal Ascot. The presence of Gossie as a visiting seamstress seems to represent the last vestiges of a world that no longer exists, although I can just remember Gossie from the depths of my memory of my own childhood: her tiny frame, her squawky voice and her alarming habit of holding dressmaking pins in a line along her mouth. The point is that great cultural change can happen in only a generation or two. And recently it truly has.

There is a 'Fox box' in the churchyard at Burghclere, where several generations of William Foxes are buried under a kind of ziggurat, the same words repeated over and over again: *William Fox of Adbury Park*. The William Fox who died in the war had a son, William Fox, my mother's brother (the one in the nursery with Nanny and Mr Keefy), who died at the age of 90 in April 2020. Another William Fox to add to the Fox box. There are two more generations of William Fox alive among my Fox cousins today: 'little William' (who is about 6' 6" tall) and his son 'Billy' (ditto).

The spirit of 'Billy Fox going on' with Lady Curre's hounds lives on.

Victory in Europe Day, seventy-five years on, was as good a day as any to remember that wartime generation: William Fox on his grey horse and Granny on her flashy-faced chestnut in those paintings by Michael Lyne. Much of what they were fighting for is depicted in the unspoilt countryside and social detail in any one of those hunting scenes. Everything they lost is in another. There is one particular painting of William Fox on his grey horse, at Adbury, with the house in the background and the Vyne hounds, who were then kennelled at Adbury, at his feet. Because of the war, nothing in that picture remains, except the stable-yard in the distance. And the trees. The house was requisitioned and later demolished, the man was killed, the horse and hounds, who knows? But at least the bloodlines of man, horse and hounds survived. And the trees. This is perhaps why hounds still matter to so many people. At some level, it would feel like a terrible betrayal to let them go.

I clearly remember Adbury standing as a ruin, and I visit it occasionally for old time's sake, and for remembrance of that one particular Fox who never lived to be old. After more than half a century of confusion and loss, Adbury is coming alive again. The Vyne and Craven Branch of the Pony Club hold their Pony Club Camp there now. William Fox, Billy Fox, the grandfather we never knew, would probably be pleased about Adbury once again seeing horse life animating the place. Billy Fox must have liked ponies, as my mother still remembers a particularly naughty one they had, called Polony, who sometimes had to wear little boots and pull the lawnmower.

Granny once told me that she hid the horses from the

Army requisition people in the war, and lied about their non-existence. Probably 'flashy face' was one of the horses she lied about, but we only found out about that painting and that horse quite recently, a hot subject of interest and discussion on the family WhatsApp group. The house was requisitioned 'for the war effort', but not the horses, not flashy-face and the grey. Mr Keefy was shot before the end of the war, because he ate so much meat that it seemed immoral, even with wild game that was not rationed. Adbury adjoins and overlooks Watership Down, so there should have been plenty of rabbits.

There is a black and white photo of my mother and Mr Keefy, taken at Adbury during the war, not one yard behind me as I write. This scene seems not just from another world but from another age. On Remembrance Day, it is to these images of Adbury that I turn in my mind, that I think of every year: Granny and her husband in the prime of life, hunting with Lady Curre's hounds, across the cream of 'the good grass country' that is still many hunting people's idea of heaven. It is a civilised world, far from the depictions of hunting to be found on Twitter.

At home, the Old Rec, as children we too were sent out hunting, on ponies handed down from the Fox cousins, hacking miles to the meet, with 10p in our pockets 'for emergencies' so we could ring for help from a red telephone box. Another generation of benign parental neglect. We had no choice in the matter of hunting. It was just something we did. There was nothing else on offer, nor any hint at hunting being optional. We were surrounded by the literature, paint-ings and printed imagery of hunting: Surtees characters, Jorrocks, Mr Sponge, *The Fox's Frolic*, *The High-Mettled Racer* and, most memorably, *The Midnight Steeplechase*, a race in which a horse crashes through a gate, its shadow spookily unbroken.

This was normal for the time and place, and many rural children of the 1970s and 1980s would have similar memories. On Christmas Eve, we cleaned our tack in front of the Aga, in preparation for the Boxing Day Meet. We always adhered to the mantra *animals first*, in terms of whose comforts were the priority after a long, cold day of what seemed like hair-raising action. (The Household Cavalry still echoes our Pony Club drill in this respect: horses first, soldiers second, officers last.)

Every Boxing Day in my life has been associated with hunting, or shooting if staying with our Fox cousins. As children we were drip-fed the ritual courtesies of hunting and the safety rules of shooting, absorbing this information almost as if by osmosis. We were taught to say *goodnight* when we left for home, even if it was in the morning. The boys probably learnt how much to tip a gamekeeper. We learnt the poem *A Father's Advice* (the one I tried to recite in French for the Belgian Mitfords), that begins, 'Never, never let your gun, pointed be at anyone . . .' and which ends with, 'All the pheasants ever bred cannot make up for one man dead'.

The Boxing Day Meet was always considered a bit different from all the other meets, and the regulars tended (and still tend) to give it a miss. An estimated 250,000 people attend their local Boxing Day Meet now, for the spectacle and the fresh air. Boxing Day was always more crowded and fraught, and now it has become a bit of a media scrum, even though the hunting ban is established and everyone adapted to it long ago. Only later did I start to associate Boxing Day with racing at Kempton, because racing (if you are not actually there on the racecourse) involves being allowed to *watch television in the middle of the afternoon*, indoors, something we never, *ever* did as children, the one notable exception being watching Red Rum.

In 1997 I voted for Tony Blair. It seemed a good idea at the time, and was partly a generational thing, a refreshing sense of change set against the theme tune of *Things Can Only Get Better*. I knew that a bill to ban hunting would be likely, and I examined my conscience long and hard about what I thought about it all.

At the time I drew the maps of all the hunting counties for the Burns Inquiry; fox hounds, harriers, beagles, bassets, and so on, all layered on separate A1 acetate sheets in those days. My book of photomontage cartoons, *Hunting Lore Lunacy*, was published. I took the day off work for the original Countryside Rally in Hyde Park on 10th July 1997. We gathered under county balloons. A total of 120,000 people attended the Countryside Rally, some of whom had walked all the way to London from the furthest corners of the UK. The media took great interest in these country people, their gently photogenic protest, and the new Countryside Alliance. The Royal Parks authorities commented that there was no litter.

Later, there was a Countryside March in London which attracted 250,000 people. Finally, there was the Liberty and Livelihood March, which had a turnout of 407,791 people, counted by sheep-counters to avoid future dispute about numbers, and was the biggest ever recorded protest march in London at the time. For comparison, e-petitions often struggle to reach 100,000 clicks. The countryside protests worked, in terms of turnout numbers, partly because we all knew each other 'in real life', and partly because there was a sense of shared loyalty, to a way of life, to each other, and in no small part, to the memory of Granny and Billy Fox going on with Lady Curre's hounds, before the war.

I kept scrapbooks of the hunting debate in parliament and among the public. I thought that later it would all be seen as interesting social history, evidence of the old ways of the countryside adapting to great change in a way not seen since the tractor replaced the horse. In some ways I was prescient. I still have my scrapbooks and my Museum of Hunting, with particular interest in the ephemera and paraphernalia arising from the protests leading up to the ban. It is stored in the cobwebby room above the tack room at the Old Rec: the old tack room from which we set off in those distant days not all that long ago, with 10p in our pockets, the old tack room from which I learnt everything I have ever known first-hand about hunting.

My scrapbook habit included Rural Issues, and I have fired it up again, collecting newspaper cuttings about farming, hunting, shooting, fishing, rivers, grouse moors, pheasant, rural access, right to roam, trespass, litter, children, nature, climate change and mental health. These issues are coming round again, and this time, there is more at stake.

With hindsight, I was not 'marching for hunting' as my homemade life-size cut-out hound placards might then have implied. In fact I was really marching for *hounds*, and for their continued existence, in packs, in kennels, so that they should not become extinct.

There are demands to end the breeding of all hounds from certain quarters, but there are never any demands for an end to the breeding of all cats. Hounds are jolly and gregarious characters who cheerfully live in packs and lift the spirits. It would be a cultural loss too far for them to die out *by force* rather than by natural social change and evolution. It would be sad for the kennels at Belvoir Castle to lie empty or become a cafe and shop, as so many stable-yards have done. There may come a time when hounds are forever silent, but not yet.

As part of our own adapting to change (coastal change), we were forced to have a clear-out of our 'stuff', which led to a more far-reaching clear-out behind the closed doors of the cupboards and wardrobes at the Old Rec. Lying dormant for decades, these closed doors once opened revealed a series of set-pieces, defined by the elegant old clothes and 'kit' within, each one a vignette of a scene from another age.

John Morgan, who deals in *hunting kit, sporting paraphernalia and officers' effects*, filled the entire volume of an estate car with the paraphernalia of our collected past lives. Made-to-measure bowler hats from Lock's, regimental badges, mess kit, West Norfolk hunt evening dress, whips, top boots, debutante dresses, polo gear, it all came spilling out. This collective effort in adapting to change, from Granny and Billy Fox at Adbury and their sacrifices in the war, via my own 1970s hunting childhood, to the more visible, transparent and humane countryside of today, must count as progress, in the long term. If Rome wasn't built in a day, nor could it be demolished in a day. The same is true of long-established ways of life. It takes a generation or two to dismantle or reinvent such deeply embedded social and cultural mores, i.e. manners and mannerisms, kit and caboodle.

Dusting off these elegant relics of the past, of a way of life so very recently lived by my own family and yet now seeming so utterly distant, we loaded up the large boot of the estate car which would now take these old relics away, bearing them off in a manner slightly reminiscent of a grand hearse bearing away a distinguished body after a long life well lived, to their new 'afterlife' somewhere near Adbury, to be worn in television dramas like *Downton Abbey*, no longer needed for the everyday, no longer relevant to real life. The fever of that life is over, their work done.

In the spirit of *Powers of Ten*, as the estate car drove away down the drive, laden with those beautiful clothes, the elegant world of pre-war hunting and 1950s debutante dances seemed to recede into the distance, further and further away. Perhaps it was time to let it all go.

Fields of sea

To everything there is a season, and a time to every purpose under the heaven. A time to be born, and a time to die; a time to plant and a time to pluck up that which is planted; a time to kill, and a time to heal.

Ecclesiastes 3:1–3

12

DECEMBER, AGAIN

There is a convention at the end of a life to give thanks and to attempt to end on a positive note, even to the extent of alluding to if not quite an actual afterlife, then at least the idea that as one life ends, another begins, or is about to. It seems wise as a deliberate decision in life to try to adopt a default position of general optimism. Bring me sunshine. I can see clearly now the rain has gone. Hey there, Mr Blue Sky. And I think to myself, what a wonderful world. Every little thing's gonna be all right. That sort of idea.

Siegfried Sassoon in *Memoirs of a Fox-hunting Man* (1928) is amusingly pragmatic on the subject of an afterlife, in a passage I'd quite like as a reading at my own funeral (if I hadn't already arranged to leave my body to Cambridge University Anatomy Department, for the use of students and/or research, thence to vanish into an incinerator like a put-down pet, to be 'scattered in the garden'). Sassoon idly ruminates that for him the idea of an afterlife is simply a matter of the four seasons of the year, this summer, then autumn, then winter, and after that next spring, all bound up with a vague sense of going to church and not wanting to be dead.

The familiar phrases of Ecclesiastes are not fixed as if petrified into dusty old tomes, but are sunnily adaptable to change, to be reborn into a song by The Byrds, *Turn, Turn, Turn*, the underlying themes seeming not just time-less but actively contemporary to our particular epoch: a time to be born, a time to die, a time to kill and a time to heal. While the underlying necessity of Nature is constant change, some things remain eternal down the generations. We are now dug in to 'a time to heal', or if we aren't, we need to be.

This convention of alluding to an afterlife takes many forms and metaphors, but the basic idea is to emphasise hope, for the future to seem survivable to the newly bereaved. One reading which does the rounds at funerals is about a ship disappearing over the horizon, vanishing from view . . . But! Ahoy! While the ship may have vanished from our particular point of view, to others somewhere beyond the horizon, it is arriving. This is perhaps not the most original or inspiring metaphor, but at least it is one that introduces a trinity of natural concepts relevant to our particular 'time to heal': circular geometry, three dimensions and universal scale.

A comparable modern metaphor enabled by the Internet is the tracking of the International Space Station as it orbits Earth, or following the journeys of 'our' swallows as they fly to Africa. It is strangely uplifting to see a short piece of video filmed in sunshine, of our swallows flying over a specific pass in the Pyrenees. Of course they are our swal-lows, flying so well, we all want to believe.

Traditional funerals may also include the hymn which

begins, 'The day thou gavest, Lord, has ended ...' which all seems rather final until you come across a warming line:

'The sun that bids us rest is waking/ Our brethren in the western sky ...'

Although presumably intended as another metaphor on a theme of The Circle of Life, this is a pleasingly literal reference to real-life nature and the movement of the planets, and is therefore more comforting to those of us who don't believe in a literal afterlife, but quite enjoy the reassuring metaphors of the seasons, the agricultural year, and the unerringly reliable cycle of decay and renewal that is the essence of Nature itself. It will be a day like any other, the day that I die. The sun will still rise and the birds will still fly. There is something reassuring in the predictable natural ordinariness of that particular day, whenever it may be. It is only to humans that death is so particularly disruptive. In nature, it is simply a recycling process. *I was not, I have been, I am not, I do not mind.*

People often say things like, 'Nature is so good at recycling, unlike humans', as if Nature (often elevated in these contexts to the capital N) was somehow separate from humans. But we are just an animal, as much a part of nature as any other, and we are masters of clever recycling: earth and stone into architecture, pigments into paintings, hardy sheep fleeces into Harris Tweed, wood into literature. The problems only arise when we upturn a forest or two to make the foundations of Venice, or a barn, or a fleet of ships, or the British farmed landscape, and forget or neglect to replace what we have used. As long as we take only the sustainable surplus of any natural resource, at a rate that is less or slower than the rate at which it renews itself, then we can live in balance in perpetuity, usefully employing (not 'plundering') the plants and animals, forests and grasslands alongside us, as we have for thousands if not millions of years before. Until about a century ago.

Henry Beston, in the book *The Outermost House*, considers the nature of animals relative to us: 'They are not brethren, they are not underlings; they are other nations, caught with ourselves in the net of life and time, fellow travellers in the splendour and travail of the earth.' He also refers to the sharp senses of animals, meaning non-human animals in this context: 'For the animals shall not be measured by man. In a world older and more complete than ours, they are more finished and complete, gifted with extensions of the senses we have lost or never attained, living by voices we shall never hear.' He might have added, 'and scents we can never smell'.

The sense of smell bestowed on dogs has served us well since the first wolves hung around our caves. On the whole it has been a mutually advantageous and symbiotic partnership, the relationship between dogkind and humankind. After centuries of hunting together, we have almost entirely moved away from the historic partnership of hunting animals with dogs, towards one in which we use the scenting skills of dogs to find other useful things, or nuisances, such as truffles, escaped prisoners, drugs, bombs, diseases and dry rot. This is progress. This is compassionate human-dog social evolution happening in front of our eyes if we choose to be optimistic, to see it.

Medical Detection Dogs with the right training can now 'hunt' for cancers, Parkinson's Disease and Covid-19. Enviro-Dogs 'hunt' for dry rot in historic buildings. The hunting relationship between man and dog is essentially the same as it was a thousand years ago, but the practical uses to which we are applying the scenting skills of dogs, and human-dog communication have adapted to changes in public opinion and life in a modern urban age. Spaniels who a century ago might have been trained only as gundogs are now trained as dry rot or drug detection dogs. Perhaps there is a future career path for our historic packs of fox hounds, harriers and beagles to adapt to this new and useful line of work. They have certainly proved their superior scenting skills over the centuries, and their gregarious enjoyment of human company.

There is an enormous public appetite for change and 'a time to heal' at this stage in the twenty-first century. Our particular preoccupation is to heal the damage human activity has done to nature and the environment, as distinct from 'the planet'. We do not need to heal the planet. Planet Earth would be just fine without us. We only need to heal the damage we have done to the planet and its plants and animals, and in the process heal the harm we have concurrently done to ourselves. We have become increasingly aware of the devastation caused by unconfined economic growth and the more absurd excesses of consumerism, yet most of this news is not actually new news, and that is what makes it all the more vexatious. We have been warned of this damage for the whole of my life, and many of us have made conscious decisions for decades, in an attempt to mitigate and minimise our part in that destruction.

A brief history of environmental activism during my lifetime, coincidentally the exact era during which such catastrophic damage has been done, would start with vague memories of the Greenham Common Women, camping out for years on an airbase near Granny at Adbury. Throughout my time at school, I was a bit of an eco-worrier (as distinct from warrior), reading horror stories in the newspapers and campaigning vaguely for the rainforests or for a ban on live exports of farm animals. As a student I designed eco-friendly architecture and rubber-stamped the envelopes of all the letters I sent with a Friends of the Earth message in green ink saying *Stamp out the debt not the rainforest*, while not really understanding the precise politics of this well-intentioned sentiment. For years I wore two faded 'rainforest-saving' T-shirts, one with red-eyed tree frogs, and another with a different kind of rainforest frog with little blue hands. I didn't overthink the carbon footprint or the need for two T-shirts, but carbon footprints were not much thought of then. It was all about the ozone layer, and Prince Charles making worried but prescient speeches and talking to his plants.

My generation is old enough to remember the Earth Summit of 1992 in Rio, and a horse called Earth Summit named after it, who won the Grand National in 1998. The Greenpeace boat *Rainbow Warrior* was often on the news, doing genuinely daring deeds of derring-do in the name of the environment, Save the Whales, and so on. Before we were even born there were CND anti-nuclear protests and love-ins and bed-ins and flower power. Long before Greta and Extinction Rebellion, an unlikely alliance of people, including Jonathon Porritt, George Monbiot, Sir David Attenborough, HRH The Prince of Wales, assorted 'Slippies' (Sloane hippies) and Swampy (an anti-Newbury-bypass protester famous for living in tunnels and/or trees at the time) warned us, constantly. We listened, we stopped using CFCs, and we started recycling in earnest. But it wasn't enough.

Human concern about nature and the environment has

a long and noble history. My personal environmental hero is Thomas Wright. Thomas Wright is largely forgotten by history, but is fondly remembered in his birthplace at Byers Green in County Durham, where a memorial stone refers to him as a 'Natural Philosopher'. We could do with more Natural Philosophers now, with a *Powers of Ten* zoomed-out 'universal' view of our world in the grandest scheme of things. Thomas Wright would be fascinated by the *Powers of Ten* film and flipbook, and by our current climate crisis. He would no doubt have many imaginative (probably eccentric and possibly outlandish) ideas about how to restore balance to Earth and Nature. We recently stayed at the Thomas Wright House in Byers Green, and I walked alone in his footsteps along a range of footpaths and tracks. Little seemed to have changed since 1786. It was almost as if he was there.

The difference now, and it is a truly positive difference, is that it is not just outliers, eccentrics and people with a particular concern for 'the environment' who are taking action and changing their ways, but everyone. Nature has gone mainstream. Almost everyone cares, and even those who don't may change their minds in due course. The post-lockdown litterers are not beyond redemption. (But there will surely always be a special place reserved in hell for *people who hang plastic dog-poo bags on trees*.)

The changes we are all making now will very soon show tangible, visible results. The one thing we can have faith in is Nature and its extraordinary powers of renewal and regeneration. The whole premise of rewilding is that 'nature balances itself' and if we allow natural processes to work their magic, then biodiversity is miraculously and surprisingly quickly restored. The Knepp estate experiment (and it really was a brave and risky venture into unknown unknowns before it all went 'right') has shown us what even a short 'time to heal' can achieve.

We are in the end only one animal. Maybe there is only so much damage we can actually do. Nature tends to balance itself, but we may not always recognise it as such while it happens. We are currently living through an era of unusual floods, wildfires, localised plagues (of locusts etc.), a global pandemic and failed crops, including wheat. What more will nature do to 'balance' itself, one wonders? Tiny stories of a column inch or two in broadsheet newspapers give clues to the avoidable future: people fighting over water, people permanently abandoning islands, people fighting over food. It is happening already.

Planet-scale change requires international laws and zoomed-out universal thinking, but a billion people individually never dropping litter can still play a part. It is not just that litter is ugly, it is also a waste of a valuable recyclable resource. Litter should be seen as a minable material, not to be strewn around beaches and hedgerows, or left as crass votive offerings at the summits of the world's mountains.

Boyan Slat is a genuine modern genius in the Renaissance Man mould, combining art and science, but channelling his particular gifts of genius into the planet-wide pariah of plastic. With his remarkable one-man Ocean Cleanup (while he's still in his early twenties), Boyan Slat is miraculously demonstrating the possibilities of gathering plastic with a series of Interceptors, like a Biblical fisherman caught in *The Parable of the Plastic Fishing Nets*. The resulting harvested plastic is then recycled into beautiful and useful products, with an odd kind of authenticity about the material being ocean plastic. The generic lightweight multi-use plastic bag is actually a marvel of engineering, with extraordinary robustness and utility from a tiny amount of material. For all the merits of the circular economy, it would be vastly preferable if for the next phase of our 'Anthropocene epoch' we could simply use less plastic in the first place. Nevertheless, the Ocean Cleanup gives an optimistic glimpse of the future, not only of the innovative genius of people, but also of the qualities that might drive brand desirability in the context of an 'eco epoch-alypse'.

The majority of land in the UK is a farmed landscape of one kind or another, so farmed land is one area where landscape-scale change can be most effective, in both the scientific and spiritual aspects of 'a time to heal'. Terrestrial mainstream television viewing figures in the UK in the Covid-19 era suggest that the UK general public cares about farming and farmers: 'Viewers have been seeking out programmes about the countryside and farming, about human resilience and an escape to natural beauty, and a broader focus on locality and identity. There is a sense of connectedness which many of us don't have these days...' said Daniel Pearl, Commissioning Editor at Channel 5, whose programme *Our Yorkshire Farm* reached number one, viewed by over eight million people.

A significant constituency of farmers in Britain are and have been quietly and deliberately 'farming with nature' for some time, typically since at least around the easily identifiable baseline year 2000, and often longer. Farming with nature has more recently come to the attention of the mainstream media and the general public, largely through the hugely helpful social media and communication skills of farmers such as James Rebanks, a Cumbrian hill farmer, aka the Herdy Shepherd and author of *English Pastoral* and other books.

Hundreds of farmers and other rural people with arcane jobs and pastimes have also taken to social media like ducks to water, including professional deer managers, thatchers, hedgelayers, gamekeepers, wildfowlers and so on. Tweeting on their phones during a break from tracking deer on a Scottish hillside or laying an English hedge, these people have opened the eyes of hundreds of thousands of people all over the world. Perhaps more pertinently and usefully, they have also shared a glimpse of their everyday life and work with urban people living practically on their doorstep, who would previously have had no way to interact with or know about such things. Used wisely, social media could be a tremendous force for good, vastly increasing mutual understanding of other points of view and tolerance of things we think we may not like.

Rewilding (or wilding, or whatever word we choose to describe the idea with which we are all now familiar) is more than a passing fad. Rewilding has an important role to play in restoring ecosystems and biodiversity in the long-term, but there is a distractingly false choice being presented (often by media-orientated 'conservationists' with no personal responsibility for any land) between 'wild' and 'farmed' landscapes, as if the two were entirely separate and unconnected. We need to farm with and for nature as the norm for farming practice, everywhere that we need to farm for food, as well as setting aside special 'wild bits' to appease and assuage our guilt. One swallow does not a summer make, and one forest or released wolf does not a 'wild' place make. If we genuinely 'feel pain at every tree felled and every animal killed', that might be indicative of a disconnection from nature, rather than of being especially empathetic. Indigenous people who are truly connected with their environment use it, sustainably.

The subject of what is 'wild' is subtle and nuanced. Grassland covers about a quarter of the world's land and can be more biodiverse than rainforest. Grassland is often described as 'overgrazed' (especially by deer or sheep), but it depends on the desired outcome. Overgrazed for what? Forest, wildflower meadow or human recreation space? Amateur 'photo-ecologists' on the Internet often claim that a particular field or hillside is a green desert, an ecological disaster, based on the evidence of a single photo (usually someone else's). But without context it is impossible to see a whole ecology from a single photo, especially if it includes multiple tiny plants and hidden insects. Photo-ecologists can sow seeds of despair where there is actually hope.

Wildflower meadows might require land to be tightly grazed by sheep and then left, or cut and baled (with bales removed) to mimic the same process. Regeneration of woodland might require sheep to be taken off the land altogether. A native wildflower meadow is as wild as a naturally regenerated woodland, but less visibly spectacular. Both are beneficial habitats, but to different species. We need both/and, not either/or, just as we need heather moorland and scrub, reedbed and arable, hedges and stone walls, and probably in the next half-century much more land left largely to natural processes altogether ... ruggedly, robustly, messily wilding and rewilding itself.

There is an apocryphal rural story which illustrates the problem of an uncritical worship of all things wild and natural, to the exclusion of acknowledging any human intervention as being useful at all. The gist of the story is

279

that a man had been working hard at clearing brambles, nettles and so on from an overgrown pond on a farm, when the vicar happened to pass by and notice his work:

Vicar: You and the good Lord have made a wonderful job of that, Harry . . .

Harry: It looks a whole lot better than when He done it by Himself . . .

The reactions of traditional hill farmers to *Summit to Sea*, mentioned earlier, contain a lesson in how, in real life on the ground, rewilding will happen only with the willing participation of local communities, specifically the people who already live and work there. Those apparently empty-looking hills are not a 'blank canvas', they are someone's home. You can't just tell people to be 'eco-tourism guides' when for centuries they have been hill farmers. Being a hill farmer and shepherd is a whole way of life.

Dafydd Morris-Jones, a hill farmer/shepherd, articulated his view of a problem with rewilding succinctly: 'What we risk with rewilding is almost fetishising a very specific form of "wild" nature, and placing that at the top, and placing other natures below it, and people below that again'.

Visiting a retired shepherd's house in Northumberland not long ago, we found every surface was crammed with pictures and little models of sheep, sheepdogs, sheepdogs on quadbikes, sheepdogs with sheep, and many variations on the theme. More recently in a farmhouse on a dairy farm in Derbyshire the same principle applied, but this time the house was crammed with show-cow photographs, pictures and little models of dairy cows, specifically Holsteins. To the untrained eye, the sheep, sheepdogs and cows all looked more or less the same, an effect greatly exaggerated by the fact that all these animals were black, white, or black and white.

I empathised with this almost comical affection for seemingly identical black and white animals, as at different times in life I have known as individuals many monochrome animals who 'all look the same'. I could tell all our black and white Jacob sheep apart. I could recognise individually a few of the Household Cavalry's cavalry blacks, the big black horses. I could at one time also recognise by name many of the individual hounds in our local pack (Kestrel, Kindly and Kittiwake, Latimer and Laughter) whose descendants now 'all look the same', or at least unidentifiably similar. The cultural significance of farm animals in the countryside is deeply ingrained, not least in the dry-stone walls, barns, cowsheds and stables of the UK, a treasure house of architecture for animals scattered across the land. Rewilding certainly has a place in the British landscape, but ideally in an already quite empty place, a place where the suppression of existing cultures is not required.

An old story on the general theme of shepherding (which in the best tradition of rural yarns may or may not be true) takes as its setting a primary school in Yorkshire:

Teacher: Why do you think the Good Shepherd went in search of the Lost Sheep?
Small child: 'Appen it were tup.

The child of the shepherd instinctively understands that not only is the tup (ram) probably the most valuable sheep in the flock, but he is also the source of next year's lambs, and thus meat and wool, the whole future of the family and the farm itself.

People all over the world seem instinctively to want to be supportive of farmers, not only because it is wise not to bite the hand that feeds us, but also because we recognise how hard farming can be on the ground, especially when we are personally involved and/or surrounded by it. Simplistic solutions to global environmental problems are not always what they seem. We could start with what we put on our plates. We know in theory that we must reduce our meat consumption, but the total carbon footprint (and animal welfare hoofprint) also depends on location, and whether or not the animals are pasture-fed, mob-grazed, and so on. Equally, there are significant moral and human welfare issues associated with many 'plant-based' foods: monocultures grown on vast farms far away, conveniently ignored or hidden in plain sight under headlines such as, 'The human cost of our taste for avocados'.

We have to try to plough our own personal moral furrow. It might also be helpful if at this stage we could recognise that we are all in the same boat, or at least on the same planet. We could have a kind of collective pact to try not to be too judgemental of those whose choices, whether dietary or otherwise, may be different from our own. Some people will use private jets, while such things continue to exist. Some people will choose to have multiple 'homes' while they are still free to do so. Some people will choose to have multiple children. Some people will probably continue to hunt, shoot and fish in some form. Some people will always wear wool and leather, while others will always refuse to. Some people will probably consume rare roast beef and claret until the end of humanity itself. Many would literally rather die than live without their personal pleasures and vices. Or without a cat. Or a dog. We have to make allowances for our collectively flawed 'human nature', diversity and so on.

The issue of other people's 'devices and desires' is a pertinent one, for instance with regard to the carbon pawprints of cats and dogs. I am a dog person with a fondness for ex-racing greyhounds and Irish wolfhounds, so I have quite a big metaphorical dog in this particular race. A study by the Geosciences Department of the University of Edinburgh concluded that 49 million hectares (i.e. acres x 2.471) of agricultural land, an area roughly twice the size of the UK, is used to make dry cat and dog food. Even if we feed our dogs on butcher's offcuts and pheasant offal, we are involved. Cats are even more environmentally damaging than dogs, being obligate carnivores and competent wildlife killers. Cats are also at large under little or no human supervision for much of the time. We love our cats and dogs, but perhaps we could think a bit harder before breeding from them. After replying to HRH Prince Louis of Cambridge that his favourite animals are monkeys, Sir David Attenborough pointedly concluded that as monkeys live in forests not houses, they are unsuitable as pets, so he'd choose a puppy or a kitten as a pet . . . ending wisely, 'Puppy'.

There seems to be a great resurgence of interest in nature currently, which in turn results in a renewed effort to care for it. It has often been said that we tend to care most about what we know, and can name, so there was a particular outrage when a few years ago the Oxford University Press removed a large number of 'nature words' from the *Oxford Junior Dictionary*: acorn, adder, bluebell, buttercup, conker . . . all removed. To add insult to injury, these old nature words were replaced with immensely dull, if necessary, cyberspeak words.

To the rescue came the writer Robert Macfarlane and the artist Jackie Morris, producing first a book called *The Lost Words*, reinstating the lost nature words to a new generation of schoolchildren, followed by another book, *The Lost Spells*, which attempts to instil an almost supernatural wonderment in nature. While sceptics might suggest that children might learn more about, say, the behaviour of a real fox from a book like *The Wild Life of the Fox* by John Lewis-Stempel, it is a huge achievement to have placed such books full of nature into modern children's orbits at all. These books will be greatly treasured and may reignite a chain reaction of interest in nature, trickling down the generations, just as parents used to teach their children the names of wild flowers, trees, birds and animals as a matter of course. *The Lost Spells* has also started an unexpected craze for children learning rhymes by heart and chanting them, like odd reincarnations of Edwardian or Victorian children chanting olde worlde nursery rhymes in the days of yore and yonder, but in ye internette age.

In the same line of country, there is a proposal initiated by Mary Colwell, author of *Curlew Moon*, to introduce to the national curriculum a new GCSE in Natural History. This was seen by many as a way of introducing urban children to nature and the behaviour of native wild animals, but in fact it may be equally relevant to rural children. There are many children brought up in the countryside who are just as disconnected from nature as their urban cousins.

I would tentatively add that there is another group of rural children who are taught, too early, too often and too casually, to understand foxes, stoats, weasels, crows, magpies etc. mainly as nuisances or pests, and sometimes still as 'vermin'. I know this because I think I was one of these children. I have always thought quite independently, so I have shaken off some of the deep conditioning, almost indoctrination, that routinely rings around rural life: that it is normal to go hunting, to wear kit referred to as ratcatcher, to say 'goodnight' in the morning, to eat shot pheasants, to spit out the lead shot, to go to church, to declare that the burden of our sins is intolerable, and 'all that'. 'All that' is ingrained by the age of about nine.

This quite particular (and peculiar) kind of rural childhood education is not necessarily wrong, either in fact or in spirit, but the culture of what I call 'presumed continuity' needs constant and careful questioning, examination and criticism. I remember being told that the person who goes hunting (or shooting or fishing) is *involved* in nature as a participant, but the photographer is only an observer. And some of the 'traditional' ways of the countryside need to disappear altogether: coursing, poaching, trail hunting 'accidents', illegal raptor killing, lead shot ...

The book and later film *Ring of Bright Water* included the seemingly routine killing of Mijbil, Gavin Maxwell's pet otter, as a pest. 'I thought it was just ... an otter ...' are the words that scarred my generation for life.

In Suffolk, at roughly the same time as *Ring of Bright Water*, when we were children there was a kind of 'received wisdom' that while hares were thriving because of our especially good hare habitat, they were also an agricultural pest because three brown hares ate the same amount of crops as one sheep. Foxes, rabbits, moles etc. were also 'pests'. Hares were sometimes referred to as stubble stags, or called Puss in the familiar way that country foxes are called Charlie. But this apparently admiring and affectionate relationship was closely allied to the idea that it was acceptable, indeed necessary, to control and/or disperse hares and foxes, by hunting or shooting. Lower down the quarry hierarchy, 'pests' were controlled by ferrets, lurchers, ratting terriers and mole traps, or in less rural circles, slug pellets, mouse-traps, poison and cats.

Big East Anglian estates had hare shoots, and were rumoured to shoot three hundred hares at the end of the shooting season. Perhaps they still do. In the east of England we still see hares often, and in magnificent condition, but you need to look carefully, and have your 'eye in'. There is no doubt that human intervention is inevitable and necessary in a farmed landscape, and that children need to be introduced to life and death, but surely the behaviour, athleticism, speed, grace and beauty associated with hares, foxes, weasels, stoats, otters etc., could have come first, before the 'child's introduction to killing things'? Naturally, in those far-off days, the books we read were full of cosy and well-illustrated stories about these same rural animals, only now in their habitual literary guise they were portrayed as little people dressed up in animal costumes: Ratty (water vole), Mole, Badger, Mr Toad, Peter Rabbit, Mr Tod ...

On the other hand, I have never felt more akin to a wild animal than when galloping across the landscape on a pony as a child, surrounded by the breathing and hoof-beats of a herd of big horses and quite frightening people. Paradoxically, responsibly run field sports can teach children about life and death, food and farming, courtesy and compassion, and can spark a lifelong interest in nature.

I was appalled every spring when the wild mallard ducklings visibly reduced in number as they were marched from pond to pond (thirteen on day one, then eleven, eight, five . . .) in a brutal demonstration of the realities of natural selection. There was a sense of wonder, but also a realism in this real-life rural education that is often absent from, for example, television programmes. Country children understand The Circle of Life, and they know that 'fallen stock' often goes to the hunt kennels. On television, on the rare occasions when a lamb or other animal is allowed to be shown to have died (announced in sombre euphemisms like 'didn't make it', or 'passed away in the night'), there is a moment of reflection, how sad but that is life etc., and that is the end of it. The question of what happens next, to the body, is just left hanging in the airwaves.

The meaning and public understanding of the word 'sport' has also subtly changed over the years. The phrase 'field sports' itself therefore comes under fire in an urban age. One of the most informative natural history books I know of is an Edwardian two-volume tome called *The Encyclopaedia of Sport*, which gives detailed descriptions of the lives, habits and habitats of all the traditional quarry species, alongside the formal rules of archery, boxing, cricket, and so on.

Surtees continually has his hunting characters saying they love the fox but love the hound more, and so on. But we no longer live in Victorian or Edwardian times. It must be genuinely disconcerting to live permanently in the wrong century, reluctant to leave behind what you see as the better world of Snaffles and Surtees, a modern Mr Sponge stuck in a lifelong Sporting Tour, but in the age of motorways, barbed wire, irritating antis and interfering bans. I have some sympathy for those who really do seem to be born in the wrong century, happier living in 1720 than 2020. Perhaps 'Century Dysphoria' should be formalised as a discombobulating condition, the sufferers to be afforded empathy rather than antipathy.

While not criticising the generations before us, we recognise that times and attitudes have changed, especially since the invention of social media. It might be helpful, as an attempt at bridge-building and Venn-diagram overlap, for people to talk openly about the field sports culture in which they (we) were brought up, and how it has changed and could continue to change: the best of it, the worst of it, the future of it, and above all how to break the chain of *presumed continuity* so that certain aspects of rural life might melt away into the landscape forever.

For instance, on paper I am a Game and Wildlife Conservation Trust 'Accredited Game Shot' (96 per cent score), but I choose not to shoot live quarry, and I condemn the illegal killing of birds of prey on grouse moors or anywhere else. On the other hand, I eat game which has been shot by other people, therefore I am involved, and must take responsibility as part of the field sports community. I love hounds, but think realistically hunting must reform itself and evolve, genuinely and demonstrably, to be *only* drag hunting (as distinct from trail hunting) if our packs of hounds are to survive into the far future. Bloodhounds are a separate and less controversial alternative. I support the licensing of shooting, and a reduction in the numbers of game birds released. I believe that lead shot is poisonous and should be phased out.

These changes would be genuinely beneficial progress. We *can* change. Everything in nature changes all the time, and the British countryside and 'traditional country life' is no exception. When the evidence changes, reasonable people change their minds.

As well as all the climate science, the blue maps and the 'state of nature' reports, we have some less formal ways of comparing the past, present and future, and of finding hope in progress. The historic sea levels of Venice are recorded by the green algae tide lines against identifiable buildings, accurately rendered in the paintings of Canaletto. The quantity and quality of wildlife in the British countryside in the past is recorded in the pictures in the 1950s Ladybird Books series, *What to Look for In ... Spring, Summer, Autumn* and *Winter*, in which our native flora and fauna seem to thrive in abundant clumps, swathes and flocks alongside farming.

These Canaletto paintings and Ladybird Book pictures have unintentionally provided a human and relatable 'baseline', and for the optimist, a welcome spark of hope. While not without ecological consequence in the lagoon, it must be a small spark of hope that instead of the 'Venice in Peril Fund pizza' of my youth, we now have a working version of the MOSE flood defence, protecting Canaletto's Venice from *acqua alta*. Across the British countryside there is a huge effort to return to farming *with* nature, restoring much of what has been lost in my lifetime to something more like the pictures in the Ladybird Books. Sometimes progress needs a step backwards.

In East Anglia, the three founding landowners of Wild East UK have allocated 20 per cent of their land to a wilder landscape, rewilding and restoration of nature alongside productive farming. This has inspired thousands of 'ordinary people' (in this context meaning 'people who have not inherited an estate of several thousand acres') to allocate 20 per cent of their own smaller patches and gardens to the messiness of nature untamed. Our gardens are being left half wild. Councils are leaving verges uncut. The convention for municipal and suburban tidiness is being relinquished. Nature is genuinely being given 'a time to heal'. Some might add, about time too.

We can modernise and adapt to the enormous forthcoming changes at a zoomed-out global scale, while still retaining human character at an intensely local scale. The eccentricities of humanity are timeless. Mr Gotobed lived in Little Snoring in Norfolk in the 1970s. There is a window cleaner with Mr Bit written on his van. There is a tree surgeon who calls himself The Tree Fella. I planted a cabbage patch which accidentally became a haven for frogs, toads and cabbage white caterpillars and butterflies. There is a machine called a Grimme reaper which harvests the Benacre potatoes around us in 2020. Snipe often gather at Snape. On it all goes. Not all bad. Often amusing. Repeatedly beautiful. The land always feeding us, if we feed the land. Nature always having the upper hand in the end.

If I listen intently to what I might hear on the wind in the landscape around us, much of it could be from almost any century: the contented gruntling of a few hundred outdoor pigs, the faint hee-haw of donkeys, the clanking of animal trailers and metal feeders, the rustling of oak leaves in the wind, occasional horses, hounds, a hunting horn, a shotgun, fourteen quiet gundogs, ducks, a cock crowing, a vixen screeching at dusk, a distant dog barking, birdsong, tractors, gulls following the plough, church bells, the boom of the bittern in the reedbeds, lapwings and curlews on the stubble, oystercatchers, the honking of wild geese ... and in the background of all of it is the constant roar of the waves, eating away at the land, all too soon to transform this familiar landscape into fields of sea.

'Despite all our accomplishments, we owe our existence
to a six-inch layer of topsoil and the fact that it rains.'

JAMES WONG
Twenty-first-century ethnobotanist

TAILPIECE

Imminent imagined near-future inventions and/or likely situations, in no particular order

1. Carbon trading of personal allowance; rationing of flights, air miles, houses etc.

2. Home as multi-functional hub, working/shopping from home, changing city/office 'ecology'

3. Increased localisation of experience and use of local shops and services

4. Geothermal energy from Iceland and solar from Africa etc. exported to global energy grid

5. Mini modular nuclear reactors transportable by lorry (e.g. existing by Rolls Royce due *c.*2029)

6. Photovoltaic manufacturing costs reduce to provide highly cost-effective renewable energy

7. Plastic waste incorporated into road surfaces, concrete, foundations, paving, tennis courts etc.

8. Solar panels evolve to become road surfaces and/or transparent surfaces, windows etc.

9. Solar panels on roofs of cars, buildings, large empty surfaces etc. as standard

10. Green roofs and sedum/plants on roofs of new housing and industrial warehouses etc. as standard

11. Ocean plastic clean-up fully functioning c/o Boyan Slat and The Ocean Cleanup etc.

12. Ocean plastic recycled items for sale/industry, recycled plastic gravel in roads/buildings etc.

13. No-litter packaging jelly-balls for water, fizzy drinks, beer etc.

14. No-litter packaging jelly-balls for 'survivaball' air-dropped emergency water, food and shelter

15. Plastic and rubbish seen as a minable mineral resource providing materials, metals, fuel etc.

16. No-plastic plastic problem solved with potato starch or similar as routine alternative

17. Plant-based food, clothes and domestic items mainstream, 100 per cent ethical veganism still a minority

18. Greater appreciation of natural materials for all applications, wool etc.

19. Lab-grown meatless burgers/nuggets etc. supersedes factory farming as low-cost fast-food/protein

20. Electric cars and carbon-neutral air travel c/o Cranfield University research, e-planes etc.

21. Driverless cars, lorries, buses and trains, robot tractors and combine harvesters on farms etc.

22. Robot hoovers, lawn mowers and the Internet of 'domestic things' etc. as standard

23. Improved recycling and culture of seeing waste of anything as environmentally immoral

24. Manned missions to Mars from Moon base, leading to renewed valuing of Earth ecosystems etc.

25. Rewilding, wilder farming, wilder meat, 'wildland' safaris, wildlife-spotting/birding eco-tourism

26. Wilder 'hunting' models of shooting, emphasis on experience not numbers, sporting eco-tourism

27. Release of some 'charismatic species' – lynx, wolves etc. – to satisfy urban demand for this model of 'wild'

28. Cats may gradually be seen as less acceptable pets because of significant killing of wildlife

29. Huge improvements in state of nature and the environment, because of changes in human behaviour

ORGANISATIONS, PEOPLE AND BOOKS

These organisations, people, books etc. have been chosen because they are likely to have long-term influence and relevance. This is a small selection for simplicity, but they give a range of information and opinion on rural issues and each leads to others.

Organisations

Countryside Alliance, @CAupdates
Game & Wildlife Conservation Trust, @GameandWildlife
British Game Alliance, @BritishGame
Game To Eat, @GameToEat
National Trust, @nationaltrust
Rewilding Britain, @RewildingB
Wild East, @WildEastUK

Farming, rewilding and conservation estates/people

Knepp Estate, @kneppsafaris
Charlie Burrell, @kneppcastle
Isabella Tree, @Isabella_Tree
Holkham Estate, @HolkhamEstate
Jake Fiennes, @jake_fiennes
Somerleyton Estate, @somerleytonfarm
Hugh Somerleyton, @HughSomerleyton and @WildEastUK
Richard Negus, @TrooperSnooks
James Rebanks, @herdyshepherd1
George Monbiot, @GeorgeMonbiot

Books

Contemporary

Wilding by Isabella Tree
The Wild Life of the Fox and other books by John Lewis-Stempel
Native by Patrick Laurie
English Pastoral by James Rebanks
The Ethical Carnivore by Louise Gray
Inglorious by Mark Avery
Feral by George Monbiot

Classic

Silent Spring by Rachel Carson
Diet for a Small Planet by Frances Moore Lappé
What to Look for in Spring, Summer, Autumn, and *Winter,* Ladybird Books series
The Effluent Society and other cartoons by Norman Thelwell
The Outermost House by Henry Beston

Other Authors

Peter Scott
Gavin Maxwell
Denys Watkins Pitchford, aka 'BB'

and

The Easternmost House by Juliet Blaxland
@JulietBlaxland

www.sandstonepress.com